DOING THE DOORS

A doorman for almost twenty years, Robin Barratt was a founder member of the Worldwide Federation of Bodyguards and is author of *How To Find Work As A Bodyguard* and the *International Directory of Security and Executive Protection*.

DOING THE DOORS

Robin Barratt

MILO BOOKS

First published in February 2004 by Milo Books

ISBN 978 19038 54198

Typeset in Plantin Light by Avon DataSet Ltd,
Bidford on Avon, Warwickshire, B50 4JH

Printed and bound in Great Britain by
Cox & Wyman Ltd, Reading, Berkshire

MILO BOOKS
10 Park Street
Lytham
Lancs FY8 5LU
info@milobooks.com

Contents

Foreword

I have been doing the doors for 20 long years. I have also worked around the world as a bodyguard and as a trainer of bodyguards. Security and protection has been my life – I know nothing else. As a bodyguard I have primarily looked after businessmen in countries and areas of high risk, such as Bosnia and Croatia during the war, Israel, Nigeria, Asia, North Africa and Russia. I have also acted as a minder to celebrities and artists and I have even looked after the odd suitcase of money or briefcase of diamonds. I have been working the doors since 1984 and been a bodyguard since 1988.

Bodyguarding was a struggle at first; it took quite a while for me to establish myself as credible and trustworthy. At first I only had the occasional contract and it wasn't until after we established the Worldwide Federation of Bodyguards (WFB) that I really become known and respected in the world of close protection. Until then it was an effort to get noticed and to get work. The world of executive protection is a closed and insular world, a world of referrals and recommendations, an 'old boy network' of mainly ex-Special Forces and higher-ranking military officers. But I persevered and worked hard and in between contracts I spent a lot of time studying and training.

I was first introduced to the world of the bodyguard by Allen Waller. He was ex-SAS and tended to concentrate on private military contracts, of the likes of which I had no experience. I was considered a liability and was rarely allowed to join him or his team. But, as time passed and I studied more and attended more and more military-style training courses I slowly became immersed in the twilight work of 'Military Training and Exercises'.

Together we formed the Worldwide Federation of Bodyguards. The WFB was eventually sold to a subsidiary of SECURITAS in Iceland in 2000. I sold my shares and pretty much retired from bodyguarding, although I still retained a few select clients who I still occasionally work for.

Whenever I was not working abroad on contract, or working with the WFB, I always returned to working the doors. It was the only job I could get that allowed me time off for contracts and training. I knew I could easily return to the doors time and again, whenever my life hit rock bottom – and believe me it frequently did.

I have seen and experienced the most amazing and the most horrific, the hilariously funny and tragically sad. I have travelled the world staying in the most exclusive and expensive hotels – mixing with the elite and the wealthy – and I have lived in the most squalid of bedsits, with no money even to buy food. I have been gloriously happy but have also been admitted into a psychiatric hospital after numerous nervous breakdowns.

My life has had a lot of ups and downs. I have moved cities and countries at a moment's notice without a single possession, and not caring for a soul around me, yet I have been disturbed and tormented at not being able to give my daughter a stable and secure upbringing.

But above all of this, and in spite of it all, I am a professional – working the doors has been my life since my first door as a very innocent and naive 22 year old. I have worked on 29 doors in a total of 16 towns and cities throughout the UK, from the rough mining town of Mansfield to gang-infested

Manchester, from the provincial city of Norwich to England's capital, London. I have worked at a variety of venues – from the toughest hellholes to the poshest of wine bars – each unique in its own right and from each there are tales to tell.

I will also discuss some of the techniques of working a successful door – how to stand, what to look for, how to react and act, what to say and what not to say. Of course I have not always practised what I've preached and have sometimes suffered the consequences. When I first started the doors back in Norwich my mentor and teacher, Bob Etchells, gave me various procedures and guidelines to work with, and I have continued using them to this day. These I gladly and willingly pass on to you. Whether you are a doorman, club steward, minder, bodyguard, or just plain concerned about your everyday security and safety, some of the techniques I discuss can certainly be used to good effect in our increasingly violent society.

Most people see doormen as mere thugs and hoodlums, uneducated bouncers whose only capabilities are of intimidation and violence, and so I have also tried to highlight that yes, we live and work in a violent and aggressive environment, a world full of drunks, drugs and trouble, but for most of the time we hate the world in which we work and, when we have to go into difficult or violent situations, we feel as scared and as frightened as anyone.

Working the door is a difficult profession. Sadly we are a product of our society, and without doormen there would be mayhem on the streets and in the pubs and clubs of every town and city in the UK. Society produces alcohol, alcohol produces drunks, drunks cause trouble and generally we have to sort it all out. Yes, some doormen are thick, shaven-headed, hard, uneducated monsters, and yes some doormen are unethical and immoral, but most are not. Times have changed, and most doormen now care deeply about the work they do, use as little violence as possible, are polite, have a sense of right and wrong, never drink or take drugs and have other, more 'socially respectable', jobs.

Sadly the general public still mostly regard doormen as pieces of shit – mere thick thugs. But we are still the first person they turn to when they have a complaint, or when their girlfriend gets her handbag stolen, or when a fight breaks out, or when the building needs evacuating because of fire, or when a customer is unconscious and need resuscitating, or when an ambulance needs to be called, or when their daughter's drink has been spiked, or when drugs are being pushed, or when a friend has epilepsy on the dance floor, or when... the list is endless. We are scum until an incident occurs, then we are suddenly highly regarded and indispensable but, once everything has been resolved and back to normal, we return to being scum again. No-one cares for the doorman.

Well, I am proud to be a doorman. I am proud when I put on my white shirt and black trousers, tie my tie, clip on my badge and don my jacket. I am proud when I stand on the door and welcome customers into my venue. I am proud when the night passes successfully and I am proud when everyone leaves at the end of the evening having enjoyed a pleasant, safe and trouble-free night.

But a doorman's life can frequently be aggressive, violent and fraught with danger. Tragically doormen have died doing the job. There are doormen that have been disabled and many that are permanently injured or scarred. It is not a job for the weak, insecure, timid or fainthearted.

And so I dedicate this book to the hundreds of thousands of doormen that work on the doors in pubs and clubs around the world. I also dedicate this book to all the doormen that have been killed or injured whilst on the doors as well as to all the doormen whose customers leave their venues safe and sound. We sometimes do a shit job in some shitty places but at the end of the day we are all one big team.

NB: I have used the word 'doormen' throughout this book as it is easier than using 'doormen and doorwomen' each time, but I know there are also some excellent and dedicated doorwomen working the pubs and clubs – and to you I also dedicate this book.

And to all the scumbags and arseholes, to all the scrotes and knobheads whose intellect is barely measurable and whose only desire is to cause trouble on the door and inside a venue: FUCK OFF.

Robin Barratt
Christmas 2003

PROLOGUE

Bosnia, Summer 1993

'I'll drive,' I argued. I wasn't in a good mood that morning. Robert had woken me up at about 3 a.m., coming into my room pissed and wanting a chat. He always got pissed when he was feeling low. It was his escape. There were many times when the pressures on us were just too great, the problems too insurmountable, the experiences too horrific, so turning to alcohol seemed the only way out and the only way to forget. Temporarily anyway.

We were both tired, we needed a break and had decided that after this trip we would go back to our apartment on the Island of Krk for a couple of days of rest, then drive back to the UK for a week or two off.

Krk was great – our sunny little haven away from the daily atrocities and carnage we witnessed in this disgusting war in Bosnia. In Krk we could rest, go swimming, sailing and scuba diving, sit in the restaurants and bars at night and drink and talk, and go back and fuck our Croatian girlfriends. But we were both exhausted, we desperately needed to just get away from everything and everyone, we both desperately needed a rest.

Krk hadn't really been affected too much by the war. There hadn't been much fighting on the island itself, although there were various tales of the occasional spurt of gunfire, but so little compared with much of Croatia. However there were many hundreds of refugees continually streaming onto the island and the Red Cross centres were running at full steam trying to house and feed them as well as getting medical treatment to those that required it, and trying to search for lost relatives and friends. But walking through Krk, even during the height of the war, it was hard to imagine that just a few miles away men were fighting, women were being systematically raped and children were being slaughtered. It was a contrast that was almost impossible to comprehend.

We felt that by getting away from Krk we would be getting away from everything – a kind of cleansing of our minds. We wanted to get back to normality, to the security and stability that only our own country and our own environment could give us. Just one more job then we could go home and we were both looking forward to it so very much.

'No, listen – I'll drive there and you drive back, ok?' Robert replied. He was also getting annoyed – neither of us was in the mood to argue. Robert was moody at the best of times so, feeling as I knew he did that morning, I decided to end this conversation once and for all.

'Look,' I said firmly, 'it was you that was on the piss last night, you're the one feeling like shit this morning, you sleep now, I'll drive there and you drive back. No more arguments, ok?' Then I added for good measure, but with a touch of sarcasm, 'Pisshead.'

'Pisshead' was the last word Robert heard.

We had just finished strapping down our load. The journey we were to take was not a long one and we had already completed it a couple of times previously, but it was probably one of the most dangerous journeys at that time during the conflict in Bosnia. Like the previous two trips, it was making us both a little edgy and a little nervous. It was going to be another mad dash down the motorway that led from Zagreb, the capital of Croatia, to Belgrade the capital of Serbia. For about 70 miles we had to drive straight along the front line. Few, apart from us, were stupid enough to take such a journey.

The evidence of those that had was left by the side of the road: burned-out buses, bullet-ridden cars, dead and decomposing bodies.

Most people wanting to get to the eastern side of Croatia took the long route; turning north at Kutina, then east at Virovitica over the conflict zone to Nasice or Osijek and back down, but that added about four to six hours onto the journey each way which we were not prepared to take.

As per the previous two trips, we were tasked to take medicine into a town near to Brod, about 120 miles down the motorway from Zagreb. This small, once pretty town was divided into two by the river, one side in Bosnia and in Serbian territory and the other side in Croatia.

A little ornamental bridge, long since demolished, used to span the river and for decades both sides lived peacefully with each other. But now the two were divided – those who were friends were now enemies, those who were loved were now hated.

We were delivering aid into the Croatian side, directly on the front line and under continual mortar bombardment, which kept everyone but the most foolhardy sheltered in their cellars or bunkers. Few people had an opportunity to safely enter or leave this little town – it was effectively cut off because of the continual and indiscriminate mortar attacks.

The first time we had arrived, about two months ago, Robert got out of the pickup and said, 'Where the fuck is everyone?'

We had found our way to the centre of the town looking for the hospital, where we were to deliver our consignment. Typically in eastern Europe, the centre consisted of a large paved square, which became the main meeting place; children could play, lovers could meet, the old could reminisce and friends could sit over a coffee and watch the world go by.

However, the day we first arrived the town was deserted. We didn't fully understand why until another barrage of mortars rocked the town, causing us to run frantically for cover. We lay flat against a low wall which was the boundary to what we imagined was once a bustling café and restaurant but now just a burnt-out, blackened, shrapnel-scarred, windowless shell.

We had planned this first trip in advance so we knew roughly where the hospital was. We had both had extensive experience in the protection and security industry, taking us into many strange and sometimes hostile countries around the world. We were used to forward planning and total preparation, and realized its absolute importance in the success of any mission, and on this first trip to Brod we had made no exception.

The bombardment lasted about ten minutes. We lay cowering with our hands over our heads, praying that a mortar shell wouldn't blow us to pieces.

Then there seemed to be more time between explosions – it seemed to have calmed a little – so I signalled to Robert and we dashed back to our vehicle, which thankfully had not been hit, and raced towards what we had hoped was the general direction of the hospital. We had become a little disoriented and so it was purely by chance that we saw the hospital sign.

The town's hospital wasn't a big building and looked to have once had two or three floors, but most of the upper levels had been destroyed. The ground floor was surrounded and enveloped by a wall of sandbags to the height of the top of the ground floor windows. There was a makeshift vehicle ramp running under a canopy to an open, doorless entrance.

As we turned into the hospital gates, raced across the short drive and up the ramp to the entrance it seemed that most of the medical staff were waiting at the doorway.

As we pulled up to the doors, medics rushed urgently round our vehicle thinking we were the first casualties of this barrage. We quickly told them of our delivery, and the look of urgency and confusion in their faces rapidly turned to relief and delight.

We jumped out of our vehicle, raced round to the sides and, as quickly as we could, untied the straps and pulled off the tarpaulin. The doctor in charge ordered the staff to unload the vehicle, which took just a few minutes as they all ran with the boxes inside the building and down to a lower floor. The ground floor was just an empty shell too.

The doctor ordered an orderly to get us some tea.

However, almost as soon as the pickup was unloaded the casualties started to arrive. Standing at the entrance to the hospital we could hear them before we saw them; the screeching of tyres, the high revs and the crunching of gears as vehicles, with their bleeding and dying casualties inside, made their mad dash to the hospital. Brothers, wives, husbands, sons, daughters and friends: they just kept coming. We rushed to the Toyota and quickly moved it off the ramp just in time to see the first vehicle come through the hospital gates. We jumped out and stood briefly at the entrance as we watched the car pull up.

A man, his white shirt and bare arms completely covered in blood, jumped out of the back seat screaming and crying and clutching what must have been his seven- or eight-year-old daughter. She lay motionless in his arms. We looked at her pretty little face, bright yellow ribbons tied neatly in her braided hair, her beautiful yellow and blue flowery summer dress and a bloody pulpy mess where the base of her legs should have been.

In stunned silence we got back into our vehicle, fighting back our tears and quickly drove off. We promised ourselves that if we were ever asked to come here again, we would. Without hesitation or doubt and regardless of whether we might ourselves one day be a casualty in a vehicle screeching its way to hospital. We would return . . .

So this was now our third trip and after securing our load

with a final tug of the rope, we jumped into the Toyota Hi-Lux and set off out of the compound. Although the load capacity wasn't great, the Toyota was an ideal vehicle for much of the terrain in Bosnia as it enabled us to deliver emergency aid and supplies into places to where most other vehicles struggled to get.

We also had our fake Red Cross ID cards and documents, as well as having Red Cross symbols stuck on the car doors and bonnet. We'd had the fake documents prepared on a previous brief trip to the UK for a special operation we had been asked to do; smuggling an elderly Croatian family from the front line back through Bosnia to their family and children in Croatia.

Apart from delivering aid to various Red Cross officers throughout Bosnia and Croatia, we were not nor had ever been members of the Red Cross, nor had we ever worked for the Red Cross, but we thought that by pretending to be their UK representatives in the Balkans it would give us immunity to being targeted and attacked. We were right, and it had saved our lives on more than one occasion and had helped us immeasurably on many others. However if we had ever been found out we would have been shot on the spot.

Our normal routine, once we had left Zagreb and had passed the last UN checkpoint before entering no man's land, was to open the windows fully, open the doors on to the first catch and drive as fast as we could with music blaring until we got to the other end. The reason for opening the windows was to minimize injuries from flying glass should we be shot at, and by opening the doors to the first latch, it dispersed the pressure inside the vehicle slightly should we drive over a land mine. Instead of the explosion being contained inside the vehicle it would be forced out. However, we would still be pretty fucked.

Also, on both previous trips, we had turned the radio up loud and sung at the tops of our voices throughout the journey, both to humour ourselves and to keep our minds off the possible dangers ahead. Not only were we travelling along the front line, but also we were going into a town under heavy bombardment. For some reason neither of us felt like singing that morning; Robert was nursing a bad hangover and felt unusually low and depressed and I was unnervingly preoccupied with my thoughts. For some reason this trip didn't feel right.

We had got to know the Lebanese UN soldiers at the last checkpoint quite well. We had always stopped and joined them for a tea – both on the way out and on our return – as on our last two visits the same guys had been on duty on both occasions. We would chat and laugh and swap photos of girlfriends and family and then, just before setting off, they would always gravely warn us not to take the trip, telling us that we were foolish and stupid. As we left and warmly shook hands they would call us their stupid and crazy British friends. Later in the evening, on our way home, they would view us zooming towards them through their binoculars. They would all cheer, put a pot of water on their one-ringed stove and have sweet, hot, black tea ready and waiting as we arrived.

But today was different. As we approached our friends at the UN checkpoint for the third time Robert and I still hadn't said a word to each other but we were both looking forward to a nice cup of tea before commencing our journey. It would put us at ease but as we approached the barrier immediately rose. We looked at each other confused, shrugged and drove slowly past the bunker looking in, hoping we would be stopped and beckoned over for our traditional cuppa.

But we didn't recognize any of the soldiers on duty, they didn't even stop us, they just stood at the entrance, nodded sternly and waved us through. My instinct told me something wasn't right. Our routine had been disturbed and it worried me that things were not as usual.

The most critical and dangerous time on this motorway

route was as we passed the tollbooths. All the booths were destroyed and of course abandoned, and it was here that we saw most burnt-out vehicles and dead bodies. Although the booths themselves were all but destroyed, the concrete bollards for the cars to pass between remained. The gap was too small to drive through at speed; an error of just a few centimetres would have been catastrophic. There was no way to pass through quickly, and we had no choice but to slow right down to around ten miles an hour and squeeze through.

The first booth was about seven miles past the last UN checkpoint, and we passed through it without problems. As we sped up I turned the radio on to give us some background music, as driving along this stretch of road was unnerving and uncomfortable. Even if neither of us were in the mood to sing, I still wanted something to listen to.

The second booth was about 30 miles further down the motorway. I slowed right down, inched through the narrow gap and suddenly I heard a sharp 'crack' and felt a splash of wetness on my cheek and neck.

'Fuck!' I shouted as we went through the booth. The car jolted and I felt what must have been another round slam into it. We were being shot at.

'Fuck!' I shouted, 'Fuck, lets get the fuck out of here!' Concentrating on the road ahead, I slammed my foot hard on the accelerator as we went through the gap.

I didn't understand what had splashed against my cheek, it didn't register until I looked round at Robert. He was lying back, eyes wide open, and the front part of his forehead was missing. The back window was red with his blood. Robert had been shot in the head.

'No!' I shouted, over and over again. I wiped my cheek with my hand and looked down at it. It was covered with his blood and brains.

'Robert!' I screamed and turned to look at him once more. There was a tear running down his cheek.

I didn't know what to do. I wouldn't stop; I couldn't. I reached down and turned the music on loud and I just drove and drove, as fast as I could.

I drove for what seemed like an eternity. I drove with my best friend dead next to me. I could smell his death. With tears streaming down my cheeks, and fixated on the road ahead, I cried uncontrollably until I reached Brod. I didn't want to look round, I didn't want to look at him again, I couldn't accept that my dear friend and colleague was dead next to me with his blood and brains dribbling down my shoulder.

As I approached the hospital entrance the staff immediately recognized our vehicle. They waved and smiled. They were eagerly awaiting their next delivery of medicine and supplies.

As I slowed in front of the hospital entrance the same doctor, who always seemed to be on duty, walked to the vehicle. He waved happily and smiled at first, before opening the door and finding my new delivery.

I came home soon after.

CHAPTER ONE

Nowhere Boy

Being out on the streets seemed infinitely better than being at home. I hated being at home. I was never a happy child. Looking back, many years later, the only memories I have of my childhood are sad, depressed and miserable. I didn't have a happy childhood and I envied those that did. I desperately wanted happiness, to have a family that loved and cared for me, that inspired me and that I could look up to and respect. Instead I felt lonely and alone. Sure I had friends, but I needed so much more – I needed the love of my parents. I desperately needed to be hugged and looked after. I can never remember my mother hugging me, not ever.

I also wanted a father that I could adore and look up to. I wanted a father that would inspire me to do great things, to be someone special. Instead my father left while I was too young to have any memories of him; I have no memories at all of us living together as a family. He committed adultery, went to prison for fraud and then fucked off to Australia leaving us alone and virtually destitute.

I was born at an RAF hospital. My father was a fireman in the RAF, stationed just outside a small sleepy town called Donnington – famous for its racetrack. My mother said that I was an accident; a result of one of the first nights of passion with my father. She was 20 years old and only just married when I was born. My father told me he was there at my birth, comforting and reassuring her, but my mother said he wasn't

– I am sure she would know who was and wasn't standing staring at her as she pushed me into this ugly world. My father has always lied. He lied about everything and anything, all the time. My brother Mark popped into this world 18 months later – I presume the result of another accident. My father left us shortly after.

I never knew the truth exactly but according to my mother, my father took out a loan to buy a speedboat. He then sold the boat for cash and forgot all about repaying the bank. He fucked off to Australia taking all the money with him, leaving us in poverty.

He eventually ran out of money and returned to the UK a year or so later, when he was caught and sent to prison.

At any rate, that was the story that my mother told me one day in her seething hatred for my father; what actually happened I never really knew. I do remember my mother showing me their divorce certificate, which cited adultery as the cause of their separation, although I didn't know who my father was adulterous with.

I never really knew what my father did for a living once he left the RAF. He was always in and out of jobs, ducking and diving. One day he would have a sailing shop, the next a mobile grocery shop. He worked in an office for a rubber stamp company, as a builder and carpenter and he once had a sweet shop. I could never keep up with what he was and wasn't doing.

We moved from Donnington to Ealing, west London, where my brother was born, and then to a caravan in the village of Langley, near Slough. On occasion we struggled to eat properly. We were poor – my mother was desperately trying to make ends meet.

About a year later my mother, Mark and I moved to Norwich, where we eventually settled. My mother wanted to be near her family – her mother, father and both her brothers lived in Norwich and could provide support.

My grandfather was Polish and a real character. He flew Spitfires during the Second World War and was stationed at an RAF base nearby. He became quite a decorated fighter pilot, the first to fly alongside the German flying bombs (Doodlebugs) and tip them away from inhabited areas with the wings of his aircraft. He had my mother's name – Halinka – proudly written on the side of his aircraft next to the tally of his German hits. He was a lively and proud man full of interesting and exciting stories. But he was also an aggressive man and occasionally quite violent. After the war he left the RAF and worked as a printer at Jarrold's, a local printing company.

It seemed he hated the civilian world in which he now lived and began to drink heavily, which fuelled his aggression and violence. He was a strong man too, and once broke my grandmother's ribs giving her a passionate hug.

Both my grandmother and grandfather lived in an adorable little bungalow on Catton Grove Road, just a few minutes' walk from our council house. As children, and before my grandfather drank heavily, we would pop round after school and play on his old motorcycle or watch as he built his canoe in his shed at the side of the house.

Being Polish, we had wonderful parties and gatherings, full of song and good cheer. My grandfather loved to play the guitar, and we would all joyfully sit in a big semi-circle around him as he sang and played. My mother and grandmother were great cooks and there would always be plenty of good Polish food: cabbages, meatballs, soup, casseroles, steamed fish, pike, and of course, lots of vodka which sadly normally resulted in my grandfather ending up either asleep and snoring loudly in the middle of the living room or being rude and aggressive.

As time wore on, and as he drank more, we spent less time with him. He preferred the solitude of his bottle over us. The last time I saw my grandfather alive was one afternoon after school. I had popped round for something and he answered the door drunk. As I stepped inside the hall he immediately started shouting, accusing me of not looking after my mother, of being a bad son and a bad grandson. He had become an alcoholic and was in a rage. I told him to fuck off and slammed the door hard behind me as I stormed out.

Shortly after, he had a stroke and spent the following few years paralysed in hospital, unable to move or speak. He eventually died.

I saw him one more time; in the coffin at the undertakers. My mother asked me to go with her. He was lying there, ashen, still, devoid of life, emotion and feeling. It was hard to imagine that this was once a wonderful, enchanting, fun, happy man, a daring and brave man who flew alongside German flying bombs – quite possibly saving hundreds of lives – and who sang his heart out with his grandchildren around him. What had this once great man come to?

At the end of the runway at RAF Coltishall in Norfolk is a tiny graveyard solely dedicated to fighter pilots. As we stood huddled around his gravestone on a bleak, cold and windy day, three Harrier jets flew over as a mark of respect as my grandfather's ashes were placed into the ground. Pilots of the present honouring a pilot of the past.

I was never a violent child. Like most kids hanging round the streets, I had had a few run-ins with the police for small things like breaking windows and petty vandalism, but nothing serious. I was in a small gang with a few school friends and would hang around the streets near the local shops, stealing what we could when we dared, or we would go to Woodcock Road council estate, about ten minutes away from my house, and taunt other local gangs and vandalize empty houses. Woodcock Road was a hill that ran from the mostly privately owned semi-detached wealthier properties up to a large and quite rough council estate. The top of Woodcock Road joined

Aylsham Road, and all along Aylsham Road, going out of the city were other, smaller estates.

For some reason on our way home, we regularly picked on one specific house near the bottom of Woodcock Rd. We would throw stones at the windows and doors and run off laughing. On the fourth or fifth time we didn't notice that the police were waiting in the dark and just as I rose my arm holding a big stone we heard a loud 'Oi you lot!' and looked round to see two policemen rushing towards us. One of the policemen grabbed my hand as I tried to throw this huge boulder through the living room window, and the other copper grabbed Christopher O'Callaghan as he tried to run off.

They gave us a most severe telling off and took our names and addresses, threatening to arrest us later. Every day for about two weeks I was petrified that the police would turn up at my front door, handcuff me and march me off to the police station, but thankfully they never came.

We would also hang around the church at the top of Aylsham Road. The church and graveyard tended to attract youngsters from the other estates nearby too. We would all sit, drink, smoke, be abusive and lark around until it was time for us to go home.

One night a kid from a nearby estate tried to join our small gang. He nervously came over to us and tried to chat. We didn't like him much and decided to play a cruel joke. We had an empty cider bottle which we all pissed in. We told him he could become a member of our gang if he could pass the initiation test. He would have to drink a bottle of cider in one go, which of course he boasted he could do. The poor kid took a few big mouthfuls of our piss, spluttered and spewed. We laughed and ran off.

I wasn't a tough child, neither hard nor aggressive, and I never had fights with anyone. I wasn't a leader – I would follow the other kids and do what they did because I wanted to be accepted as part of their gang. I knew a lot of what they did was wrong and I was always a nervous and reluctant participant.

As a teenage prank one evening we decided to put burning paper down the petrol tank of a car parked in a side street not far from my house. We lit the paper and shoved it down the tank, pushing it as far as it would go with a twig. We all stood back and waited, eagerly expecting the car to blow up like in the movies, but nothing happened. One of the lads, Tim, decided to look down the spout to see if the paper had got stuck, when suddenly a flash and a fireball of burning petrol exploded in his face. I was standing next to him at the time and I can remember his face blistering and bubbling, and the smell of burnt flesh as he ran home screaming in agony. I cried when I got home, and even more the next day when the police arrived.

But generally I thought myself relatively well-behaved considering I wasn't the brightest of children and my friends weren't the nicest of lads.

It was hard for my mother, bringing my brother and me up on her own. We were desperately poor – my father didn't pay my mother maintenance, although he swore blind he did. It wasn't until many years later, when he had re-married, that he started paying – but only because his wife gave him the money to do so.

We were so poor I remember having to sit on cardboard boxes to eat our dinner as we had no chairs. We certainly didn't have a TV, only an old radio and record player that my grandfather had given us.

Every time the ice cream van came by my mother turned the radio up loud. She didn't even have enough to buy us an ice cream and didn't want us to hear the van's melody.

Once, as a special treat, my mother bought my brother and me a packet of chocolate sweets. We could rarely afford sweets and looked longingly at the beautifully coloured packet as our mother waved it in our faces, warning us that we were only allowed one sweet a day. But of course we couldn't resist and, when my mother was at work, we greedily wolfed them all down and hid the empty packet with all the wrappers under the chair, thinking it would never be found.

Sadly, the next day my mother decided to sweep the living room carpet (we didn't have a vacuum). We had a look of absolute horror and fear as she moved the chair aside to reveal the empty packet and dozens of empty sweet wrappers. We were both scolded and sent to our rooms.

My mother had originally trained to be a nurse but after we were born she had various jobs including working as a waitress at a steak house, selling coffee in a department store, as a receptionist at a builder's merchant and as a barmaid.

My mother had various boyfriends but it was while working as a barmaid that she met and later married one of her customers, a man named Donny. I detested Donny from the minute I set eyes on him. She laughingly told me years later that the first time she met him she couldn't stand him either. He was an odd character but she said she felt a bit sorry for him as he had just broken his arm. They got chatting, started dating, one thing led to another and before I knew it they were getting married. I thought he was awful, strange and slimy but my mother seemed happy.

From the moment he came into her life, my brother Mark and I felt cut off and excluded from their lives. All our mother's love and attention was now focussed on Donny – everything my mother did, she did for him. He got whatever he wanted to the almost total exclusion of my brother and me. We felt we no longer figured in my mother's life, as her priority was now to make Donny happy and we came a very distant second.

Back then I only understood that firstly I didn't have a father permanently in my life and I desperately wanted one, and secondly I now despised the man that came into the house acting as my 'father'. Both Mark and I hated the fact that my mother was now showing so much love and affection towards Donny and yet nothing towards us.

My mother had suffered years of poverty, struggle and hardship. She was so desperate not to lose what she now had. She could now have all the things she could never dream about having: a holiday, new clothes, new furniture, better food. She even had a car, as Donny was a used car salesman.

My mother was happy, Donny was happy but my brother and I were desperately unhappy and we weren't even noticed. I remember having to cover my ears, crying with both anger and sadness as I could hear Donny noisily make love to my mother night after night. I was jealous as my mother held Donny – hugged him and kissed him while we received no affection at all. He bought us new beds, a TV, sofa, new chairs, a table, he decorated and renovated the house and took us on holiday but I would have gone back to sitting on cardboard boxes rather than have him in my life.

I wanted to get him out of this house and away from my mother. But of course he stayed, and my mother was totally oblivious to the sadness and despair both my brother and I felt, because her life was now and will always be with Donny.

I once asked my mother for £5 to buy food as my dole cheque was late and I had nothing to eat. She refused and I went hungry for two days. Another time, many years later when I had a family of my own, we were about to be evicted as I was severely in arrears with my mortgage. My mother had plenty of money and recently had large inheritances from both my godmother and my grandmother. I asked to borrow £800 for two weeks to pay off my arrears and to stall eviction until we could sell the house. She refused, saying that the DSS would house us if we got evicted. She would have preferred to see us evicted and living in a DSS bed and breakfast than lend us a relatively paltry amount for just a few weeks. But that was my mother – her sons were never a priority.

My brother was so miserable that he first tried to run away

when he was twelve. It was during an afternoon we spent at the Castle Museum. We would often go to the castle while we were waiting for mother to finish her afternoon shift. Normally Mark and I did our own thing – we would look around a bit, have a drink in the cafeteria and try and nick books from the castle bookshop. We would then arrange to meet near the entrance and go together to meet mother but that afternoon my brother didn't turn up. I waited a while and then went back inside, looking for him everywhere. Not finding him I rushed to meet my mother at our pre-arranged place and time. For about an hour we searched the castle together, sporadically returning to the meeting point. We waited and waited and, just as we had decided to go to the police station, he eventually returned. Initially we thought he had got lost. But he was so terribly unhappy he had just decided to run away. Being so young, he didn't really know what to do or where to go, so he thought he should come back. My mother wasn't concerned about finding out why he did what he did or why he felt the way he felt – he just got shouted at and smacked, probably because of the inconvenience he had caused her – and sent to bed without supper.

I had my first nervous breakdown at 15. It came when Donny, Mum, Mark and I went to my uncle's birthday party at his house in Great Plumstead, about ten miles from Norwich.

I don't remember much about the evening apart from standing in the kitchen, tears flowing down my cheeks as I watched them laughing and joking, drinking and enjoying themselves in the living room. I couldn't stand their happiness. I asked myself what on earth have I done in this miserable life not to be happy? Why couldn't I be happy? Why couldn't I laugh and joke and enjoy myself like everyone else? I tried to fight back my tears, to control myself but I couldn't. I left the house and walked and walked, crying for hours and hours. The party had ended, Mum and Don had finally realized I was not there and come searching for me – finally finding me huddled by the side of the road. I broke down. That evening I sat at home with a knife to my wrist, rocking backwards and forwards, crying like a baby. I was so immensely sad and miserable that at 15 I could have easily taken my own life. Suicide is something I have thought about many times since.

My father re-married. Mark and I never had much regular contact with Dad and his new wife Jean but every summer we almost always spent a week or so with them on holiday. It was fun and we generally had a great time.

We would either go to a caravan or campsite, or take their small motorboat out from Poole Harbour, or just spend time at their house in Wiltshire.

My mother hated my father and she would call him every name under the sun. She resented the fact that we had a great time with him on holiday. We had such good holidays that we never wanted to leave and my mother hated that. We would return home with gifts and presents, things which Mum and Don said they could not afford to buy us themselves. My mother would tell us day after day what a waster Father was, how badly he had treated her and how he never paid her any money. A lot of what she said was true: my father was and will always be a waster. He has always been full of shit and a compulsive liar but when I was that age, above all, he was my father. He was still better that having no father at all and considerably better than Donny.

I got on quite well with my father's new wife Jean. She was a schoolteacher and taught maths at a grammar school in Bath. My brother is great with all things practical whereas I had trouble even wiring a plug, but he struggled at school whereas I was quite the opposite, and more academic than he was. I actually loved school and would have done much better had I enjoyed a more stable and happy home environment. I studied hard, enjoyed what I was studying and really wanted to go on to further education. I knew I had the ability, I just didn't have the environment. There were too many other pressures and distractions. As the pressures of school and exams drew nearer I slowly distanced myself from the hoodlums on the street and developed a more discerning base of friends, some of whom I still have the occasional contact with, 25 years later.

I joined the after-school drama class and was involved in a couple of school productions. In one I played the lead role, Tark. It was a futuristic play called *The Dream Machine*. I loved to be up on stage, I loved to perform and I loved looking out into the audience knowing that everyone was looking straight at me. Standing on stage I was someone, I was different, unique and I couldn't believe my ears when I first heard applause – were these people actually clapping something I had said and done? That elated me more than anything in the world, it overcame my sadness and desperation at home, it overcame my anger and resentment towards my stepfather, it overcame the fact that I had no love and affection from my mother. I had the adoration of an audience and that was worth more than anything, even at my young and tender age.

Finally I started to develop some direction in my life; I really started to believe in myself and who I was. I knew inside I was going to be an actor. I sent off applications for drama school. I had already decided that I would study hard and once I had finished my O levels I would then do my A levels and then I would go to RADA and eventually become a famous actor.

However, I just couldn't stand living at home any longer. A few days after my sixteenth birthday I came home from school and decided there and then to go and live with my father. It was an impulsive decision yet I was absolutely sure that my father would welcome me with open arms, and that Jean too wouldn't mind if I came to stay. After all he was my father, wasn't he? And I did get on very well with Jean.

Before my mother and Donny returned from work I called my father. He said yes, of course, if I was unhappy at home and needed a break then I would be more than welcome to stay for as long as I liked. That evening I told Mum and Donny I was going to live with Dad. Initially mother seemed a little upset but she didn't ask any questions or try to find out why. In a way I think she was actually pleased I was going – one less intrusion in their life. I packed my bags, finished school and caught the first coach early Saturday morning to Bath.

Once at Dad's things were great. I was finally finding myself – I was feeling good and happier than I had been in a very long time. Dad had transformed the attic into a bedroom, complete with my own kettle, tea and coffee. I managed to get a temporary YTS job placement as a technical assistant at a local college and Dad bought me a little moped to get me to work and back. I still had my dreams of acting and managed to join a local theatrical club. They were halfway through a production so there was no role for me apart from as a stage assistant but it was just good to be part of the production. I met a couple of nice 'cultured' friends, one of whom I realized was gay when, one evening after a rehearsal, he came over and stood next to me, holding my hand. I was a totally naive 16-year-old virgin holding hands with a thirty-something gay man and didn't know what to do or where to go. I froze with fear. After a few seconds he let go and wandered off chatting to other members of the cast. Needless to say I became very wary of him in future and kept as far away from him as possible.

As Dad began spending more and more time with me, Jean became more and more possessive and jealous. He was enjoying my company as much as I was enjoying his. We would make things together in his workshop at the bottom of the garden – he was always a good carpenter and craftsman. He would improve the house and I would be his interested and eager apprentice. A couple of nights a week we would also pop across to the local pub and have a drink. I had never had a relationship like this with my father and it was great. I felt so good and so happy.

However one evening, after we'd been out together in his workshop making a wooden box for my records, Jean became hysterical. She shouted and screamed at me, telling me I was splitting the both of them up and that I had to go. She couldn't stand me in the house any longer. Later that night, after I had gone to bed, she gave Dad an ultimatum – either I went or she went. Of course it was me that had to go. I was devastated. I managed to stay for a couple more days, calling the Samaritans every night from the callbox down the road. I had finally found a home and a family life only for it to be cruelly and abruptly taken away three months later.

I was 16 years old and now had nowhere to live. I couldn't live with Mum and Donny because I hated Donny and I couldn't live with Dad and Jean, as Jean hated me. I had nowhere to go and no money and I didn't even have the support of my family.

I decided to go back to Norwich, as I had more friends there than I had in Wiltshire. I found a small, seedy, undecorated bedsit on Valentine Road for just £10 a week. Valentine Road was at the beginning of bedsit land, populated by students and the hard up. It wasn't a particularly rough area, but not that nice either.

I quickly befriended a couple, Rick and Jan, living in one of the rooms upstairs. They were always screaming, shouting and hurling abuse at each other and doors would be slammed as one of them stormed out swearing, but I think they took pity on me as they were always helpful and kind. They would cook a little extra for me, or help me out occasionally with a little money.

Rick, a rough but quite good-looking guy, had just been released from prison. As we sat together over a beer one evening before Jan came home from work he told me he was so hard up one drunken afternoon he tried to rob a bank. Needless to say he didn't manage to steal anything and quickly got caught as he staggered off down the road. Apparently he got five years but only served three.

I spent the first night at the bedsit frozen and huddled up on a dirty, smelly, well-used mattress listening to Rick and Jan shouting at each other upstairs. I had nothing – no furniture, no bedding, no money, no food, nothing. I wondered again that night whether I should continue with this awful and rotten life. Was it really worth living if it was going to be like this?

CHAPTER TWO

The Doors

For the next six years I went from job to job, dole queue to dole queue, bedsit to bedsit and from girl to girl. I could never stay in one place for long – whenever I felt slightly settled I would simply pack up and move on, without reason or warning. I would just quit my job or move house or tell my girlfriend to piss off. As soon as I became happy and things started to look better I would simply step away. I would tell myself time and again that I simply did not deserve anything good and stable in my life and that life for me was meant to be full of shit.

I never had any problems meeting girls. As a teenager and into my early twenties I could pick up almost any girl, and frequently did, just for fun. I was quite good-looking, and, although I was emotionally unstable, I had a good personality, good looks and I could make women laugh easily. I would frequently go out on my own as I knew I could go into almost any bar and get chatting to almost anyone. I wasn't frightened of women, and met them easily. I loved the company of women. In fact I had more women friends than I did men – I tended to get on far better with women and felt much more comfortable in their company. I had women both as friends and as lovers, but I never allowed myself to go any further. I wanted to fall in love, to be with that one special person but I was so frightened of being hurt I abandoned any relationship before it got that far. I always had a deep fear that the love I would eventually have for someone would be quickly taken away.

At 21, I met Michelle and within six months we were married. Michelle was simply stunning. She was a kind-hearted, warm, affectionate and beautiful girl. Half-Irish and half-Afro-Caribbean, she had an Irish mother who just couldn't look after her – especially in the Catholic Republic of Ireland, where a mixed-race child was then an oddity – so she was orphaned and brought up by her foster mother.

One night, in my quest for her love and adoration, I asked Michelle to marry me. She agreed and before I knew it everything had been arranged. I didn't have the strength to say no and so I got married. I was happy for a while but needless to say our marriage didn't last long.

I was unemployed, on my own and in a bad way – I had no job and no money and was back living in a shitty bedsit. I was 22 and my life had gone nowhere. I was desperate. And then I saw a job advert that was to change my life forever.

As I was walking down Theatre Street in the centre of Norwich, I casually glanced into the window of the job centre. A big sign seemed to stand out, beckoning me to read it: 'Night Club Door Supervisors Wanted – URGENTLY.' I was unemployed, completely broke and desperate for a job so I popped in and asked the girl on the front desk to give me more information. The words 'urgently' and 'nightclub' grabbed my attention, but in my naivety I didn't actually know what a door supervisor was. Of course I knew what a bouncer was – everyone knew what a bouncer was. They were the hard-looking older men that worked on the door of nightclubs and that beat you senseless for looking at them the wrong way. But what was a door supervisor? I wasn't a violent person and I knew I could never work as a bouncer, but a Door Supervisor didn't sound anything like a bouncer and so I listened with mild interest as the girl on the desk read out the job description.

The job was at a 'trendy' nightclub which was opening in the centre of Norwich. It would involve welcoming customers at the front door, sorting out any problems they might have inside the venue, locking up at the end of the night and helping with security as and when required. I knew I could do that job and certainly fancied the idea of working in a nightclub. I was just thinking of all the women I could meet.

I applied there and then. The girl called the club and asked if there were still positions available. There were. She then asked if she could make an appointment for me. I waited hesitantly. Could I come for an interview on Thursday? I thought I could go now if it meant getting a job, but I didn't want to sound desperate so I said yes, Thursday would be fine and yes, 10 a.m. would also be fine. My appointment was with the general manager. I dressed as smartly as I could considering I didn't have enough money to feed myself, let alone afford a decent suit and tie.

The Ritzy was going to be a new glamorous nightclub, taking the place of the old Samson and Hercules. The Samson was one of the oldest nightclubs in Norwich and had been notorious in its heyday.

I was extremely nervous going to the interview but the general manager seemed a decent and very friendly person. I felt the interview went well – he seemed to like what I said and how I answered his questions as, at the end of the interview, I was told that I had got the job and was to report for staff training at 9 sharp the following Monday morning. I was elated. I couldn't believe that I would soon be working as a Door Supervisor (whatever that might be) at the new Ritzy nightclub. That night I went out celebrating, got blind drunk with what little money I had and ended up vomiting all over my bed.

All new employees, from the bar staff and glass collectors to the cloak room attendants and door supervisors, had to attend a three-day training and induction course before the grand opening Thursday night. At the end of the first day's training, the general manager presented the door supervisors with their new uniforms. The trousers were a nice dark grey colour and looked great. The tie was nice too, the same grey as the trousers but with a lighter grey stripe through the centre. But the jacket! They expected us to wear bright yellow jackets. I was naive and didn't really understand what was happening when Bob, the head door supervisor, held up the jacket and said to the manager, 'You are joking aren't you?' I didn't understand why, but he looked very concerned. 'We can't wear those,' he continued, 'we would look ridiculous, like fucking canaries.'

I didn't say anything even though I did agree. Who was I to say anything? I was timid and quiet and wouldn't dare cough loudly, let alone voice any opinion – especially on the first day of a new job that I so desperately needed.

I soon learned that Bob was the local hard-man in Norwich. He told us that he had been a doorman for quite a few years prior to starting at the Ritzy and, as I soon found out, he had a fearsome reputation in the city. Bob knew just about every criminal and con-man, every hard-man and nutter, and he fought hard to maintain his reputation. For some reason Bob and I clicked and got on well from the very first meeting. He could tell I was a beginner and very naive, that I was nervous and tense but for some reason he took me under his wing and guided me through the first few weeks of my life on the doors. We grew to be great friends and excellent working partners.

Away from the doors Bob was a kind-hearted and caring father but on the doors he was ruthless. He was frightened of no-one and would take on, and beat, the most daunting of opponents. He would always fight dirty, tearing at his opponents' eyes, biting off their ears and nose, ripping their bollocks. Bob taught me my first very important lesson, a lesson that I have carried with me throughout my career both as a doorman and out in the field as a bodyguard. It was that

I must never, ever get beaten. I should do what ever I had to do, but I must never lose. Once beaten, he said, I would lose all confidence in myself and all respect – both self-respect and the respect of others. Once beaten, I would never be able to effectively work the doors again. Throughout my career on the doors I have come pretty close to being beaten, and have seen a great many others beaten senseless. I have seen hard-men reduced to tears, on the floor curled up crying out for mercy. But thankfully to date I have been lucky and have never got into that frightening and soul-destroying situation. Never allowing myself to be beaten has been my philosophy throughout my life on the doors and it has stayed with me. I have been in a great many extremely violent situations and every time things have started to look grim and I could see no way out, I have recalled Bob's odd eyes staring at me and drumming home this first lesson: 'Never get beaten Robin, never.'

The product of a broken home, Bob adored his mother, who lived on her own, and would visit her two or three times a week. He would often say, 'Mind if I just pop and say hi to my mum?' before we went off to give someone a good hiding, or some other criminal activity. I would sit and wait in the car, knowing he wouldn't be long, and watching him close the door to his mum's apartment tucking a cosh or baton under his coat.

I once asked Bob why he didn't want to do any other job apart from the doors, and I was amazed at his reply. Bob could read, and enjoyed all sorts of books, but he couldn't write or spell. He told me he tried to complete an application form for one job and was so embarrassed that he quickly left the building, leaving the form uncompleted on the table. He said he never wanted to go through that frustration again so he never bothered applying for any other job.

Being with Bob was like being with a minor celebrity. Norwich is not a big place and the nightlife scene is comparatively small, so everyone involved in the clubs knew Bob.

He once told me a story of when his house was burgled. He had come home after a night at work and found all his possessions in a pile in the living room. The burglars had simply left everything in a heap once they saw Bob's picture on the mantelpiece. He was pretty pissed off, as he had to return everything to their original places in his house, but not as pissed off as the burglars would have been had they completed their task.

Bob was as strong as an ox, yet never lifted a weight in his life. He was short and stocky and as blind as a bat. If he wasn't wearing his glasses – and he never did – driving with him was a nightmare. He would quite literally have his nose up against the windscreen, braking suddenly as he approached the car ahead or traffic lights. To make matters worse he was also banned, had no insurance and invariably drove stolen vehicles. He also hated anyone else driving. But at least he could never get done for drunk driving – Bob was teetotal. He never drank any alcohol whatsoever.

'Head office, nothing to do with us,' replied the manager to Bob's comments regarding the awful yellow jackets. The manager seemed a decent guy – he was from the old school of club managers and had been running nightclubs and bars for most of his working life. He got on well with all of the doormen – in fact he had started his career on the doors ten years previously, running a door in the East End of London, so he had a great affinity for all of us. Even though many of us were new to the business and he could see we really didn't have a clue about anything, he would always back us up and help us out.

I could see that Bob really didn't like the idea of us wearing these awful yellow jackets and we all felt roughly the same. They were not practical, they were not reasonable considering the job we were going to undertake and – most importantly for me being blond – yellow didn't go with my complexion.

Bob was right – wearing yellow on the door was not a good idea. To most people yellow gives an impression of cowardice, and that is not the image we needed. The first excuse he had, Bob privately told us later, he would get rid of them.

I was soon to realize that door supervisor and bouncer were one and the same.

I realized this when I went to Ritzy that first Monday morning and looked around at my fellow 'door supervisors'. Some were average-looking guys but most looked like real doormen. In my naivety I had stepped into the world of the nightclub bouncer.

We would soon learn that we were all going to have to work for our money at the Ritzy. It was not going to be the glamorous venue that everyone expected it to be. There were simply not 1,000 glamorous people in Norwich to fill a club of that size one night a week, let alone four. Standards would soon drop but by that time I had turned into a fairly good doorman as well as an average fighter. On the opening night I hadn't even thrown a punch, and certainly hadn't fought anyone, ever. I didn't consider myself a coward mainly because I had not ever been in a situation where this could be judged but in my everyday life I had always stayed clear of violence. Even as a teenager roaming the streets, I never had a fight, not a proper fight with fists, only the occasional scuffle, pushing and shoving. I didn't even know how to throw a proper punch without breaking my fingers or wrist and I hadn't a clue how to block or defend myself. However I did get punched in the mouth once, leaving a rough nightclub called the Festival House when I was about 18. I was with Michael Pepperell, a school friend, and we were both really drunk. I must have said something abusive to a couple of other lads leaving the club at the same time, as one turned round and punched me on the lip, cutting it. I lay on the floor for a while, moaning and groaning and drumming up enough confidence to stand up for myself and retaliate, but by the time I had got up they were gone. I stormed about with fists clenched vowing revenge but Michael just thought what a knob I was and walked off.

On the first night I was nervous, especially when I saw some of the customers coming through the door. I thought a lot of them looked fairly tough and I didn't have a clue how I would ever get them out of the club let alone fight them.

I had applied for the position because I saw this job as just a bit of fun, a laugh and an excellent way of pulling women and getting paid for it. I was neither big nor strong, and I had no martial arts experience. I suppose I just hoped that nothing bad would happen. It was just going to be a temporary job while I looked around for something better. I would have been horrified if you told me back then that I would still be doing the doors when I was 40 years old.

Even now, there are many people entering this business just for a bit of fun. They don't understand the seriousness and responsibilities of the job and the consequences if it isn't done properly. I am not saying that doing the doors is as important as, say, a fireman, but with both jobs the wrong decision can lead to injury or even death, not just to the customer but also to the doorman.

I just had to bullshit and bluff my way through the first few nights and hope my innocence and inexperience wouldn't get me found out. My thoughts were of just getting though the first few weeks. I would train hard in the gym during the day and go to self-defence classes two or three evenings a week – when I was not working – and hopefully, by the time something major did happen, I would be stronger, a bit bigger and would feel more confident with my fighting ability. I would also carefully watch and learn from the more experienced doormen, especially Bob, how to deal with potential trouble.

Thursday was the grand opening night. Entrance was by invitation only. We had about 500 fairly decent and respectable people through the doors, all owners and managers of local businesses, shops, restaurants, record shops as well as local DJs, radio presenters, celebrities, footballers, etc.

I had no experience working the front door so I was to work inside. No-one was allowed to work the club alone so we had to work in twos, and I teamed up with a guy called Julian. Although I knew Julian's face, I had actually met him for the first time a few days earlier at Chris Roberts's gym. Julian had been training for about a year at Chris's and was quite a bit bigger, and a lot stronger, than me. Chris Roberts had held various bodybuilding titles including Mr Britain and was quite well known around Norwich. I remember seeing him walking down a street one afternoon and, as he walked past, I stared in awe at his physique. His arms were huge, popping out of his blue and white striped tight t-shirt. I immediately knew I wanted to look like that.

Chris was a decent, down to earth guy and heavily into his bodybuilding. Before owning his own health club he taught physical education at a local private boys' boarding school and his gym was probably the most recognized bodybuilding gym in the area. Arnold Schwarzenegger had just entered the movie world and was every bodybuilder's mentor. Weight training and bodybuilding was slowly becoming more popular and more understood by the general public. More men had started to use weights to change the shape of their physique and it was becoming more acceptable to do so. However, real hard-core bodybuilding was still considered a sport for freaks, and, after seeing Chris Roberts's arms, decided I wanted to be part of that freaky scene. I wanted to walk down the street and have people turn and stare at me. I wanted to be looked at and talked about.

The day after watching Chris walk through town, with his arms bulging out of his t-shirt, I decided to join his gym. It was called the Burlington Health Club and was above a tyre warehouse on Ber Street, the notorious late-night haunt for the city's prostitutes.

I was almost six foot tall but weighed less than ten stone. My ribs were poking out, my legs were thin and my knees and elbows were bony. I was skinny and weak and had never lifted a weight in my life. I never ate properly, I drank too much and I never took any form of vitamin or protein supplement, in fact I didn't know what those words meant and was frequently appalled when I caught a glimpse of my physique in the mirror.

I nervously walked up the stairs and immediately heard the clank of metal on metal and smelled that characteristic odour of a health club – the showers, the sweat, old clothes, all fusing together to produce that distinctive gym smell.

Turning left at the top of the stairs into the gym I could see it was empty apart from Chris working out with another bodybuilder at the far corner in front of a large full-length mirror. I stood for a few minutes in the doorway watching in awe at these two men working out. The other bodybuilder, wearing briefs and painted completely silver, was exercising with a barbell for a few seconds, then posing in front of the mirror. It was freaky and slightly odd, but fascinating nevertheless. They both looked hugely muscular – I was truly inspired and stood watching in admiration and wonder.

After a few minutes Chris noticed me standing in the doorway and rushed over.

'Hi, can I help you?' he asked, slightly out of breath.

'Yes, I want to join,' I replied. He beckoned me into the office and we sat down.

'We are preparing for a show,' Chris said, noticing that I was still staring at the silver bodybuilder flexing his biceps in the mirror. 'So, what do you want to achieve?' he asked, getting out a programme sheet from a card box.

'Oh, er . . . I want to look like that,' I said and pointed out of the office window to the bodybuilder in the corner, and quickly added 'but not silver.' Chris laughed.

'How often can you train?' he asked.

'Every day,' I replied – I was eager.

'Well, firstly don't train with weights every day, train three times a week here at the gym and if you really want to train every day then find something else to do like biking, running, anything but weight-training.' He went on to explain how the muscle needs time to recover and that training three times a week is optimum for a beginner like me.

I paid my first month's membership in cash, almost all the money I had, and he wrote me out a programme designed for putting on muscle. Day one squats, day two dead lift and day three bench press. I would have a day off in between each workout day. I was told I could go to self-defence or other 'soft' forms of exercise, but I should not do any other weightlifting. I should follow his programme for at least two months, and by that time I should have put on at least a stone and I could then start to incorporate different exercises and training routines. He stressed that if I wanted to put on weight – and I did desperately – I should follow his programme strictly. He also told me I must change my eating pattern, making sure I ate at least five small, high-protein meals a day, sticking to mainly eggs and chicken, with plenty of water and to stay away from beer. He also suggested I bought weight-gain powder and substituted one or two meals with that if I couldn't cook five times a day. I would have to wait for my next dole cheque to buy the powder as I wasn't even sure where I would get the money to buy myself food. But I didn't care, I was told that nutrition and proper eating was the key to successful growth so I would also have to buy a couple of good books on nutrition – vitamins, minerals and protein supplements. He also gave me an old copy of *Bodybuilding Monthly* to read.

Walking out and down the stairs with the magazine tucked under my arm and listening to the clang of the barbells, I promised myself that I would be back the following afternoon.

I had been training for just a couple of weeks when I applied for the job at the Ritzy. I had seen Julian a few times training at the gym, but we didn't speak as I was just a shy beginner. I always thought he was a bit big-headed. He used to strut around the gym with his training partner, wearing shorts and a vest and would work out noisily in the mirror while I did my own thing quietly in the corner. It wasn't until we met at the Ritzy that we got talking and became friends. I told him I had seen him at the gym. We promised to meet there the following day. Because we both worked the same hours we soon became training partners.

Most people mistakenly thought Julian and I were brothers. We went around together all the time, we were roughly the same height, blond, blue-eyed and neither of us had any problems attracting women. We later formed a private club, which involved us competing with each other and screwing as many women as we could. We only ever invited one other to the 'brotherhood', a guy called Billy.

Billy also worked at the Ritzy, but only Friday and Saturday nights, as he had a full-time job as a welder at an engineering company. He and I shared a house at that time — I moved in with him shortly after starting at the Ritzy. One evening, he went up to his room with one woman and came down the following morning with another. I couldn't believe my eyes. I hurriedly asked him how he managed such an incredible accomplishment. He told me that the first woman was married and had to get back home to her husband, so she had to leave in the middle of the night. But instead of going to sleep Billy – being Billy – called another girl who came round in the middle of the night and stayed until the morning. I had known the married woman quite well as I had seen her at the house a few times, but I hadn't seen the second girl and was surprised when she and Billy came into the kitchen that morning to make some tea.

Back at the Ritzy, I got through the first Thursday night without incident. I had actually enjoyed the job. We just spent the evening wandering round and round the venue patrolling, checking the exits, the toilets, the restaurant area and the dance floor. We also had static positions at key areas inside the venue where we could also stand and observe. At the end of the first night I was feeling a lot more comfortable; I was still nervous and worried about my performance should I have to deal with an aggressive situation, but after that first night I felt more at ease and thought the job was going to be fun.

On the Friday night the Ritzy was open to the general public. I arrived for work half an hour before opening, and there were hundreds of people waiting in a queue outside. I banged the front door and the receptionist let me in, closing the door hurriedly behind me. It was going to be a busy night and I was to have my first experience of working as a 'real' doorman with the paying public. I didn't count the previous night as it was more like a private party. Tonight was my first night of what was going to be a long, turbulent and sometimes very violent career on the door.

I signed in at the front door and went to the staff room where the other doormen would meet. Most of the doormen were already there, sitting chatting and drinking coffee. I was just starting to get to know the other guys: Bob Etchalls, Billy Waters, Julian, Bob Fitzgerald – elder brother of Steven, a guy I knew well from junior school – Daroush and his brother Kouresh, both Iranian and really hard tough-guys, Garry Dunmow, skinny and small but as fast as lighting, Big Clive, Tattooed Tony – a postman by day and martial arts expert, whose arms were completely covered in brightly coloured tattoos – and other doormen whose names I cannot remember. Looking around at everyone I wondered what the hell I was doing there. I felt out of place, an alien in a horribly hostile world. I certainly knew I was practically incapable of defending myself, let alone anyone else. I also knew that I didn't have the strength to grapple or manhandle anyone the same size or bigger than me out of the venue. I was dearly hoping I wouldn't have to. We were a big team and I was hoping we had strength in numbers. I was nervous but tried not to show it.

We didn't have radios, but there were emergency buttons on each bar and in the DJ booth. When activated they registered on a panel at the front door. There was also a small white strobe-light placed strategically between the reception area and the club itself, which could be seen from almost anywhere inside the venue, so those of us inside could immediately see that an emergency button somewhere in the club had been activated. We wouldn't know where until we encountered the guys from the door running in, but then we would just follow them.

There were ten doormen working at Ritzy that first Friday night, four on the front door and six inside working in pairs. There were also two more doormen working on the door up at Central Park, a feeder bar and part of the same complex. From a balcony in Central Park you could look down into the nightclub through a large glass window, but there was no admission to Ritzy from within Central Park so customers had to go out of the building and round to the Ritzy door. Central Park closed at midnight and the doormen would then join us in the Ritzy for the remainder of the evening.

On one hand I was uneasy about doing such a job, not really knowing whether I was capable or not, but on the other hand I wanted to prove myself to the guys. In a perverse sort of way one side of me actually wanted something to happen so I could at least try to deal with it and show the others I was ready, willing and able. I liked all the guys – they were all fun and enjoyed a good laugh. Some of them looked hard and menacing but that interested me, I wanted to be part of that scene and to be accepted. Doing the doors seemed an exciting world, a glamorous and seductive world, a world of violence and crime, a world which one side of me felt drawn to.

Working full-time on the doors seemed like a perfect job. I could wake up late, spend my days in the gym and going to self-defence, laze around, watch movies and have the pick of many women. What more could anyone ask for in a job?

After the first day on the training course I was proud to tell people that I was working as a door supervisor at the newest and best venue in Norwich. In a shallow and egotistical way I felt as though I was suddenly someone in this small town.

I was loving that first night – the atmosphere was great, people were drinking, the women looked good, and I was enjoying the music. I could see myself really enjoying this kind of work, if only I was actually able to do the job. I was praying that, when the shit did hit the fan, I could handle things and I could fight alongside the best of them. I was apprehensively waiting for the first time I was called to prove myself, and I didn't have to wait long.

Julian and I were patrolling towards the lobby area when the strobe light flashed. The doormen at the front door shouted for us to go up to Central Park. They couldn't leave the front door at the Ritzy, as it was getting very busy, so we were quickly beckoned upstairs.

We raced as fast as we could up the back stairs and into Central Park with Daroush and Kouresh following close behind.

There was a circular bar in the centre of Central Park, and a sectioned seating area with tables and chairs on a raised platform at the back of the room. This was the glass windowed section, which overlooked the Ritzy dance floor below.

Last orders had been called and the bar was closed. One doorman was kicking out upstairs, while the other remained on the door at the entrance at the bottom of the stairway stopping anyone else from coming in.

Tony, the doorman inside, met us at the back door as we

rushed into the bar. He told us that there were a group of five guys in the raised seated area being rude to other customers as well as to the bar staff. When Tony had gone over to ask them to drink up and leave they just told him to piss off. He knew it would have been foolish to try to deal with the situation alone so he asked the barmaid to press the panic button, which registered downstairs at the Ritzy reception.

I was scared. My adrenalin was rushing through me wildly as the four of us piled out of the back door and into Central Park. We could immediately see five guys causing problems. Two were seated while the other three stood at the window making abusive gestures to the customers dancing below. They didn't realize it was one-way glass and you could see down into the club but they couldn't see up into Central Park.

I caught eye contact with one of the guys seated – he grabbed his crotch with one hand and gave me a wanker sign with the other, and laughed to his mate. I had a millisecond to decide what to do. Was I just going to ignore it and try to get them out verbally and diplomatically, or was I going to step in with both feet and have a go, bearing in mind I have never had a fight in my life and here were five guys all wanting to have a go at these cowardly doormen wearing stupid canary-yellow jackets?

This was my time. Should I step into the world of violence and aggression, of brutality and bloodshed or should I step away, back down? Was the yellow jacket really mine to wear? I was frightened but was I a coward?

In an instant I decided the route I was going to take. My life would change forever. I was going to enter the world of violence. I raced over to the guy sitting in the chair and, before he managed to get up, grabbed his hair with my left hand and punched him in the face three times as hard as I possibly could with my right hand. I didn't know what I was doing, I just swung at him wildly. I let go of his hair and he fell backwards off the chair, smashing his head hard against the floor.

'Stay down!' I shouted and turned to see what the others were doing.

Daroush had pinned one of the guys against the window and was smashing his head repeatedly against the glass. Blood was splashing everywhere as Daroush tried to break the glass with his head.

The other arseholes had run off and the doormen were chasing them down the stairs. I looked down at the guy I had hit. He looked deformed. I had broken his nose and his jaw and smashed his eye; there was blood everywhere, all over his face and seeping out onto the floor.

He cowered as I looked down at him and shouted, 'Don't ever fuck with me again.' I then kicked him hard in the ribs.

The Central Park manager was quickly on the scene. 'Fuck, you've destroyed him,' he worryingly said as he looked down at my handiwork. He swiftly ushered me away from the scene. 'You don't fuck around, do you?' he said as he rushed me up the back stairs to the office.

An ambulance was called as I sat with a coffee trying to calm down. My mouth was dry and I was shaking but tried not to let it show. It was my first taste of violence and it was extreme. I was worried that I was going to be arrested on my first night. But the police were not called and, once I had eventually calmed down, I resumed working the rest of the night.

As I went to bed that night I could visualize his face, bloodied and frightened, and wondered if I had gone too far. I was amazed at what damage one human could do to another. I had never experienced anything like that before, I had not even seen that kind of violence, let alone been the cause of it.

When I looked down at the broken face of the person I had battered, at first I did feel a little sorry him. But at the end of the day my reasoning was that it was his fault, he was an idiot and he deserved to be taught a lesson. I was judge and executioner in one and I felt good about myself. I never bragged but I knew where I was going and what sort of person I was going to be. I realized that violence didn't worry me in the slightest. In fact I actually enjoyed it – the thrill, the anticipation of the outcome and especially the rush of adrenalin. I wanted to have the experience again and again. And with the Ritzy being the Ritzy, I didn't have to wait long.

A week or so later I saw the guy walking towards me in the centre of town. I could see that his jaw was wired and he still looked bruised and battered. As he saw me approaching he quickly crossed to the other side of the road. I had nothing more to prove and pretended I didn't see him.

If I had caused those kinds of injuries working the doors now, it is almost certain that I would have been arrested, charged and quite possibly put in prison. But things were different back then. Doormen rarely got arrested and people rarely pressed charges. Those that caused trouble seemed to accept the consequences. Nowadays it seems that customers can say or do anything they want and if a doorman retaliates the police are called and the doorman arrested. I have known so many doormen that have simply retaliated and then have themselves ended up being arrested. Doormen sometimes have to put up with so much shit. I liked it the old way when, if someone caused trouble, they got taught a lesson – simple.

After the incident on that first Friday, word soon spread that I was ok. The other doormen knew I was dependable and could mix it when needed. Above all people soon realized that I was not to be messed with. Doormen at Ritzy and soon doormen on the other pubs and clubs in Norwich began to realize that I had few morals and ethics when it came to violence. Word spread that I just didn't care. I had started to develop a reputation.

Weeks and months passed and I found that with every violent situation I encountered, I grew more confident in my abilities. I began to understand what worked and what didn't, which locks and grips caused the most pain and what were the most effective ways of disabling an opponent and successfully getting them out of the club. I would go into any situation without having much fear, just excitement and anticipation.

However I would always try to remain humble and modest and I would never brag about what had happened. I had destroyed those that were braggarts and knew that I could just as easily be destroyed should I start bragging myself.

Most incidents at the Ritzy were alcohol-fuelled arguments between groups of blokes or were sparked by stupid, giggly, drunken girls. Whenever there was an incident, my goal was not to try and split them up and escort them out peacefully using the least violence possible, but to cause the greatest of pain and shock to frighten them. They would then either realize they were out of their league and leave, or turn to have a go at us, and if they did they would then get a severe beating. We would even provoke them into having a go at us sometimes, egging them on, urging them to retaliate.

Each doorman had his own techniques. The martial artists would use two or three punches and perhaps a roundhouse kick or two. Big Clive would just pick them up and carry them out, while Ian and Billy used their heads, disabling any opponent in an instant. I followed Bob's practice of fighting dirty. I would almost always go for the throat or knees, for neither of which is there any defence. A quick strike to the side of the knee can disable an opponent immediately and render him disabled for weeks and a grab to the throat can put them to sleep in seconds. I would then follow up with a gouge to the eyes, a headbutt or break their nose. These few techniques would guarantee to disable almost any opponent in an instant. No man, however hard or strong, can withstand his knees being broken or his eyes being gouged. However, there are many boxers and street fighters that can take their noses being broken or a good punch to the face, and this is one reason why I would never ever punch or headbutt first.

One Saturday night a group of posers came into the club, the kind of wealthy, well-dressed customers that looked immediately out of place but whom the manager would have liked a lot more of. They were local young businessmen, one of whom – I shall call him Steve, though that's not his real name – was quite well known in Norwich. His father was very wealthy and he was very arrogant. He drove a sports car, dressed immaculately and was tanned and good-looking, with not one strand of hair out of place. He was also hated by most of the doormen. Rumour went round Norwich that one evening a few weeks ago, Steve had met a girl at Hy's nightclub, directly across the road from the Ritzy, and taken her back to his place. Apparently she didn't want to sleep with him, but he insisted and ended up raping her. She refused to press charges, saying that she was a little drunk, he did meet her at the nightclub and she did end up at his place. In a strange, unjust way she felt it was her fault.

She was the best friend of one of the doormen's girlfriends and he was in a rage once he noticed him in the club, standing arrogantly at the bar, eyeing up the women, laughing with his friends.

The two Iranians, Julian, Billy, Ian – whose girlfriend's friend was allegedly raped by Steve – and I stood milling around not far from the posers, but far enough not to be noticed. The plan was to confront Steve when he went to the toilet. We were trying to keep an eye on the club as well as on Steve, and hoping he would have to take a piss soon. We weren't disappointed, and it wasn't long before we noticed him nod to his friends and walk towards the toilets. As Steve walked in, six doormen followed him.

Steve was standing with his back towards us taking a piss into a urinal. Billy blocked anyone from coming in and the two Iranians told everyone in the toilets to fuck off.

'Did you, or did you not rape Carol?' Ian called as Steve was desperately trying to finish pissing.

'Listen, I don't know what you mean,' said Steve, shaking. He was scared.

'I'll ask you once more,' said Ian, getting close to Steve. 'Did you, or did you not rape Carol?'

'Who is Carol?' Steve replied turning round, zipping up his fly.

'So you don't even know the names of those you rape?' replied Ian. He was visibly getting angrier and angrier. Ian is a brute, a menacing-looking doorman with a big flat forehead who tends to lose his temper in a flash and uses his forehead with frightening accuracy and force.

'I didn't rape anyone.'

'So now you are saying my friend is a liar?' Ian screamed into Steve's face. 'Is that what you are fucking saying, that my friends are liars?'

Steve had no way out – either he would admit to raping Ian's friend or calling her a liar. Either way he was going to get a beating and he knew it. Ian grabbed Steve's throat and slammed him back against the urinal wall. He then butted him hard across the nose and mouth, breaking his nose and splitting his lip. Steve fell to his knees and Ian slammed his face into the urinal as it started to flush, with blood and piss running down the plug.

'Let's go,' he said, ushering us out and wiping his forehead with his sleeve.

At the end of the night we were all called into the manager's office. Apparently one of his customers got a severe beating in the toilets, but strangely no-one saw a thing. We promised the manager that we would keep a closer eye on the toilets in future.

Bob was right, the yellow jackets didn't last long. It wasn't just because they were an awful colour but with the amount of fighting and violence there was at the Ritzy, we had to frequently work without jackets as they kept on getting more and more blood-stained and dirty. The yellow jackets were eventually replaced with dark blue ones, which were much nicer and a lot simpler to keep clean.

The Ritzy was a wild place, both from a customers' and a doorman's point of view. From the customers' point of view it was a cattle market, where even a fat, ugly, bald-headed moron could pull.

Back then, men didn't dance as much as they do now, so the girls would tend to dance by themselves on the dance floor and the blokes would stand in groups around the perimeter, staring. The dance floor was directly in the centre of the building, so most people would just cruise round and round, like horses in a circus ring.

From a doormen's point of view the Ritzy was not just a wild place because of the violence but because it was so easy to meet a different woman almost every night. Near the back exit was a small room, empty except for a large, stained mattress. This was the 'shagging room', where many a doorman would take women for a quick shag. I have to say that I wasn't as bad or as prolific as some doormen and never actually used the shagging room, and although I did take some girl there once, it was already in use. I wondered who was inside and looked through a small hole in the door to see a girl kneeling down giving one of the doormen a blowjob. I couldn't see which doorman it was, only his dick!

As well as shagging the customers, the doormen also shagged most of the staff. There was one time when we were all sitting in the staff room before the club opened, talking about women, as you do. Bob Fitzgerald said he had taken a girl named Julie home the previous night. Julie worked on reception. He was quite proud; she was a pretty girl, with long blond hair and a slim figure. I had also fucked her the previous week. I told him that, and then Julian butted in and said he had also taken her home the day before me. In fact every one of the doormen, except one, had had her, all within the first couple of weeks of her starting work. We were all rolling around the floor laughing. The funniest thing was that she said the same thing to each and every one of us; that she never normally did that sort of thing on the first night.

And that was what the Ritzy was like. Fucking and fighting occupied our lives and it was great. I loved it. This was my world, the world in which I belonged. This was where I was going to make my name and build my future.

CHAPTER THREE

Steroids

I first started taking steroids about a month after starting at the Ritzy.

Two things happened within a very short space of time that led me to my first injection. Firstly, I had been going out with Debbie, one of the instructors at Chris's gym. She had one of the most beautiful bodies that I can ever remember seeing. It was perfect, and she was a fitness fanatic who kept herself in wonderful shape. As well as a tiny waist and a perfect round arse, she also had wonderfully shaped breasts. They were perfect and I can still visualize them, all these years later.

Debbie had been looking for something in Chris's office and came across some tablets. I was training in the gym at the time, and she came over and said, 'Look what I have found in Chris's desk, what do you think they are?' She gave me a few of each. They were different sizes, two with some sort of a pattern on one side and the other plain.

I presumed they were steroids, as I was sure Chris wouldn't have anything poisonous in the drawers at the gym. At that time everyone in the gym was talking about steroids. They were of interest to almost every bodybuilder and weightlifter, but back in the mid-1980s it was still extremely hush-hush. Nobody talked openly about steroids and no-one really believed that the physiques on stage and screen were a product of drugs. It was still widely assumed that most bodybuilders built their physiques solely by training hard and eating correctly and most of the general public didn't even know what the word steroid meant. Now it is widely understood that every good, well-muscled physique is a product of steroids and hormones and that it is virtually impossible to build any decent physique without using them. It is also widely known and reported that many athletes in most sports use some form of enhancement drug. But back then steroids were virtually unheard of and even the top bodybuilders denied their use.

I looked at the small white tablets and, not knowing what they were or what they did, decided to swallow them. Needless to say, nothing happened, although for the next few days I was paranoid, thinking that at any moment I would double over, crippled with pain and sickness. But nothing, I didn't even grow!

The second thing that happened was that I was slowly getting pissed off with training with Julian. He was always stronger and bigger than me. I couldn't keep up. Although I had not been training long I felt I was making slow progress yet he was zooming ahead. It didn't take long for me to get onto the subject of steroids.

'What are steroids and what do they do?' I asked quietly as we were training together in the gym. I had never talked to anyone that had actually used them.

'They make you big,' Julian replied a little sarcastically, 'and strong,' he added as he curled with a weight I could never imagine lifting. 'See,' he said as he put the barbell down. 'Why? Are you interested in getting hold of some?'

'Of course,' I replied, 'I want to get big. Are you on steroids?' I asked, curling a much lighter weight.

'Yeah,' he said, hesitated, then continued, 'but not much.'

'What sort?' I was fascinated, this was the first person I knew that admitted taking drugs and I wanted to learn more. He told me he took a drug called Deca Durabolin – whatever that was. I wanted to know more: what they did, how they worked and if there were any side effects.

'The only side effect is that you get big and strong.' He laughed as he picked up the heavy barbell again. He was being his usual sarcastic self and I was impatient.

'Can you get me some?' I asked eagerly.

He said he could easily get 'gear', although it would be quite expensive.

'Doesn't matter how much they are,' I pleaded. 'Just get me some as soon as you can.' I never told him about the drugs I had found a week earlier in Chris's drawer. So I asked him to order me some Deca Durabolin as soon as he could. I wanted to grow faster and get stronger and knew I didn't want to do it naturally.

Finally, after just over a week, Julian called me and told me it was here and for us to meet and train together later that day. I couldn't wait.

I met him at the gym and we sat in the corner of the empty changing rooms, like a couple of drug dealers, as he explained that I should take one 200mg injection of Deca Durabolin a week for six weeks.

'You don't fucking inject it do you?' I almost yelled as he took from his bag the needles and syringes.

He looked at me and laughed. 'What do you think you fucking do with it?' he asked.

'Fuck!' I exclaimed.

I paid Julian £8 for each 200mg injection. Back then, £8 was an awful lot of money and it wasn't until a lot later that I realized just how much profit Julian, my best friend, was making buying from his supplier and selling on to me. 'Friends are friends but business is business,' he laughingly told me later when I reminded him about my first steroid purchases. But at the time I was very naive and knew nothing about gear, its availability, what it did or its price.

Julian produced from his kit bag six tiny bottles of Deca Durabolin. I couldn't understand how the products contained in those little glass vials could change the shape of a person's physique. But I was eager to find out.

'I thought they were tablets,' I said, worried.

'You asked me to get you what I took, and this is what I took. I can keep these and get you some tablets if you like, but it'll take another week, maybe longer.'

I thought about it for a few seconds then said, 'No, fuck it. Show me what I have to do.'

We went to the toilet in Chris's gym and he showed me how to inject myself. He showed me how to draw the liquid up, tap the syringe to get rid of any air bubbles and indicated where to put the needle – in either your leg muscle or top right of the buttock. Julian gave me my first ever injection of an anabolic steroid, but told me I would have to do the others on my own.

The first injection wasn't too bad. I was a bit sore for a day and I had a little lump at the injection site, but it soon dissipated and I could train and walk with only mild discomfort. But when I had to do it myself a week later, I was shaking like a leaf.

I got everything ready in a line in my bathroom: vial, swab, needle and syringe. I kept looking at the needle – it looked huge. I flipped off the small metal top of the vial to reveal a rubber cap. I placed the vial down and put the monstrous green needle on the syringe. There are various sizes of needle and Julian had given me a 2-inch green. However, he failed to tell me that I should have used different needles to draw the liquid and inject, as pushing through the rubber cap blunts the end of the needle considerably, making it a lot more painful and harder to pierce the skin. I plunged the needle through the rubber cap and I drew the liquid up into the syringe. That was the easy bit. I then got rid of the air bubbles by flicking the liquid as Julian had shown me.

I was holding the syringe with my right hand and trembling. As soon as the point of the needle touched my skin, I hesitated.

I just couldn't put it in. I tried again, and again. Every time as I touched the skin with the needle my bottle went and I just couldn't push it home. By now I had numerous spots of blood on my arse and it felt like a pin cushion.

Then I thought, maybe I could drink the Deca and not inject it, which would be much easier and a lot less uncomfortable. Luckily I never went through with that idea, as it would have made me very ill.

'Ok,' I said aloud to myself, 'one last time.' If I didn't have the bottle this time I would give up the idea of injecting and ask Julian to get me tablets. I rolled up a cloth, put it between my teeth and bit as hard as I could as I skewered the needle in and depressed the plunger. Fuck, I thought, I can't be doing this every week. I didn't quickly jab it in, as one is supposed to, but skewered it slowly, which hurt like hell. When I pulled the needle out blood oozed from the hole. I dropped the needle on the floor as I frantically rushed to grab some toilet roll to stop the bleeding. My arse was sore for well over a week.

Injecting oneself intramuscularly is not an easy thing to get used to, and it took me quite a few months to get the hang of it.

After Julian's first injection I had waited with anticipation, expecting to grow immediately. When I say immediately, I did actually think I would grow there and then, right before my eyes. But of course I didn't, not for at least two or three weeks, but then I did start to see an increase in strength and I was starting to put on a little weight. By the end of the six-week course I had put on about a stone and was absolutely elated. I wanted more, but Julian cautiously advised me to have six weeks off.

Again I took his advice, but I had started doing some of my own research and I was reading every book I could find on the subject. I was slowly getting more and more information on different products, their effects, side effects and dosages.

When I first started working at Ritzy I wore a jumper or sweatshirt under my shirt to make me look bigger, but after a few weeks on gear I no longer needed to – I was getting bigger and I was getting stronger.

Over six months I bought two or three courses from Julian but it wasn't long before I started to make my own contacts for gear. I could get it a lot cheaper and was soon doubling and even trebling the dose. I also started experimenting with other products: Parabolon, Dianabol, Testosterone, Primobolon, and Anapolon 50. And I was getting bigger – after every course I was at least a stone heavier.

I started to buy off a guy up in Yorkshire, who later got arrested for selling repackaged out-of-date animal products. I didn't know at the time and I wasn't supplying anyone else, but I was taking larger and larger quantities of almost every product he sold.

I rarely had time off steroids, just alternating from one product to another. From my initial dose of just one Deca a week for six weeks and then a break of six weeks, I was taking steroids almost every single day, without a break, and this went on for years. I would take three or four 200mg Deca a week, fifteen to twenty 5mg tablets of Dianabol a day and four or five 250mg injections of Sustanon a week. I would do this for six to eight weeks, and then change the products, swapping Deca for Parabolon, the Sustanon for another Testosterone such as Enanthate and the Dianabol for Anapolon 50. I would try Equipoise, a veterinary product for cattle and horses, Esqilline direct into a specific muscle for isolated growth, as well as Nolvadex to ease water retention and HCG, a product to stop your body shutting down its own testosterone production: I was chemically built.

Although I wasn't particularly defined, I was soon one of the biggest and strongest bodybuilders in Norwich. I would frequently draw a crowd in the gym when I was lifting huge poundage. People stopped their workouts to stand and stare.

My blood pressure shot up, and I would frequently have nosebleeds when lifting heavily. I was getting quite bad acne on my back and my balls had shrivelled but I didn't give a fuck. I was strong and big and that was all I cared about.

I also had a reputation on the doors. Most people knew me, if not by name, by face. I was beginning to be somebody and it felt good. But the steroids also changed me mentally. I was becoming more aggressive and would lose my temper in an instant and fly into a rage. I would also become impatient and more prone to depression. I found the worst drug for depression was Anapolon 50. It was the strongest drug on the market but also the most toxic with the most severe side effects, and it made me depressed literally overnight. I could only take Anapolon 50 for three or four weeks; if I had taken it any longer I am sure I would not be here now, as it made me almost suicidal. One time, while in the middle of a course of Anapolon 50, I seriously considered driving my car into a motorway bridge after a girlfriend had left me.

I had access to a lot of gear and it wasn't long before I was supplementing my wage on the door by selling it. At first I would deal to other doormen and bodybuilders in and around Norwich, but quickly moved to selling gear via mail order. I would advertise in all the bodybuilding magazines – not blatantly but by using subtle wording and phrases, something along the lines that I had fast-acting bodybuilding supplements available at excellent prices. The magazines must have known that I was selling steroids but always seemed to accept my adverts. I soon had hundreds of pounds of orders coming in every day.

I never stayed in one place for long and at this time I was living in a flat on Yarmouth Road, just outside Norwich. My flat was packed with steroids. I had everything and anything, hundreds and hundreds of boxes of injections and tens of thousands of tablets. I kept a big order book and generally kept enough stock to send most orders back out to customers that same day. I had a great customer base, as everyone knew that by ordering from me they would receive their products within the week.

I would first send customers a price list of normal protein supplements available from any health food shop, but a day later I would send them a separate steroid price list with a different return address.

Most regular customers sent cash via registered post, as mail did sometimes go missing – especially when whoever was sorting my mail at the Post Office realized that most of the envelopes coming to me contained money. I couldn't complain. I was big, I was strong, I was working the doors and I was one probably of the biggest mail order steroid dealers in the UK. I was doing very well. I had worked hard to develop this business and was earning quite a lot of money when, one Monday morning, there was a loud knock on my door.

I wasn't expecting anyone that early and the postman had already been, so I opened the door carefully. There were two guys standing before me: a 40-year-old with a note pad in one hand and pencil in the other, and an older, frightened-looking smaller man standing behind him. The second man had a camera round his neck.

'Yes, can I help you?' I asked suspiciously.

'My name is Goodbody.'

'Good for you,' I said and started to close the door.

'I work for *The Times* newspaper. We are writing a story on steroids in sport.'

'Sorry I can't help you,' I said and was just about to close the door.

'Before you close the door on us, we have already written a story about you, and to be honest it doesn't look good.'

I was shocked. 'What the fuck do you mean?'

'About ten days ago we bought steroids from you by mail order. We wrote a letter with the order saying that we were competitive athletes and asked your advice. You wrote back and told us what we should take.' I had many inquiries, people often asked my advice on courses and dosages and I did remember recently writing such a letter.

'We also have some photos of you leaving your house. We think it might be better if you talk to us and tell us your side before we publish our story.' He finished and waited for my reply.

Why did this happen to me, I thought? Why couldn't I just get on with my life and my business. I wasn't hurting anyone. I certainly didn't force steroids onto anyone. I was always careful to tell people about possible side effects as well as advising them on stacking their steroids and what products worked best together and in what quantities. I had become quite an authority on drugs and frequently used myself as a human guinea pig with new products and alternative stacking methods.

I thought for a few seconds. Should I tell them to piss off and let them write their story, or should I invite them in and put my case? I couldn't deny that they had bought gear from me, and I am sure they had taken some photos, but would they actually write my story if I gave one to them or not? Should I take the chance?

'Ok, best you come in then.'

We sat down in the living room and talked.

Following a high-profile athlete recently failing a drugs test, Mr Goodbody was researching the availability of steroids and hormones within the athletic community. He had me set up. He told me that he had approached a friend of mine who was already buying gear from me. Whether this story was true I never knew and I never discovered who this 'friend' was. If I had he certainly wouldn't be walking the same way. This Mr Goodbody had asked where he could get hold of some gear as he had just started training. This 'friend' of mine suggested me. Knowing that it would be doubtful whether I would sell directly to him without knowing him, he decided to request a price list via the mail, which of course I sent.

He then sent the money by registered post, which I had signed for. He also requested I post the stuff to him via registered post, which I did, putting my return address on the back of the envelope – I didn't want his gear going missing.

I realized how foolish I was because I had not applied my normal procedures of covering my tracks and this knob Goodbody had turned up on my doorstep with all the evidence he needed for a great story.

My lounge was full of gear: on the floor next to his chair I had a carrier bag with at least 20,000 Dianabol tablets, and nearby a crisp box with hundreds and hundreds of ampoules. I was caught good and proper.

I decided to give him a story. I told him how important I thought it was in educating athletes on the use of drugs rather than cover it all up. I talked about how prevalent the use of steroids was in almost every sport, that almost every sportsman from amateur track athletes to professional footballers and rugby players took steroids. I said it was now impossible to rid sport of drugs and was important not to abuse them, so why not teach people how to use them properly? I also talked about counterfeiting and fake drugs; there were many un-scrupulous suppliers out there selling vegetable oil in ampoules and talcum power in tablets, with no positive effects and quite possibly lots of damaging ones. At least I sold genuine products.

I chatted for about 90 minutes, but did he publish anything that I had said? Of course not. He just wrote that I was a big dealer making lots of money selling hundreds of thousands of pounds' worth of steroids and how I was corrupting innocent athletes and youngsters.

Having a photograph of myself, some of the steroids I sold and a price list, with a detailed description of my business on the second page of *The Times*, was just about the worst publicity anyone could wish for. I first knew about the story a few days later when someone had called my mother, who had then called me. I rushed out of the house to the newsagent and bought the newspaper. I couldn't believe what they had written after everything I had talked to them about, after all my moralizing and discussion of what athletes and the public should be told and not told. The media were again talking about steroids as a drug in line with others such as cocaine and heroin and portrayed me as a criminal underworld drug dealer. I carefully read through the article, word by word, sentence by sentence – they didn't print one word of what we had discussed. Not one.

From about midday that day and for the next three days, I must have had almost every newspaper in the UK camped outside my apartment. They were popping business cards through my letterbox and knocking on my door. The phone rang and rang and after the first hour I took the plug out of the wall. I was besieged and had to hide in my apartment with the curtains drawn and the blinds down. For a few days I was a prisoner in my own home.

I carefully burnt my order book with the names and addresses of all my customers and the receipts I had for all the registered and recorded delivery items. I didn't know quite what to do with all the gear I had in the house. I didn't want to get rid of it as it was worth too much money and I knew I couldn't safely leave the house with it either, so I boxed it up and placed it behind a panel under the bath. An obvious place but I couldn't find anywhere else.

After a couple of days, when things had died down and there were fewer knocks on the door, I decided to venture out. I needed some fresh air and food. I cautiously looked through all the windows. There seemed to be no-one suspicious loitering around. I opened the door and looked around again. Nothing. I thought I would now be left alone. I went back inside, packed my gym bags and decided to go training.

Just as I was getting into my car, I was stopped. The

Ministry of Agriculture, Fisheries and Food, in conjunction with the police, had apparently been waiting for me since the story broke. They arrested me and charged me there and then with selling a prescribed drug without a prescription. They had obtained all the information they needed from *The Times*.

They asked if they could take a statement in my apartment. I said no, I hadn't seen my girlfriend for almost a week and I was expecting her that afternoon. She had a key and I really didn't want her finding me sitting there with the officers from the Ministry of Agriculture, Fisheries and Food. She was an air hostess and I was worried that all the bad publicity would affect her job. I told them about her and managed to persuade them to take the statement in their car.

I sat in the back with one official sitting next to me and another in the passenger side. I told them that it was just an exaggerated story I gave the newspaper and that I had only just started selling steroids when I got caught. I had only sold a couple of hundred tablets before Goodbody started his investigation and picked on me. I couldn't blag it too much as they did have evidence from the sale of items to *The Times*.

They charged me with five counts of supplying a drug without prescription. However it would be a civil and not a criminal prosecution, for which I was thankful. This was the reason they didn't need to take me to the police station. The police car sitting opposite was, I presumed, just for backup. I suppose arresting an 18-stone, steroid-dealing doorman was considered fairly high risk.

The guy sitting next to me told me they had to search the house and asked whether I currently had any steroids at home. I thought about it for a few seconds and then said yes, of course but they were for my own use only. He asked where they were, and I told him that they were in the bathroom cabinet. I had always kept a small amount of stock for my own use separate to those I sold.

'What do you have?' He asked.

'Some Deca, about ten vials, some Primobolon, probably five ampoules and some Anavar tablets, maybe about 100 tablets, nothing much.'

I forgot to tell them about the 20-odd thousand tablets and more than 500 ampoules and vials hiding under the bath.

'Any others, anywhere else?' He asked suspiciously.

'No, just in the cabinet,' I replied, light-heartedly. 'Like I said, they are for my own use, it's not illegal and I certainly don't supply any more,' I answered.

'Ok, but we have to check and list those in your possession and take them for testing,' he replied.

'All of them?' I asked, worried that I might lose some stock.

'Afraid so,' he replied.

'But they are for my own use; can't you just leave me a few?' I pleaded, 'I am in the middle of a course and you know how dangerous it is to just stop half way through a course.'

He thought about it briefly and then said, 'Ok, but we have to take one of each item for testing.'

So I led them into the house and straight to the bathroom where I opened the cabinet and showed them what I had. I sat on the bath rim while one of the men counted and named each product while the other made notes. They also listed the batch number and expiry date. He took one of each item, and I had to sign that he was taking it. I was sweating – I really didn't want them looking any further.

'Can we go now?' I asked. 'No offence, but I really don't want my girlfriend coming home and finding you here'.

'Ok, you will be hearing from us again shortly when you will be summoned to court.'

As I bid them farewell, and closed the front door, I almost collapsed with relief. What would I have done, I thought, if they had found the rest of the gear?

When I got to the gym later that day, Chris wasn't there. One of his assistants nervously said hello as I went through to change. He was normally quite chatty, but he said nothing that afternoon so I just changed and started training.

As soon as Chris arrived he literally ran over to me and said that he was sorry but I was barred. I was no longer welcome to train at his health club. He was worried about the reputation of the club, having a known steroid dealer training there. Chris must have known I was taking and selling steroids. He also regularly competed at national level, which was virtually impossible for most athletes to do without taking steroids. Chris liked me training there, we often ate breakfast and trained together, I even had a free membership. But I was now barred.

I finished my workout at my leisure, showered and left without saying another word. I was pissed off but didn't want any trouble. It hadn't been a good day and I didn't want to make it worse by being arrested for battering a gym owner the day I was arrested for selling gear. That wouldn't look too good.

Chris was a decent guy. It was his business, his livelihood and, although I was extremely pissed off, I did understand his dilemma. I was a friend yet business was business and I had no right to take his livelihood away.

I tried another gym nearby. The owner also said the same thing. In fact few places in Norwich would allow me to train. Most barred me – about the only place I could train was in the basement of the Church of England Young Men's Society (CEYMS). They had a really basic dungeon-type dusty gym. It had little machinery, mainly free weights, but it was better than nothing and Julian and I ended up becoming members of CEYMS for many years thereafter. Maybe a Christian charity was more forgiving than everyone else. CEYMS was actually great as after training we could have lunch in the canteen and play a few games of snooker. It was also in the centre of Norwich, which made it very convenient.

I was sick of all the bad attention I was having and so a few weeks after I was nicked and after I had sold all the gear I had hidden in the bathroom, I went to New Zealand. Initially I intended to spend two or three weeks on holiday but I ended up staying a bit longer. A friend and his wife had moved to Hawkes Bay, on the east of the North Island, a year previously. I called and asked if the invitation was still on for a holiday. He said it was, and I packed my things and left.

I went to court about two years later, when they eventually managed to find and serve notice on me. I had evaded them for quite a while, continually moving house and changing address, but eventually they caught up with me and I was fined £2,000.

When leaving the court I had to dodge the local TV cameras and rush to a friend's waiting car. I was on the local TV news again that evening as well as in most major newspapers, including of course *The Times*, the following day.

Being one of the biggest and strongest bodybuilders in Norwich, a doorman and one of the biggest and best-known steroid dealers, I had developed quite a reputation. I set out with the intention of being known in Norwich, of having the reputation of being a bit of a hard-man, somebody – but I exceeded even my own expectations. I was never sure whether people wanted to get to know me because of my reputation or because I was a decent guy. If ever I had a night off I would go out and never have to pay for a thing, I would drink free, get into every club free and would even eat at some restaurants free.

I would be continually acknowledging people as I walked down the street, nodding and waving and saying 'hi'. I was becoming quite a big fish in a relatively little pond and I was enjoying it.

I involved myself in small-time criminality, but nothing major. I wasn't really interested in crime and had no interest in any other drugs apart from steroids. Norwich had its fair share of villains – car thieves, prostitution rings and drug dealers – but I was happy being a known doorman and bodybuilder and was not eager to push into the seriously criminal world. Many of the doormen were known criminals but most eventually got arrested and served time, something I have never done in the UK.

I had quickly moved from working inside the Ritzy to working the front door with Bob Etchalls, which was much better. I didn't mind working inside, it was fun a lot of the time and there was much more going on, but the front door was much better as I had more control over the 'unit' and the customers. I was good at my job. While other doormen came and went, I stayed and became part of the furniture. It was a good job and it enabled me to train hard during the day, play snooker and concentrate on other 'business' activities.

I would steal a few cars, handle occasional goods stolen from warehouses, and issue a few punishments as and when required.

One of the staff at the Ritzy wanted her old car stolen and burnt. She wanted the insurance money so I arranged with her to steal it and set fire to it in a car park in the centre of Norwich. I don't know why I didn't choose a quiet secluded spot but, as usual, I wanted to make a bit of a show.

I had arranged to steal the keys from her handbag and take the car to St Andrew's car park where Billy was to meet me on his motorbike. This job ended up being a farce, where everything that could go wrong, went wrong.

I came to work as usual, signed in and had a chat to the other doormen. I then went to see the woman in question and had a chat to her for a few minutes. Conveniently she had to pop out for something, leaving her bag open on a desk, so I managed to 'steal' her keys without much of a problem.

The car was parked down the street directly opposite, but out of sight of the club. I left my jacket in the staff room and slipped out the back door and rushed round to where her car was parked. I jumped in and turned the key. It didn't start. I tried again and it still didn't start. I was stealing a car to set fire to it and the bloody thing wouldn't start. I had to ask a couple of lads passing by to give me a push.

'You work at the Ritzy don't you?' one of the lads asked.

'Yeah, why?'

'Let us in free and we'll push it for you,' the other said.

'Ok, but you'll have to leave it until after eleven as I have to pop out,' I said. 'Oh, and you didn't see me tonight, did you?'

'See who?' they said and pushed me. I managed to bump start the car and drove the short distance to the car park.

The car park was only a few hundred yards from where the car was parked, and I could have pushed the thing there myself. I finally arrived but couldn't see Billy. I parked and waited. Although it was a Thursday night, thankfully there were not many cars parked nearby. At last Billy roared in and stopped next to me.

'Sorry I am late,' he said over the rumble of the bike's engine, 'fucking bike wouldn't start.'

'Yeah, had the same problem,' I said, tapping the roof of the car. 'Got the petrol?'

'I thought you were getting it?' he said.

'How can I get it? I'm fucking working – you were supposed to get the petrol.'

'No, you said you would.'

'What, and bring a fucking can of petrol to work with me?'

He shrugged. 'Fuck. Ok, jump on, let's go and get some.' So I took out the spare crash helmet from the pannier, put it on, jumped on the back of Billy's bike and set off to the nearest petrol station. We pretended our car had broken down and bought a small jerry can and filled it with petrol.

Finally we got back with a full can, matches and a running motorbike for a quick getaway. We saturated the car, inside and out and led a trail of petrol to where the bike was.

In the distance we saw flashing police lights coming our way. Someone had probably noticed us splashing petrol everywhere and called the police. Billy hurriedly tried to light the match. It wouldn't light. He tried again and again it didn't light. The flashing lights of the police car were getting closer, we could see them turn into the car park.

'Give the fucking matches to me,' I said as I grabbed them off him. Billy jumped on the bike and revved the engine while I lit the last match and threw it onto the path of petrol.

'Let's go!' Billy shouted as the car whooshed into a ball of flame. A car ablaze is phenomenal, and it illuminated everything in sight, including us as we sped away past the police just as they pulled into the car park.

I jumped off the bike at the side of Ritzy and walked round to the front door and calmly stood next to the doormen as though I was working.

'What's that?' one of them asked me as I stood there, probably smelling of petrol and sweat.

'Fire, I expect,' I replied and walked past him into the club, with vapour rising gently from my shirt.

We were lucky to have got away and vowed that we would be more prepared next time, but we never set any more cars on fire after that night.

CHAPTER FOUR

Knowledge

Being threatened is part of working the doors. We would always have threats against us, either from those that we turned away or from those we would throw out or batter. Most threats were made in drunken anger and nothing ever came from them. Things were quickly forgotten once those that had made the threats sobered up or realized they had been wrong. Threats against us were part of the job and we rarely took any notice.

However there were occasions when Bob Etchalls and I were threatened on the front door at the Ritzy and these threats, we felt, were real.

One such threat came when Bob and I turned away two brothers of a big family in Norwich. We decided we had to strike first, before the threats against us went any further and got out of hand. This family were quite well known, farmers and factory workers, scumbags and dumb idiots. Individually they are nothing but in their family pack they were a force to be reckoned with. Altogether there were eight brothers, two of which Bob turned away from the Ritzy. They weren't that drunk but we didn't want them in the club as they really were troublemakers, so we gave the excuse that they were both too drunk. They were immediately abusive on the door and made the usual threats but left without trouble. However they must have taken offence at something Bob had said (probably the bit about them all being scumbags, inbred knobs who fuck each other as well as their mother), as word on the street spread that they were coming back the following weekend in force to storm the door. Even though we had a good strong team, eight brothers plus their uncles, cousins, aunties, scumbag friends, friends of scumbag friends and their mother would be too much for us all to handle. It would be a bloodbath, a huge brawl that we didn't really want, so Bob decided to pay a little visit to the eldest brother and warn him off.

'What are you doing this morning?' Bob asked on the phone early one Tuesday.

'Training, then nothing much. Why?' I replied sleepily. I had just woken up.

'Fancy going for a little drive?'

'Now or later?'

'I can pick you up in town after you've been training, say eleven-thirty?'

'I'll be at CEYMS so pick me up at twelve.'

In the car Bob told me what he intended to do. We would go and have a quiet chat to the eldest brother, who seemed to control all the others. We would talk to him 'civilly' and 'politely' tell him the facts – that his brothers were indeed drunk and abusive and so we couldn't let them in the Ritzy. They had threatened us and now we were coming to resolve the situation before it got out of hand. We would tell him that we didn't really want any trouble with their family.

'And where are we meeting him?' I asked, slightly confused.

'Well . . .' Bob hesitated, 'we are not actually going to meet him.' He laughed. I shook my head in despair – I knew that Bob was up to something. Civil? Polite? That wasn't at all like the Bob I knew.

'So, where are we going then?'

'We are going to where he works.'

'And?' I asked.

'And, well let's see,' he replied.

Bob had found that the eldest brother worked as a machinist at a factory on a large industrial estate on the outskirts of Norwich. We were going to check it out and see if we could visit him where he worked.

'That would really piss him off, wouldn't it?' Bob laughed.

It didn't look a big place. The factory had a small reception office to the left of the building and a loading bay to the far right which faced the road. The loading bay seemed to lead straight into the factory, as we could see people working through thick strips of plastic that hung over an opening. There were a couple of small trucks parked outside, and quite a few cars and bikes in the car park on the left of the building. We also noticed there was no CCTV.

'How are we going to find him in there?' I asked Bob, pointing at the building.

'We just go in and ask.'

'What, just go straight in and ask where he is?' I couldn't believe we were actually going into the factory.

'Let's try and blag it,' he said. 'Same time tomorrow?'

'Ok, why not,' I answered. I could think of other things I would prefer to be doing Wednesday morning but it was going to be a laugh.

'And wear shirt and trousers, we have to look official,' he added.

'Bob, how can you ever look official?' Bob was the most unofficial guy I knew and at 18 stone it was also hard for me to look business-like.

The next day Bob picked me up at the same time and place. He had brought a couple of clipboards, some blank sheets of paper and a couple of pens. He also brought a torch.

I looked at him and laughed.

'We have to try to look the part.' He smiled, but I was right. Looking at Bob in his white shirt and grey doorman's trousers, he could never look official.

We drove to the industrial estate and parked the car down

the road a little and walked to the main entrance. We took a deep breath, went through the main doors and swiftly passed the receptionist, greeting her with a warm, 'Good afternoon.' We walked straight through and into the factory, not giving her any time to ask questions – we gave her the impression we knew where we were going.

Once inside it seemed as though no-one really took any notice of us, they all seemed preoccupied with their factory work. There were about 20 men and women operating different types of machinery. I went up to the first person I saw walking down an aisle and said smilingly, 'Err, excuse me.'

'Yes?'

'Do you know where we can find err . . .' I looked down at my blank sheet of paper, 'Mr Sammy Greaves,' and looked up at her.

'Sammy who?' she said.

'Sammy G– .'

'Well, I know he isn't on this section, try sheet metal, through the screen over there,' she said, pointing to a clear plastic screen dividing the unit into a separate section.

'Thank you.'

We walked off, through the screen and into sheet metal. Again, no-one seemed to be bothered as to who we were, they looked up at us with brief curiosity and continued with their tasks. Without looking too suspicious we carefully scanned the area for the man. Suddenly Bob tapped me on the shoulder. He had noticed Sammy in a far corner operating a drill bit. He was concentrating on drilling patterned holes on a square sheet of metal. He was wearing eye goggles and didn't notice us approaching.

At the same time as Bob noticed Sammy, I noticed two guys in a glass-partitioned office at the far end of the factory look over and point at us. I could see that they were talking, probably wondering who we were. I noticed one of them shrugged as they both turned and left the office.

'We've got company,' I whispered to Bob and we stood behind Sammy.

Sammy must have sensed someone was behind him as he looked round. He was seated on a low stool and turned to see Bob and myself towering over him. He had a look of absolute fear on his face. He could not believe we had come straight into the factory, passed everyone and had found him at work.

'We need to chat,' Bob started. 'Your brothers were turned away because they were drunk and yet you have threatened to come back and sort us all out. Who the fuck do you think you are? If you want a fucking war we will give you a fucking war. Is that what you want, a fucking war? Because if it is, we will fuck you. We know where you live, what cars you drive, where you all work, if it is a war you want then a war you will fucking have. Do you fucking understand?' Bob's voice was raised.

'No, no, no, I didn't mean it,' he squealed. He had nowhere to run. 'Please, everything's cool.'

'Everything's not fucking cool,' Bob continued. He was making the most of the limited time we had to make our point. 'So unless you and your brothers back off we will give you more fucking grief than you can ever fucking imagine, do you understand?'

He cowered down, covering his head with his hands as Bob got closer to him. Some hard-man he was. Just as Bob was going to smack him we heard from behind us, 'Can I help you lads?' We turned to see a couple of suited men, probably managers or supervisors, standing behind us.

'No, just having a quick word with our pal here,' Bob said in a cheerful voice, patting Sammy's back hard. 'We were just leaving,' and then Bob quickly turned to Sammy and said, 'If you want to take it further we will be back, or you can just leave it, it is up to you.'

'Excuse me,' one of the suits said.

'Yes?' I replied.

'Who gave you permission to come onto the shop floor?'

'He did,' Bob butted in, pointing to Sammy. 'Said we could come to see him any time we wanted.' As we turned to leave Bob said to the two supervisors, 'Can you show us the way out please?' The smaller of the two pointed down the aisle we had come from.

'Thanks,' Bob said and we walked. Just as we were leaving the sheet metal section we turned to look at Sammy. He seemed in confrontation with the two supervisors – probably being questioned or being given a good bollocking.

'So we were going to "calmly" and "politely" resolve the situation before it got out of hand?' I laughed at Bob as we left the factory.

'Did I say that?' Bob replied. I knew that nothing was ever calm and polite with Bob.

I had been at the Ritzy for just over a year when the old general manager got moved on and a new one started. Like many new managers, he was immediately disliked by most of the staff. He had his own way of running *his* business, which was completely different from the previous manager. There were many of us at the Ritzy that just didn't like change, but most of all the doormen.

In my experience general managers that have worked the doors are completely different in style and character to general managers that have come from university or from a liquor and bar background. I can tell them apart almost instantly. This new manager had just graduated and this was his second unit, the first when he was deputy manager in Nottingham. It was evident from the very beginning that he knew nothing about running the doors. From the onset he seemed to want to make his mark, to show us that he was the boss. He was an arrogant, high-handed knob that thought he was a lot better than he was. But he was our manager nevertheless and while we were still working we had a duty to him and to the club. Well, sort of.

The second weekend there, he had asked three of the doormen to help him move house. They would have to go with him to Nottingham in a hired van, pack and load his things and return to Norwich that same day. The doormen he chose were not the most ethical of guys and when they realized they couldn't take their own car, as the manager refused to pay them petrol, they got pissed off. It was made worse by the fact that they had to travel in the back of the van. Although he had thoughtfully included a couple of old mattresses, the van was empty on the journey there so every time it took a turn the doormen would roll around the back uncomfortably. Coming back the van was almost full which made them cramped and even more uncomfortable. They were not happy bunnies.

To cap it all, at the end of a very long day and tiring day, after they had unloaded all his things and placed them neatly in his new house, the manager said 'thanks guys' and that he would add the hours worked that day onto their wages the following week. That meant it wouldn't be cash, as they expected. It wasn't looking good for the new manager as the doormen vowed to take revenge.

A few evenings later, while the manager was at work, a couple of the doormen decided to burgle his house. They had both signed in for work as usual, then immediately disappeared out the back exit. It was a big unit and everyone was preoccupied with their own tasks – no-one would notice two missing doormen for a couple of hours.

It was true, no-one had noticed they had gone, no-one had asked where they were, no-one tried to find them for any reason and equally no-one noticed when they were back, they just calmly returned and continued working as normal, signing out at the end of the night. However that night they went home with most of the manager's household possessions in the back of their cars. They stole his TV, video recorder, videos, camera, money, some credit cards, various household utensils, watches and some jewellery, a fax machine and other bits.

The manager was devastated. He could not believe that had been burgled a few days after moving to Norwich. Being the concerned and friendly chap I was I tried to console him a little and told him that Norwich did indeed have quite a high crime rate, but worse was to come.

The new manager decided to start a kids' night on Monday evenings. From the very beginning it proved extremely popular. There were no other kids' nights at any other nightclub in Norwich, and having such an event at the Ritzy, the biggest and most well-known venue in the area, attracted hundreds of children from all over the region.

We wanted to appear fairly casual that night and so were very relaxed in attitude and appearance. We didn't wear the normal uniform, just jeans and sweatshirts with the word 'security' on the back. Also, of course, we could not be as aggressive and forceful as we could on normal trading nights – but we certainly felt like it as sometimes the kids were murder. It was a very busy event and sometimes fairly hard to control.

Apart from the opening night, the manager never actually worked the kids' nights, he just assigned an assistant to run the evening. They were pissed off and resentful for having to work and spent most of the evening in the office playing solitaire on the computer.

One condition for the council granting a licence to hold a kids' night was that all alcohol had to be taken off the shelves and stored safely. All the bottled beers were to be kept in the cellar, the spirits in a separate store cupboard.

On the third Monday, the doormen decided that burgling the manager's house wasn't enough, so they decided to steal all the kegs and bottled beer from the packed cellar. The cellar was near the rear exit doors. Because of the huge turnover, a cellar-man normally worked full-time on normal nights and managed and re-stocked the cellar during the day. Because no alcohol could be served on Monday nights there was no need for him to work so there was no-one looking after the cellar and its contents.

One of the doormen worked during the day delivering meats throughout the county, so he had access to a large truck. Once the night was in full swing and the assistant manager was tucked away up in his office playing on his computer, the doormen smashed the lock of the cellar and quickly loaded the wagon that had been reversed up against the back door. They completely cleared it of all its contents. There was nothing left; they even took the gas bottles.

Apparently they took about 20 full kegs of beer and around 50 cases of bottled beer. The police were called, we all gave statements but of course no-one witnessed a thing – all the doormen were busy minding the rowdy children and CCTV wasn't widely used in nightclubs at that time. We were all bollocked severely for not noticing what had happened. However, to compensate we all had a wonderful Christmas drinking bottled beer and watching some very good films on video.

I couldn't imagine why, but the new manager was getting pissed off with what was going on at the Ritzy. He couldn't blame anybody specifically because he had neither proof nor evidence. There were no fingerprints and obviously everyone denied everything. He couldn't easily get rid of us as many had been there for over a year and we had certain rights. So he decided to make things very difficult for everyone instead.

He took more control of all of his staff, but above all the doormen. He obviously thought that we were the ones most likely to accomplish these kinds of criminal acts (I don't know how he came to that conclusion).

Instead of touring the unit in pairs, he allocated us positions and we had to remain in those positions all night. We were only allowed to change or move position when he authorized us to do so. In this way he knew where the doormen were all the time. If we weren't where we were supposed to be he would immediately notice and come looking for us. He was on our backs even when we went to take a piss.

He also cut our hours. Instead of all the doormen starting at 8.30 p.m., he would stagger our starting times, which meant some doormen lost up to ten hours a week from their already meagre wages. He also did away with staff dinners. To doormen, staff dinners were important and we particularly appreciated them. For those of us that were heavily into our training, five or six hours without food was a hardship that we just could not endure. Lastly, he stopped free drinks, allowing us only squash. However, we were now no longer allowed to be seen drinking on the nightclub floor and we had to go to the staff room every time we wanted refreshment, but we couldn't leave our designated spot without his permission. It was becoming a nightmare but we all knew what he was up to – he wanted to get rid of all the old doormen. Once we had all gone he would relax the unrealistic and unnecessary restrictions.

It did the trick – one by one we all left.

By that time I had a good reputation in Norwich; almost everyone knew who I was and what I was capably of doing. I was training hard and studying full contact karate three days a week – technically I was getting better and better and emotionally harder and harder. I could certainly handle myself, although I always tried to remain humble and modest. I have never believed in exaggeration or boastfulness. What made me particularly cruel was that I really didn't care what I did to any opponent – I had no morals when it came to violence and I would do anything as long as I never lost a fight.

Bob Etchalls was my mentor. He taught me everything I needed to know, and over the years I have refined and developed my knowledge and experience based on his initial instruction and good advice. Over the years I have remained good friends with Bob and, like me, he is still doing the doors.

Bob taught me many important things, things that I still use to this day and which I adapt and adjust according to my situation or environment. These basic, simple procedures have assisted me time and again and without some of his initial instruction I would have surely taken more beatings than I had, especially at the beginning of my career. Bob was a good teacher and I learnt fast. I suppose without Bob I would have learnt eventually, but it would have been harder and a lot more painful.

Time and again he would advise me never to stand directly in front of an opponent in a confrontation. Most people are right handed and will throw the first punch with their right arm. If you stand directly in front of an aggressor, his first punch can be thrown quickly, on target and with little warning. However, by standing slightly to the attacker's left, fractionally more time is given to react, as well as the attacker having slightly further to throw their punch.

Bob also showed me that the best way to escort someone out of the club was by walking behind them to their right and by holding their right arm, just above the elbow, with my left hand. If they attempted something it was possible to feel it happen early. Also their right arm is being controlled, which leaves my right arm free to punch, throw or grab as necessary to stop the attack.

Another very useful tip when confronting two or three opponents was to always take out the biggest or hardest-looking first – even if he was not the one mouthing off. By taking him out, Bob said, it frightens the others and they may not retaliate if their hard, tough-looking mate is out cold on the floor.

I enjoyed martial arts and studied karate primarily to improve my fitness and general fighting skills, but I soon found that on the door karate is practically useless. As a sport most martial arts such as karate, kung fu, and tae kwon do are fantastic. They are great catalysts for personal growth and development and excellent for learning self-control, self-discipline and respect. But in a street fight martial arts are only helpful if the practitioner is particularly skilful and with very high grades. Street fighting is totally different. Street fighting is vicious – martial arts are not, at least not in training. In a street fight there are no rules, you must do what you must to survive. I once saw two third dan wing chun experts beaten by one good streetfighter with three swift and devastating punches.

When I first started at Ritzy, Bob told me that I should practise two or three good holds and locks time and time again. He said that in most situations on the door there would rarely be any need to use more. By mastering two or three, onlookers would think that I had greater skills than I actually had. And that is exactly what I did when I first started.

Bob also told me, time and again, that is was so important when stopping two or three people on the door for the doormen not to stand together. Although standing together initially seems like a good idea, it can give an aggressor one bigger and easier target, as opposed to two smaller ones. So, when I worked with Bob, we always stood away from each other, keeping an eye on both the aggressors and ourselves.

In a potentially violent situation, too many doormen can sometimes provoke aggression and aggravate problems, turning what could have been a simple affair into a brawl. Sometimes it is wise for just one doorman to go into potential trouble and to try and diplomatically quell any disturbance, with the other doormen stood slightly aside carefully watching and assessing what is going on. The other doormen can then quickly step in if aggression escalates.

It is also very wise to have some sort of silent signal between doormen, a signal that alerts others that assistance is immediately required. By scratching my head and keeping my hand on my head, my colleagues knew that I needed help, and that it wasn't just a normal scratch.

There are many doormen with huge egos and these are the ones that cause the most problems. Younger doormen are the worst – they seem to think they have something to prove. I was extremely violent on the doors but I rarely started trouble. Bob was the same. He was a really hard man and a nasty fighter but I never once saw him start trouble. He would always have a great deal of respect for everyone and in return everyone had great respect for Bob.

I had offers from most other clubs and pubs in Norwich to run their doors, but, until the new manager at the Ritzy arrived, I was quite happy where I was. I was earning a wage, there were always plenty of women, I had plenty of free time and it was a fun and lively place to work. It was never boring. But I'd had enough of the Ritzy, and it was time to move on.

Julian and I moved across the road to Hy's nightclub, where we spent a boring and not particularly active six months. The nightclub was named after its owner, Hy Kurzner, a local Jewish businessman who also owned a couple of other restaurants in Norwich as well as a pizza place next to the club. As our supper we were allowed to have a free pizza any night we worked. I just loved ham and pineapple pizza, so every single night my supper consisted of pizza and, coupled with the lack of activity in the club, I quickly put on weight.

As usual I was still screwing around. Working in the clubs was my idea of heaven. I didn't meet different women every night, but almost every week there would be someone new in my bed. Blondes, brunettes, black, white, fat, thin – I didn't care.

I started seeing a girl called Tamsin who was working at the pizza restaurant attached to the nightclub. I had been out with her for a couple of weeks when I met another girl called Stephanie. They were both nice girls and very attractive and I didn't want to leave either of them so I thought that I could quite easily see them both. Why not? They wouldn't find out, why should they? Tamsin worked evenings at the restaurant and Stephanie had a day job. I thought they could come and go at different times of the day and night and never meet. I hadn't yet slept with either of them but had got past the first hurdle.

One afternoon I arranged to meet Tamsin at Brambles, a decent local café in the centre of town, at 4 p.m. before she started her shift at the restaurant. I then arranged to meet Stephanie later at around 6 p.m. when she finished work. Things were looking good.

The café was upstairs, while downstairs was a card and gift shop. Entrance to the café was through the shop. Before going up to meet Tamsin, I paused at the shop and bought two cards, both exactly the same. I thought I would write something nice and romantic to both of them – actually I thought I'd write the same thing in both cards and post them later.

After paying for the cards I walked up the stairs and into the café. As I walked in, sitting together at the same table by the door, were both girls.

Oh fuck, I thought. What was I going to do? There was no escape. They had both seen me come in – I couldn't do anything apart from sit with them.

'Coffee?' I nervously asked.

'No,' Tamsin replied with a look to kill, 'you're not staying.' That was telling me, wasn't it?

'You know, I called my best friend Steph this morning,' Tamsin said, indicating across the table, 'and told her of my new boyfriend. I told her he worked with me at Hy's. She also told me about her new boyfriend who funnily enough also worked at Hy's. So we decided to meet for a girlie chat and . . .'

'How could you?' Stephanie butted in. She looked both sad and angry.

'What's in here?' Tamsin demanded, snatching the paper bag. She turned it upside-down and out dropped the two cards.

I was stuck for words. I had been caught red-handed and there was nothing I could do. I was red with embarrassment and wished the ground would just open up and swallow me.

'So you don't want a coffee then?' I stammered.

'Fuck off,' Stephanie said, and I did.

I got bored very quickly at Hy's, as there was never any trouble. I needed action, a challenge, and it was not going to be found at this venue. The guys I worked with were great, but there was just nothing happening. We ran the door from a small dingy reception area, which was at the bottom of a flight of stairs leading up to the club. It kept us separate from the noise, atmosphere and customers. After about 11.30 p.m. and once everyone was in, it was a long, boring and very quiet night. The manager, a camp, slimy-looking, bald headed queen took a fancy to me and once slapped my arse as I walked in front of him up the stairs into the club.

'Do that ever again and I will rip your fucking head off,' I threatened. I was never racist or sexist or any other '-ist' come to think of it – anyone can be whoever and whatever they want to be as long as they didn't affect or interfere with my life – but it was obvious he wanted my arse, which made me uncomfortable and embarrassed. He never slapped my arse again but continued giving me snide and suggestive comments. Needless to say he was another manager I didn't like much.

Once he had left the Ritzy, Bob Etchalls started up a small door security company and asked me to join him. At that time in Norwich there were no other security companies – every venue employed its own doormen. There were never any women working the door either. Back in the mid-1980s the doors were an extremely violent environment and I doubt there were many women that could have of coped or enjoyed working in such places. The door was a purely male domain and it wasn't until much later, in Manchester, that I came across doorwomen.

Bob formed the first door company in Norwich and began to provide doormen to various clubs and pubs around the city. Apart from the guys Bob sent to work the doors, the clubs paid for his name. Having Bob Etchalls running the door was a deterrent itself. Bob also had a couple of pubs that just paid him a weekly fee without the provision of any doormen. They rarely had problems but felt safer with the knowledge that, should there ever be a problem, they could call Bob and he would turn up in force.

Norwich is a quiet and pretty city of about 120,000 residents. It has a Church of England and Roman Catholic cathedral, a Norman castle and a big market in the centre of the city. It has a massive student population, as the University of East Anglia is situated on the outskirts, and there are two major hospitals as well as two large psychiatric hospitals and a BUPA private hospital, so there is also a large nursing population. It is the home of Norwich Union, one of the largest insurance companies in the UK, and the city is surrounded by lots of small market towns and villages.

Its primary industries are blue-collar and agricultural but Norwich also attracts quite a high number of tourists in the summer, both to the city and to the Norfolk Broads, as well as overspill tourists from the coastal resort of Great Yarmouth, Norfolk's answer to Blackpool. At that time Norwich also had about ten nightclubs and, they say, a pub for every day of the week.

Like any other big city, Norwich has its hoodlums, yobs, drunks and drug addicts, its prostitution and organized crime, but neither Bob nor myself got involved with the darker side of Norwich's crime scene. We were big fish in the small world of the doors, but that was about it. We neither cared about nor bothered with major crime or drugs. We knew of those that did – acquaintances that were involved in bank fraud or counterfeit money, in car ringing and drug pushing, but we had little to do with them, other than an occasional polite acknowledgment. They didn't interfere with the doors, and we didn't interfere with their business. Sometimes crime overlapped and we would hear of a big criminal working the door, but it was rare. However one such person is worthy of note as we had no idea of the true nature of his business until after he had left the doors.

Charlie was a good-looking, slightly built, 30-something, tough-looking doorman who joined us for a short while at the Ritzy. He was a quietly-spoken, humble guy who rarely got into trouble. I realized he wasn't working at the Ritzy because he needed the money or a job when I walked back with him to his car one evening after work.

As we chatted he took out his car keys and initially I thought he was getting into a clapped-out old Mini. But he walked straight past the Mini and stood next to a brand new Lotus Esprit. My jaw dropped.

'Is this yours?' I asked incredulously.

'Uh huh,' replied Charlie quietly unlocking the door.

'So what the fuck are you doing at the Ritzy?' I asked. It would have probably taken ten years working there to save for a car like his.

'I have my reasons,' said Charlie.

'Well it isn't money,' I laughed. 'Can I sit in it?' I had always wanted a Lotus, ever since I lovingly put a poster of an Esprit on my wall at my father's house.

I sat in the car, looked around, fiddled with the controls and marvelled at the leather interior.

'So?' I asked Charlie.

'So?'

It was hard to get two words out of Charlie – he just came,

did the job and went home again. He was a nice guy but rarely said a word.

'So?' I asked again.

'So, I have to go, it's late. See you next week.'

Charlie never told me why he worked at Ritzy, and a few weeks later he left. About a month after that, I was casually chatting to an acquaintance at the gym, who knew everyone and everything, and Charlie's name cropped up. It appeared that Charlie had to show the Inland Revenue some sort of a legal and legitimate job, as they were making a meticulous investigation into his activities. He lived in a beautiful detached house on Newmarket Road, the most expensive road in Norwich. He drove a new Lotus and had a couple of other more modest but still fairly expensive cars. He also had a small villa in Spain, but he didn't have a job. Until he started at Ritzy, he was claiming the dole.

Apparently Charlie's uncle had a car breakers yard somewhere between Cambridge and London, with a very busy car crusher. Allegedly Charlie's uncle was making an extremely good living picking up executive cars around the UK and taking them to his uncle's yard where they would be crushed and never seen again. He charged the car's owner twenty percent of the street value of the vehicle, which would have to be paid in advance. The owners could then report the car as stolen and claim on the insurance – with a guarantee that the car would never turn up anywhere else.

Unluckily for Charlie, on the one day he bought the Lotus into town he was seen and recognized by one of the dole officers and an investigation was started. There was no evidence that he was working and earning money, and he had no bank savings, so the DHSS could not prosecute but they forwarded their file on to the Inland Revenue. Charlie had to quickly sign off and find some sort of job, anything, so he worked at the Ritzy for a short while.

I never knew what happened to Charlie or whether he eventually got caught, he simply disappeared from the Norwich scene and I never saw him around town again.

CHAPTER FIVE

The Clean-up

Bob Etchalls asked me to join him and his recently formed door company. He had a few contracts at venues in town, one of which needed some serious work. It would be rough, hard work and the money wasn't that good but working with Bob was always fun and a laugh and I said yes without hesitation. I needed some excitement and to use my fists again. I felt myself getting stale, getting complacent.

We were asked to clean up a sleazy, drug-infested shithole of a pub on the outskirts of the city. It attracted mainly the sleazier student type, as well as a small group of scumbag bikers, dope dealers and drug addicts. A new manager had been appointed to try and clean the venue up, ready for a refurbishment. It was his first unit as a manager so he was desperate to show his bosses what he could do. He also wanted to do it without bringing any undue attention to the place, as the police already knew about the type of customer it attracted.

The manager gave us carte blanche to run the door as we saw fit, but stressed that we should call the police only in a real emergency and when there was a situation we really couldn't handle. Was there such a thing, we laughingly asked ourselves? Now that was the sort of manager we all liked to work for.

The manager was quite happy to maintain and build on the student market. With cheap beer and dancing, it would be great for business if he could turn the unit into a purely student venue. But first we had to get rid of all the scum that was also getting in.

There would be three of us working the door three nights a week from Thursday until Saturday. Bob brought in another experienced ex-Ritzy doorman, Tandy. Bob knew Tandy very well – they had worked together at other doors before. Although stocky and as strong as a horse, he wasn't tall but he had a face that his mother still cried over. Tandy wasn't a handsome man and didn't say much, but when he did he had a wicked sense of humour. I liked Tandy and, like us, he didn't give a fuck about anyone. He simply did not care about anything and would go into any situation, no matter how many there were of them or how violent it got. He just loved it – he loved violence and loved using his fists. Actually he was mad, off his tiny trolley, but Bob rightly thought he would be great for this venue, as we were to soon find out.

Our first night was just an assessment night – we stood on the front door and watched carefully who was coming in. It was decided we wouldn't stop anyone, we would just observe what was going on and, after a detailed discussion at the end of the evening, plan our strategy for the following weekend. We were all appalled at some of the people that came into the venue. They were the worst kind of drugged-up scumbags anyone could imagine: drug dealers and drug addicts, bikers and the more sleazy student element. It was going to be a tough job but we were all up for it and couldn't wait for the following weekend.

At the end of that first evening we sat down with the manager and discussed exactly what he wanted for the venue and which customers he did and didn't want in. We also talked in detail about what we, as doormen, would have to do to help get him there. He didn't mind the students – we agreed that most of them were pretty harmless and provided the basis of the income for the venue – but he didn't want the dealers, addicts or any bikers whatsoever.

That first night we had witnessed three guys shoot up in the toilets as well as a line of people out of their drugged-up minds sitting outside on the pavement along the wall of the venue. We had also noticed three or four scumbag-looking dealers beckoning customers to the toilets and had seen a fight between two dirty bikers. One took out a switchblade but their friends pulled them apart and they left. Last but not least, at the end of the night there was a bottling. And this all took place on one Saturday night at a venue with a capacity of only 250, in the respectable and conservative city of Norwich. It wasn't surprising that the new manager was frightened, and I think he regretted taking on such a venue and was desperate to clean it up.

Being the idiots we were, we told him not to worry and assured him we would clean the place up as quickly as possible.

We decided from then on it would be compulsory that everyone entering the venue would be searched. In those days no-one used rubber gloves and so we had to be very cautious if we put our hands in pockets, although we would try our best not to. We would stop the searches once we had deterred most of the dealers and drug users. The main drug was cannabis; Ecstasy wasn't even known, and students could rarely afford anything else. However we would also be looking for LSD and amphetamines, as well as the occasional bit of heroin.

We decided that any drug dealer would be permanently banned and handed over to the police. The manager didn't mind us calling the police if we caught a drug dealer as that, he thought, would look good for the venue. We knew the local supplier and he was not a man to be messed with, so we would treat the dealers with caution and diplomacy. We didn't want a war with him. We also knew that some of his dealers were so desperate they would kill for their patch and hoped that searching would stop them coming in pretty quickly.

We also decided that if we found someone shooting up in the toilets we wouldn't batter them senseless, which is what we all wanted to do, but just escort them out peacefully. It wasn't worth getting into a fight with drug addicts – they would have dirty syringes which could be used as weapons and, when high, many don't feel pain.

The bikers would be a problem – with them we would definitely have to work for our money. A hard-looking bunch dressed in their leathers, steel toe-capped boots, scummy, dirty jeans and long unwashed hair. We decided the quickest and easiest way of getting rid of them was to implement a basic dress code, but this would only work in conjunction with a big 'Under New Management' sign. This would be our excuse – new manager, new rules and 'we are only doing our job mate'.

The good thing about not doing anything the first night was that no-one expected us to do anything the following night, so they were all in for a big shock.

All week the three of us were scheming and planning and we probably spoke to each other every single day leading up to that first Thursday night. None of us could wait for the week to pass, we all wanted to get stuck in. But we were also all a little nervous nevertheless.

The venue was mainly a pub, but with a dance floor and DJ downstairs. Thursday, Friday and Saturday night it had an entertainment licence until 1 a.m. Because it was primarily a pub it was also open all day but didn't get much business. The evening trade didn't start until about 8 p.m., and generally at around teatime there was no-one in the unit at all.

We arranged to meet up at 7 p.m. in the small lounge area upstairs. It was an hour before we were due to start, giving us enough time to go through anything we needed to before the customers started to arrive.

As we sat down the manager brought up some coffees. We knew we might be fighting that night so we were dressed very casually – we were all wearing black jeans, hard, military-style black boots and black sweaters with 'Security' on the back. We also had black bomber jackets, as it was getting cold in the evenings and we would be spending most of the night outside the front door. Tandy had also brought with him a small duffel bag – we were to learn that Tandy had spent most of the week hunting for suitable weapons, bless his little heart.

Once the manager left us to our coffee I looked down at Tandy's bag.

'What's in there?'

'Oh, just a few things we might be needing,' came his reply, 'I've been quite busy this week.' He sat there and sipped his coffee while we looked at him expectantly.

'Well come on, show us,' urged Bob. Tandy shrugged and picked the bag up and banged it down on the table, making a loud metallic thud. I looked at Bob, he looked at me and we started to smile.

'Well, hmm.' Tandy, a man of few words, didn't quite know where to start. 'Firstly, a couple of nice little dusters, one I have altered slightly.'

As if knuckledusters alone were not enough, on one of them Tandy had welded small metal studs. Bob picked one up, felt its weight and slipped it over his fingers. He started to laugh.

Some coshes and three extendable metal batons also came out of his little bag and were placed on the table, and this time I started laughing. 'And something I made earlier from an old toilet roll holder and condom.' By then Bob and I were in tears of laughter as we imagined Tandy out shopping. 'Three expertly crafted gloves made from the finest leather, and other things.' But these were no ordinary gloves, these little buggers were single right-hand gloves and had strips of tiny spikes sewn along the inside of the palm and fingers. 'Marvellous for giving someone a good slap,' he said, demonstrating. I don't think I have ever laughed on the doors so much as I did that first Thursday night before we started work.

Deadly serious, Tandy looked around at us crying with laughter. 'What's up?' he asked.

'How the fuck are we going to use these?' I said, waving one of the gloves in his face.

'Well, I don't know, do I?' he replied, genuinely confused and looking a bit hurt. 'I thought they might come in useful.'

'You're fucking mad,' Bob and I said in unison. Tandy smiled.

'Yeah,' he said, his broadening smile showing the gap in his front teeth. 'I know.' He was mad and both Bob and I could imagine him sitting in some dimly lit room like a madman, laughing to himself as he carefully sewed the strips of spikes onto his gloves.

We hurriedly stuffed Tandy's toys back in the bag as we noticed the manager walking over.

'Everything alright lads? What's the joke?'

'Tandy's the fucking joke,' I said, trying to calm down and stop myself laughing. With his foot, Tandy discreetly nudged the bag further under his chair.

The manager look confused, not sure what was going on.

'Ok, down to business,' said Bob, wiping tears from his eyes.

The evening started fairly calmly. Apparently Thursdays were never very busy and we had hoped that by being really strict that first night, word would quickly spread so by the time Friday and Saturday came, most scumbags would have heard that this place was under new management and there was a stricter door policy. We were hoping that the worst of the worst would realize that they would no longer be allowed in and should take their patronage elsewhere.

When we said it was a rough place, it was. About fifty percent of those that were in the venue the previous Saturday night would never get in again. The manager knew this and was fully prepared for an initial steep decline in business. The other fifty percent were ok – fairly decent students and student types, and a few generally harmless weirdoes and eccentrics.

From the minute we started work we searched everyone that came in. A queue quickly formed as both Tandy and I searched while Bob controlled the front door.

Inside we had placed two tables each side of the front door, set back slightly. This meant that Bob could usher two people in for searching, sending one over to me and the other to Tandy, while he could also hold the queue as well as monitoring what was happening outside.

We saw a number of people approach the venue, realize that we were searching and quickly disappear without actually joining the queue. We tried to clock them but soon lost track as it happened so often. It was only possible to remember those that had a particularly distinctive appearance.

We had a few sarcastic comments and a few refusals but most customers didn't actually mind us searching – a few even said it was a good idea and were fairly pleasant about it. Most people freely emptied their pockets on the tables. Those that refused we gave an ultimatum – either get searched or don't come in. We knew it wouldn't be too long before someone would be aggressive and we were constantly prepared.

The first to complain was a dealer I recognized from the previous week. He passed Bob on the door as his appearance wasn't that bad and Bob didn't recognize him. I called him over to the table for searching.

'I am a regular,' he said and attempted to walk straight past.

'I'm regular too, I shit every morning right after breakfast, now empty your pockets please.' I pointed towards the table. I wanted to remain polite but a little sarcastic.

'No, you don't understand, I come 'ere every week, I don't have to be searched.' He was talking too close to my face for comfort. I backed off and moved to his left side a little, again indicating towards the table.

'Everyone has to be searched, new manager, new rules,' I replied. We didn't have time to go through all this, we were getting busy and the queue was growing rapidly.

'Well get the manager, he knows me,' he demanded.

'I am not going to argue with you, either get searched or you don't come in, simple,' I smiled. No more talk, we would have to get rid of him soon.

'Fuck you, I'll be back in a minute,' he said aggressively and started to walk off.

'Listen mate,' I said, 'find somewhere else to drink from now on, you are not welcome here.' I was now in the mood to fuck him right off.

'What do you mean?' His voiced rose and he turned and looked straight at me, his arms straightened and away from his body a little, his fists clenched in a typically recognizable pre-fight stance. I was now on my guard. Just then another scumbag joined him. 'What's up?' he asked menacingly.

Tandy stood directly behind me with Bob slightly to my right, between me and the queue.

'Nothing is up,' I said staring at his mate. 'Your mate is no longer welcome here.'

'Why, what has he done?'

I had had enough.

'Listen, things have changed around here,' Bob said, 'you have to drink somewhere else, now piss off, ok?'

The two started swearing at us again but we ignored them. They hadn't yet pushed things so far that we felt we had to batter them, they were just being verbally abusive but nothing we couldn't easily ignore. We were not going to answer or argue with them any more – we had a queue waiting to come in.

Foolishly I turned my attention away from them for a few seconds, leaving them standing muttering together to my left.

I remained at the door while Bob walked down the queue, assessing the crowd and seeing who we might have to turn away.

'Oi, wankers,' I heard called from my left and instinctively I looked round.

'Come on then you cunt, have some of this.' I noticed a flash of silver as the guy pulled a blade from inside his jacket. I knew now why he didn't want to be searched. I looked down at the blade; it was about five inches long with a black handle, the type you would find in any kitchen. He had hesitated slightly and was holding it a few inches from my stomach. I looked back up straight in his face. I could see the fear in his eyes. He wasn't quite sure whether to use it or just turn and run.

'Now what the fuck are you going to do with that?' I asked and stepped slightly closer. I could feel the point press through my sweatshirt and against my abdomen. Bob had seen what was going on and had quickly returned, standing about an arm and a half's length to my right, near the second scumbag. In that position Bob could have immediate contact should he decide to join in. I didn't look at Bob – I knew where he was and what he would do, I didn't need to worry about him. I was just concentrating on the scumbag that had a blade pressed against my stomach.

The queue was getting agitated, they knew something was going off, but I had my back to them and they couldn't see the blade. No-one had mobile phones in those days so no-one could have called the police even if they did see what was happening.

'Either use it or fuck off, otherwise I will take the fucking blade and cut off your fucking head.' I was nervous but I knew exactly what I was going to do. If he decided to go for it or run off I was prepared to take him out but I knew I would have to be very quick, as I didn't fancy ending up in hospital or dead. But I also knew that with that weapon I could do almost anything in self-defence and probably get away with it, apart from perhaps killing him.

'Well?' I asked menacingly. It was a chilly evening but I could see sweat on his forehead. He was more scared than I was. If he stabbed me and got caught he would definitely go to prison but if he didn't stab me he knew he would get the biggest beating of his life. His only choice was to try and run for it.

He hesitated and moved back slightly, and as he did I grabbed his wrist with my left hand, forcing the blade down, at the same time I slammed my right fist upwards hard into his neck. He dropped the blade and I swiftly followed up with a punch to the side of his jaw. He crumpled against the wall. As soon as I made my first move Bob had immediately smashed the second guy's head hard into the wall.

We both stepped back – we didn't take things any further. We didn't want to get nicked nor even go to the police station to make statements. We had already decided that the venue didn't want any bad publicity or attention. They got up and staggered off. We never saw them again.

For well over an hour I was tense and shaking. The adrenalin surging round my system made calming down difficult. It is a normal thing and very difficult to control. Adrenalin primarily protects the body from injury and from pain and this recovery period is generally called the 'window' period. Roughly an hour after any stressful incident or accident the body protects itself. This is why it is so important to get medical attention during the first hour after any serious accident. It is also unwise to piss me off during this hour.

The rest of that first Thursday evening passed fairly smoothly. We turned quite a few away, had more verbal abuse, and had a few threats but nothing out of the ordinary and nothing we couldn't handle. The three of us rotated between doing the door, searching and patrolling inside. We could see that even after this first night the club looked cleaner and had a more comfortable atmosphere. Customers felt more relaxed, there was a much better attitude and we didn't see any drugs. We stopped all the dealers and searched everyone. We were looking forward to Friday.

Friday night was fight night in Norwich – always has been and I expect always will – and we were sure that the Hog (our pet name for the venue) was going to be no exception. According to the manager, Friday was also a traditional night for the bikers and he simply did not want any in. They were not pure out-and-out heavy metal bikers, but just scumbags with motorbikes trying to be bikers.

When we arrived for work Friday evening we noticed there were already three or four motorbikes parked on the pavement opposite the venue. They were not superbikes, just 250s and 400s. When we entered the building there were already around 50 customers, all sitting drinking and chatting and enjoying themselves. But where were the bikers that he desperately didn't want in the venue? Without actually searching the floor for crash helmets it was impossible to tell them apart from anyone else in the place, and everyone seemed fine.

At about 9 p.m. four more bikes drew up outside the front door of the venue. They stared at us for a few seconds then did a u-turn in the road and parked up on the pavement directly opposite.

We could see clearly that these were the type of bikers that were in the venue the previous weekend. None of the bikes had silencers and were noisy and annoying, and the bikers themselves looked like dirty, foul-mouthed yobs. Exactly the type of person we enjoyed turning away.

We watched as they parked. They took off their crash helmets, got off their bikes and crossed the road towards us. Tandy and Bob stood on the step blocking the door, and I stood directly behind them, ready to turn back anyone that wanted to leave the venue. We expected trouble from these four.

'Sorry lads,' I heard Bob say, 'new management, changing everything, new dress code and stuff so you can't come in tonight.'

'What about tomorrow night?' one of the bikers replied sarcastically.

'Not any night. Not my fault lads, just doing a job.'

'Fuck you,' I heard one say. They turned and walked nonchalantly back to their bikes. Well, that was easy. Turning away this specific section of scumbags wasn't going to be much of a problem after all, I thought.

I heard the bikes start and rev up. Bob and Tandy also relaxed a little. Bob turned to look at me and nodded as I let out a couple of customers that had been waiting to leave. He also let in a few others that were waiting to one side. The bikes didn't move, just sat revving and revving and over the engine noise we could just hear the shouts of one of the bikers. We thought that they were just being knobheads, teasing and testing us a little.

I heard the clunk as they put the bikes in gear, then they all came screeching over to our side of the road. Bob and Tandy scampered into the doorway and turned round to see the lead bike mount the pavement and aim directly for the front door.

'Fuck!' I shouted and, with the other two, backed further into the venue. The bike went up the first step and through the front door, stopping in the doorway with half the bike inside the club. The biker laughed and gave us the one finger salute. Tandy had already snatched the cosh from his bag and smashed it over the biker's crash helmet.

'Fuck!' we could hear him shout as he backed the bike out. The four of them sat just outside revving and revving for a few seconds, shouting at each other and threatening us. Tandy rushed to give us the coshes. 'Call me fucking mad!' he shouted above the sound of the motorbikes.

We stood at the door, the three of us with coshes in our hands. 'Come on!' Bob screamed at them and stepped onto the pavement slightly. 'Come on then!' he screamed again, slapping the cosh into the palm of his other hand. We had all lost the plot and were desperate to batter them senseless.

They came at us again and, like clowns, we turned and rushed back inside the venue, pushing each other through the front doors. The first bike mounted the step and roared into the venue with a second bike following, stopping halfway in the doorway. Tandy and I smacked the lead biker mercilessly over his head with our coshes. Cowering, he tried to back out, but the second biker was struggling to reverse as Bob was also bashing him again and again over his head. We heard police sirens. The second biker finally backed out but dropped his bike. As he struggled to pick it up, the first bike backed into him, knocking his bike to the ground once more. Finally, as the sirens came round the corner, all the bikes roared off.

We screamed and yelled as they raced off up the road.

As two police cars drew up outside, Tandy grabbed the coshes, stuffed them in his bag and threw the bag to the manager, who had by then joined us at the door. He rushed off and hid the bag behind the bar. The coppers jumped out of their cars and rushed over to us standing at the door.

'Having some problems?' one of the officers asked.

'Don't know what you mean,' Bob answered, sweating and panting.

'Are you sure?' He knew we were lying.

'Oh, yeah, we had a few bikers swearing and being abusive, but nothing much.'

Even by looking at us they knew we had been up to something and I am sure they could smell the exhaust fumes. But we certainly weren't going to tell them that a group of bikers had come into the venue on their bikes and that we had been bashing them over the head with coshes.

The manager had obviously looked inside the bag and seen what weapons we had brought and came storming over to us.

To say he was pissed off would be an understatement. He called us mindless thugs and, holding up one of the gloves Tandy had made, asked what the hell we were thinking about? We sat in silence, like naughty schoolchildren trying desperately not to laugh. Tandy again had that confused and hurt look on his face, which made not laughing even more difficult. We sheepishly agreed that we would never bring weapons to work again. Of course we did, but not a bagful and we never told the manager.

We ended up staying at the Hog for about nine months. Most weekends would have trouble of some sort. We had various weapons pulled on us but it happened less and less as time wore on and certainly nothing we, as a team, were not able to handle. We worked well together, and Bob and I always wondered if Tandy ever got to use his spiked gloves.

Although he worked on the door at the Hog, Bob had another few units he sent doormen to. He had two close to each other on Bedford Street. One was called Hector's House and the other Bedford's Wine Bar. I ended up working at both of them after I left the Hog. They were completely different to the Hog, attracting a decent, older, more mature and more smartly dressed clientele, with a lot more money. I wasn't bored with the Hog, it was always a fun place to work with plenty of things happening that kept us on our toes and we had done a great job cleaning the venue. It was now full almost every night and had a good student customer base, but it was time for another change.

New Year's Eve 1987. I was working at Bedford's Wine Bar. The entrance was on the right down a small alley off Bedford Street. The foyer led to an upstairs wine bar and a downstairs cellar bar. I stayed in the foyer on my own working the front door. Entry was by ticket only – it wasn't a hard venue to work. Like New Year's Eve everywhere it was a very busy night. I had got to know many of the customers very well and was having more and more drinks bought for me. I was slowly getting more and more drunk.

Bearing in mind I could hardly walk in a straight line let alone up and down stairs, in my drunken wisdom I decided to take a walk around the venue. The stairs down to the cellar bar were steep and the third step proved just too much of a challenge in the state I was in. I tripped and fell the rest of the way down the stairs – rolling and tumbling into the cellar bar. As I landed flat on my back at the foot of the stairs, the whole of the bar fell silent and watched horrified. Drunkenly I looked up and grinned stupidly at the faces staring back at me. A couple of regulars helped me to my feet as everyone burst out laughing. I didn't remember any more of that night but woke up with an almighty hangover on New Year's Day. I lay in my bed, curled up, my head thumping and feeling sick and very sorry for myself. Suddenly I heard what sounded like a snore coming from beside me. The sorrowful look of sadness on my face turned to a look of horror as I struggled to recall what else had happened that night and who the fuck was lying next to me. As I lay there trying not to move, I tried to put the pieces together. I remembered staggering home with someone, but I couldn't remember what she looked like. I remembered being on top of her. Lying there I looked at the clock: 11.30. I also remembered I was supposed to be having one of my rare lunches at my mother's house and she was picking me up at midday. I knew I had to get whoever was in my bed out of my bed and out of the house. Hoping not to wake whoever it was next to me, I turned to face the snoring. Looking at her sleeping with her mouth open, her shaved head and pierced nose, I thought she looked just like a pig. I didn't even know her name and had no idea how I was going to get her out of the house before my mother arrived. At times I am not particularly proud, but even I couldn't let my mother see this.

I wondered whether I should wake her gently, or just bang

about the room noisily. Looking at her lying there, mouth open and snoring, I decided to take the noisy option and so bounced out of bed and opened the wardrobe door, banging the door hard on the wall. She was still snoring. I turned the radio on – it was getting later and I didn't have much time. Just as I was about to shake her shoulders, her eyes opened.

'Hi,' she said in a soft and delicate voice. 'Did you sleep well? You were pretty drunk.' She giggled and turned to face me, letting the covers slip from her shoulders revealing two large, beautifully shaped breasts. She was ugly but had a soft and friendly voice and I didn't have the heart to tell her she was so ugly she just had to leave before my mother saw her.

Staring at her breasts I said, 'Listen, I am sorry but . . .'

'I know,' she interrupted sadly, 'I have to go.'

'No,' I said quickly, 'well, yes, you do, but take your time. My mother is coming round and I have to go to hers for lunch and I won't be back until late, but take your time, sleep a little, there's a little food in the cupboard and leave when you want, just make sure the door is closed on your way out.'

I couldn't believe I was leaving a girl whose name I didn't know and who I had drunkenly met the night before, alone in my flat. But after hearing the softness of her voice I was sure it would be ok. That day I made sure I stayed at my mother's longer than I normally would and finally got home at about 6 p.m. There was a note on the table that simply said, 'Thanks XXX.'

CHAPTER SIX

Bodyguarding

I had been doing the doors in Norwich for about four years. I was a good doorman and strong in the gym. I was well known and had a good reputation. It was about this time I went on a six-week bodyguarding course run by Allen, an SAS officer.

Allen had joined the Parachute Regiment when he was 20 years old and, after a few years, applied for and was accepted into the SAS. He was a couple of years older than me, but we happened to get on very well and every time he was back in Norwich we would meet, have a few drinks and a good laugh. Although I was fascinated with his life, he never talked about where he had been or what he had been doing – he would just turn up out of the blue, hyperactive and a little bit crazy, wanting a good time.

He had been back a couple of days and I was at his apartment waiting for him to get ready. We were going out for a few drinks and to try to get laid. After a couple of drinks he invited me to attend a six-week bodyguard training course. The SAS were having a special course in about three months and, if he could get me on, would I be interested? Of course I would. I knew nothing about the real world of bodyguards, only from the movies and books and from the occasional newspaper and magazine article, but I fancied myself in the job – it seemed a natural extension of the doors. Immediately my imagination took me to far-off places, living in five-star hotels and driving luxury vehicles with the rich and famous.

I thought I was a pretty tough guy and thought I knew a thing or two, but Allen stressed that it wasn't going to be a normal bodyguard training course. Those six weeks, Allen smilingly said, would unquestionably be among the hardest of my life.

'First you must lose about two stone,' he said.

'Two stone!' I cried. 'Do you know how many drugs I have had to take and how hard I have had to train to get where I am?' I was joking, but also serious.

'You are just too heavy. It will be a hard enough job getting you on the course – they will all be professional soldiers – and I will have to work on the commanding officer. But he will just laugh at me if I brought a 17-stone bodybuilder along with me. No, you will have to lose at least two stone and get fit, I mean really fit. I want you fitter than me.' He laughed, tapping his belly. He didn't look fit in jeans and shirt, but I knew it would take three months' hard training just to get to his level.

I promised him that I would get fit and lose two stone if he would try his best to get me on the course. He assured me he would but I must be prepared.

A few days later I called his apartment and he had gone. He departed as he arrived, with no word, no warning, leaving his usual message on his answer machine saying that he was out of town and would be back shortly.

I loved my life in Norwich and loved doing the doors, but deep down I knew they were kind of a dead-end job. I had no other skills and experience. I could fight and was good to open a door and say 'good evening' but that was about it; that didn't qualify me for much else in the world of work.

I knew I had to do more with my life, so I saw this opportunity of becoming a bodyguard as a path to a new world. Days and weeks passed and I still had no word from Allen but I was training hard, running almost every day and doing more aerobics. I even joined an aerobics class. At first I felt overweight and clumsy but I soon become fitter and much more supple. I was still studying martial arts twice a week, which helped.

About two months after Allen disappeared I arrived home and pressed the flashing light on my answer machine.

'It's me, it's on. Got you a place. Book yourself six weeks off work from July 14. I'll be back in Norwich a day before.' And then he hung up.

I looked at my diary and saw I had just over three weeks to go. I felt butterflies in my stomach and wasn't sure if I could go through with it. After hearing Allen's voice I realized that this illusion was now reality. Allen had probably moved mountains to get me on the course and I couldn't let him down; I wouldn't dare. So I stepped up my training, ate better food and grew more nervous as the day drew closer.

'Ready?' said Allen as I answered the phone.

'Where are you?' I asked. It was about nine in the morning and I had been fast asleep when the phone rang.

'Outside your fucking door – let me in.'

I opened it to Allen's smiling face.

'Come on, get up,' he said cheerfully, bursting in. 'We have a lot to do today.' He thumped his something down on the coffee table. I picked it up and stared.

'What is it, a mobile phone?' I had known friends with carphones but had not seen an actual mobile before.

That day we spent planning and preparing. It was July 12, and we were to leave on the morning of July 14. Allen advised me precisely what I would need to take: two business suits, two white shirts, three plain ties, two matching pairs of shoes with matching socks, two tracksuits, two pairs of training shoes, two pairs of jeans and two other sweatshirts, four pairs of underwear, heavy duty waterproof boots, waterproof coat and two hats, spare buttons, needle and cotton, basic first aid kit, torch with spare batteries, multi-tool kit, pencils, pens and writing paper, small notepad, sleeping bag, light tracksuit bottoms and t-shirt for sleeping in, toothbrush, toothpaste, soap, no shampoo – I could wash my hair with soap – disposable razors, no shaving foam – I could shave with soap. I should pack it in two bags, one large one and one small kit bag.

'What about what we wear to travel in – is that extra or included in the kit?' I asked.

'We take nothing more apart from what I just detailed. We wash one set and wear the other. We make sure that one is clean and ready to wear at all times, so we must wash our clothes, trainers and shoes every evening.'

'What are the suits for?'

'For work – we will do a couple of real close protection assignments during the six weeks' training. We will be training but the training will consist of both exercises and real assignments.'

I must have sounded like an excited boy on his first day at school. During that day I bombarded Allen with all sorts of questions, most of which he replied to with just a brief, 'You'll see.'

On the morning of July 14, Allen drew up outside my apartment and sounded his horn loudly. I was standing in the living room almost sick with fear and wondering whether I should have yet another shit before I left.

It was a long drive and I hardly uttered a word. I was preoccupied. I was determined to make both myself and Allen proud. Inside I felt I could do as well as any of the other guys on the course. I knew the SAS was tough. I knew they were fit and both mentally and physically incredibly resilient. Everyone knew that the SAS were probably the best-trained soldiers in the world but I would try to keep up with them and felt I could compete. We were all made of the same substance at the end of the day, and in some that substance can be broken quickly and in others never. I was determined to be one of the 'never' category.

Allen chatted a little, occasionally to break the silence in the car. He told me that we would generally train from Monday to Friday and have the weekends off. It was a long drive back to Norwich, and I had no real reason to come back anyway so I said I would probably stay.

Allen would also be attending the course but said he would be coming and going throughout the six weeks as he had another project on the go, but most of the other students would be staying for the duration. Most actually lived nearby at Hereford and would probably return home at weekends so I would probably be alone, but that was good, he said, as it gave me time to re-read my notes. He could tell I was nervous and took the piss.

The training camp used to be owned by the Ministry of Defence but had been sold about five years previously to a group of ex-SAS soldiers who had started their own private security company. It had been disused for about ten years prior to its sale and needed extensive renovation and so it was sold off very cheaply. The company provided private security consultants to companies, organizations and governments worldwide and rarely used anyone other than ex-members of the regiment. It was a very tight, closed community.

At first the instructors point blank refused to accept me but Allen badgered them to give me a chance. Eventually, and with a great deal of persuasion, I was allowed to attend on the condition that I would not be given any second chances and would be sent home if I failed in any way, at any time. Another stipulation was that everything I was taught should remain confidential – I was not to tell anyone about the style or standards of their training. I was made to sign a declaration to that effect. I was also told that, being a civilian, there might be information that I simply could not be told and if that was the case I would have to 'fuck off somewhere else'.

Just as we passed the village of Llandrindod Wells, and without warning, we turned left, through a rickety open wooden gate and onto a rough dirt track that seemed to lead nowhere. There were various 'Private Property' signs along the track, and we bumped and jolted our way for about a mile when we approached a high metal gate and barbed wire perimeter fence with large warning signs on both sides stating 'Warning – Private Property, Trespassers Will Be Prosecuted'.

Allen stopped his car and got out, signalling that I should get out with him. We both walked over to the gate and I heard a whirr as a camera, positioned on a pole above the gate, followed us from the vehicle to the small intercom mounted on the metal pole separating the gate from the fence. Allen pressed the intercom and said his initials followed by a five-digit number. The gate clicked and Allen pushed it open. We drove through, stopping briefly while he jumped back out and closed the gate behind us.

The camp was situated roughly in the middle of a large open space of land. There were two buildings, the main house where most of the instruction would take place, and a separate smaller, wooden building that was the dormitory. In front of the main house was a large gravel parking area. There were already a few cars parked neatly in a line. There was also a Mercedes 600 on its own at the far end of the car park.

'Who's that?' I asked.

'The boss,' said Allen.

We parked beside the other cars and, with our kit bags slung over our shoulders, walked up the steps and through the doors to the main building. My heart was racing; I would rather have fought a battalion of homosexual Vikings than walked through those doors that afternoon. While Allen was cheerfully greeted, I was ignored by every one of the seven guys lounging on the seats in the small lounge area. I just put my kit bag on the floor near the door and stood like a dummy, not knowing what to say or where to go. I thought to myself, what the fuck am I doing here? Once Allen had finished his greetings he wandered over and whispered 'Don't worry, the first few days are the worst, you'll be alright. Coffee?'

I nodded.

I was going to keep myself to myself and quietly show everyone that I was as capable as they were. I would study and learn but I would not force myself or my friendship on anyone. They didn't want me there – it was obvious from the first few minutes – so I would try to gain their respect by working hard and not giving in. I was in their territory and it was a long walk home.

Being the only civilian on a military course would have been bad enough, but being the only civilian on an SAS course was almost unbearable. Many times I nearly quit.

I had to work twice as hard as the other students. When the others did 24 hours' 'resistance to interrogation', they made me do 48 hours. When the rest of the students finished their morning run and went to breakfast, I was made to turn around and do it again. At first they wanted me to fail, but I stuck with it and they could see my determination. I was fit, I could fight and I had the intelligence to learn what was being taught but I wasn't a soldier and I wasn't in the regiment and that was my only hindrance to being even acknowledged by some of the students. But as time passed, I made a basic friendship with a couple of soldiers who were fairly new to the regiment. They didn't help me with anything much, but occasionally guided me with technical details only a soldier or specialist would know – how atmospherics affect communication systems or fundamental topography.

We were all given a basic schedule at the start of the first day. This was mainly for the soldiers who were tasked on other 'projects' or 'assignments' as some had to miss some aspects of the course and would have to catch up later.

I waited silently in the lounge that first evening, ignored by everyone. At precisely 6 p.m. and after the remaining two students had turned up, the boss and four instructors came in to the room.

'Evening girls and boys,' said the instructor looking around, 'and those we are not yet sure about.' He looked directly at me. There were chuckles and laughter from the other students, including Allen. I wanted to walk out. In fact I would have walked all the way back to Norwich if I'd had the guts to stand up and leave, but I stayed sat down and silent.

No-one sitting there looked any different to an average person in the street. No-one looked hard or tough; some had an arrogant air but mostly they looked like everyone else. I was sitting there feeling intimidated but I knew I had no need. These were all just normal guys with special skills.

The boss, the owner of the company and an ex-commanding officer in the SAS, stood silently looking at everyone while the instructor welcomed us all and gave commands for the coming week. He gave each of us a folder containing the schedule for the duration of the course.

We trained from Monday to Friday, from 6 a.m. until around 6 p.m., although occasionally there would be classes in the evening, but this was rare. Most soldiers would then leave the barracks to go home as most lived around Hereford, which was no more than an hour away. The two soldiers I eventually got to know were the ones that stayed on site. Like Allen and me, they lived too far to drive home every evening although they generally went home at weekends. For most of the course I was on my own and had little contact with any of the group, including Allen. During the team exercises I participated silently, speaking only when I had to but always working hard. I understood that the instructors were looking at each individual and assessing them and their skills and merits and I knew that 'leadership' for me was going to be my lowest score. I would never shine as any kind of leader amongst these exceptionally qualified and experienced soldiers, so I decided not to push this element but to try for higher scores in other areas including endurance, aptitude, fitness, unarmed combat and team spirit.

Every morning at 6 a.m. sharp we had to be outside for a 10km run. Then we would shower, have breakfast and start formal classes. The course was a mixture of classroom-style discussions and seminars and practical work and practice. In total we covered 42 separate subjects – some would just be a 30-minute seminar while others took one or two days of practice. We were taught everything from surveillance to the terrorist thought process, from leadership to working protocol, from resource management to equipment and logistical support, from para-medicine to ballistics, from unarmed combat to offensive driving, and from bomb recognition to administration.

We spent one whole day practising a three-man embus and debus. We spent another whole day just learning to j-turn a car. The wonderful thing about being on a six-week course was that we had the time to learn everything thoroughly and to practise. Everything practical became instinctive.

The worst and one of the most mentally and physically demanding times of my entire life was during the second week. In the middle of the night I was woken by three soldiers wearing balaclavas and shouting in Arabic. Towering over me, they fired live rounds into the pillow next to my head. They grabbed my ankles and dragged me off the bed, down the corridor and outside, shouting and screaming and firing live rounds into the earth near my head and into the air. One of the soldiers slammed his muddy boot on my neck while a second put the barrel of the gun in my mouth. It was still hot from being fired and the taste of gunpowder almost made me retch. All three screamed and shouted at me, asking me questions that I simply did not understand. He pressed harder with his boot and shoved the barrel even further down my throat. I was choking.

'Stop,' I heard. The boot came off my throat and I turned to the side coughing, my stomach heaving.

'What the fuck do you think you are doing here?' a voice

asked. I said nothing. I couldn't have even if I had wanted to. My throat and mouth were raw from the heat and gunpowder and my stomach was heaving.

'I asked you a fucking question, you fucking poofter. What the fuck do you think you are doing here?' I looked up at the person standing towering above me – he too had a hood over his face. 'Answer the fucking question, queer, what the fuck are you doing here?' He shouted closer to my face. 'Are you here to fuck us?' The other three were circled around me, their weapons pointed at my head. I knew I should not say one word; no matter what was going to happen I knew I could and would get through it. One of the soldiers fired into the earth a few centimetres from my head. 'Answer the fucking question. Are you here to fuck us?' he shouted, spitting saliva over my face. I remained silent, shaking and almost sick with fear. I kept telling myself over and over again it was part of the course and I would get through it, but a part of me knew that none of them wanted me on the course and no-one at home back in Norwich knew where I was. Maybe I would just disappear.

'Take him away and teach the cunt a lesson,' the guy said quietly, turning and walking away. I was racked with fear and as desperate as any man has ever been. I knew this lesson wasn't going to be enjoyable.

One of the soldiers rolled me onto my front while another tied my hands behind my back with masking tape. I was then forced up onto my legs, a hood was placed over my head and masking tape was wrapped round my eyes. I was walked back in the direction of the main house, but we didn't go up the stairs. We went round to the side and down into the cellar. I could sense it was empty from the echo of the boots on the concrete floor and it smelled damp and dirty. I was pushed down onto the floor and rolled back onto my stomach. A boot was placed hard against the back of my head as my feet were tied together, first with tape as I could hear the sound as it unwound round my feet, and then with a rope. I then heard a pulley sound and I realized I was going to be hung up upside down. The rope tightened, I felt my legs straighten and the blood rushed to my head. I was lifted and left swinging by my legs. I heard the door shut and realized I was alone.

Swinging there silently as my head pounded with blood I certainly questioned my life, what I had done and why and whether it was now all coming to an end. For the first time in my life I was really frightened. Looking back I realized they would not have actually killed me, but at the time, swinging silently upside-down, blindfolded and with my hands tied, I really thought my life was ending. I hoped it would end quickly but I had no idea what was yet to come.

Time passed, I had no idea how long but with every minute I was feeling more and more sick and my head was pounding painfully. I heard the door creak open and footsteps approach. I could hear a lever being unlocked and I was lowered slowly to the ground. I then heard the sound of water, like a shower being turned on. My feet were grabbed and without a word they dragged me towards the sound of the running water. My head was reeling; I thought they were going to drown me. I was pulled under a freezing cold shower and again left lying flat on the floor with a strong jet of water pounding my body and freezing my very soul. I lay there shivering violently as water seeped through my clothes. The hood was becoming more and more saturated and I started to panic as the cloth began to stick in my mouth. With each breath I choked. I just wanted this to stop, I wanted out, I would have happily walked back to Norwich rather than put up with this any longer. But I couldn't talk and there was no-one to listen. I tried to calm myself, to think of things logically and breathed slowly through my nose. After a while I felt less panicky but just very cold. I tried to shut myself off from my environment, disregard what was happening to me. I tried to separate myself from the intense pain and discomfort. My arms and hands felt numb, my body convulsed with the cold, my mouth was full of water-soaked cloth but I slowly felt in control. I could still breathe through my nose. I had found a way out.

After what felt like hours I heard those familiar footsteps approach and felt immediate relief as the water was turned off. Again I thought it had all ended, and that it was a little test. I was hoping they were going to take off my hood and pat me joyfully on the back, but I was disappointed. Again they dragged me silently into another room. I lay on the floor and I could feel intense heat immediately envelop me. I could actually feel the steam rise off my clothes and my hood. For a few short seconds it was heaven, I was in an incredibly hot sauna and would soon dry. Then the sound came. A high-pitched screeching sound that pierced my eardrums and dug a deep hole in my head. A sound that made me moan out loud with pain. This was worse than being hung upside-down and far worse than lying for hours under the cold shower. This was utterly and absolutely painful. I felt myself slipping in and out of consciousness. Blackness would envelop me and pull me forward, but the sound and the heat wouldn't let me go. It kept me there, barely conscious.

Finally it stopped, the door opened and I was pulled out and seated on a chair. The hood was pulled away from my mouth and I let out a gasp and breathed a deep and wonderful gulp of air.

'I asked you a question, are you here to fuck us?' the same voice asked. The question was menacing but I was thankful to hear a human voice. I wanted to talk, to tell them I had had enough, I wanted out. I wanted to pack my things and go home, but I didn't say it. Instead I simply said, 'Fuck off.'

I was dragged over to a barrel of water and my head was pushed under. I thought 'Robin, you really have fucked up now.' In and out of the water my head went, time and time again. When one of them tired the other took over, in and out time and again, each time I was struggling to breathe, to catch my breath before being plunged back in.

Finally it ended and I was dragged outside. I could feel the warmth of the sun's rays. I wondered how long this had taken as it was the middle of the night when it had all started.

But it still wasn't finished. I heard the sound of a metal door unlocking and then I was lifted up off my feet and lowered into a hole in the ground. My hands and legs were still tied but, before the metal door was shut, they took off my hood and tape from my eyes. The blinding sunshine made me squint painfully but before I could see a thing the door was slammed shut and I was left alone in this space in the ground.

It was a metal box no more than a metre square. There was no room to sit, I could just stand. It was incredibly hot and smelled of human shit. I immediately vomited down my clothes and onto the wall directly in front of me. This made the stench even worse, which made me gag and vomit again. I looked up and saw a few small holes which allowed in a tiny amount of air, which I desperately tried to stretch my neck and face towards.

The day passed and evening came and the searing heat of the metal box turned to cold. Darkness fell and I started to shiver. I tried to sleep by leaning up against the wall, but couldn't, the cold and the stench kept me awake. I pissed myself numerous times and shit myself once. I knew what it was like to really want to die. Morning came and I heard footsteps. My heart leapt. I could see the vague shadow of someone bending down, peering in. Water was then poured through the holes which I desperately tried to catch in my mouth. He walked silently away and I almost cried. I knew that if I survived I would quietly pack my things and go home. They had taught me a lesson. I was not part of their world and I would walk away without uttering a word.

Darkness fell, I was slipping in and out of consciousness when I heard a shuffling outside. The door was opened and I could see the faces of the three instructors bending down. They smiled and said, 'Fuck you smell bad.'

I was carefully lifted out. The students and instructors were standing in a semi-circle around me and they all started to applaud as my hands and feet were cut free.

It was early Friday evening – I had been there almost 48 hours. Allen told me later than the normal time was 24 hours but they decided to double it because I was a civilian. He was proud. I was just able to have a hot shower and eat one banana and then slept until Sunday evening.

I passed the final assessment at a level equal to some of the other SAS students. I wasn't the best and I wasn't the worst, but I passed and I was proud. I was soon to start a career in close protection, which would eventually take me around the world.

About six months after the course Allen and Peter – another SAS officer – and I founded the Worldwide Federation of Bodyguards. The idea came at dinner one evening at Allen's apartment in Norwich. He was due to leave the regiment the following year and wanted to start his own full-time security company. Like many serving soldiers, he had already completed a few assignments but he knew he could make a lot more money working full-time for himself. He loved the regiment but he wanted out. He had already formed a small private company called Personal Security Services (International) that handled the occasional contract he did while still serving, but he wanted to expand and operate globally on a more permanent basis. Alongside his company he also had an idea about forming a non-profit-making organization dedicated to training and uniting close protection officers around the world. As he had travelled he quickly realized that, at that time, there were few standards of operation within the civilian close protection environment. Everyone tended to do his own thing. The training in the UK would differ to the training in the US, which would differ again to the training in

South America or Asia and it was a nightmare when teams from different countries had to work together. His goal was to implement global standards of operation and training within the civilian close protection environment so that teams from around the world could work together immediately, effectively and efficiently. Initially he decided to call it 'The Federation' but soon it became apparent that that term was also used for Star Trek enthusiasts, so the name was changed to the Worldwide Federation of Bodyguards.

Out of the blue as usual, Allen called. 'Want your first contract?' He never asked how I was, or what I had been up to, he just called after months of silence and asked a direct question.

'Is the Pope Catholic?' I replied. 'Where and when?'

'Northern Ireland, next week. One week. Not great pay but better than jack shit and it'll be good experience for you. Easy job.' I shuddered when Allen said something was easy, in fact, after those six weeks, I shuddered every time I heard Allen's voice at the other end of the telephone line. I always knew that, whenever I heard Allen's dulcet tones, I was in for an exciting, challenging and unique time.

It was a few months after the course and I had only just got myself back to normal. I had started training again, after losing another stone during the course, and was working back on the doors for Bob Etchalls at Hector's House.

'I'll book your flights from this end and fax over full details.'

'But I don't have a fax,' I replied.

'Well go and fucking buy one!' he exclaimed. He was never one to mince words. He arranged to call back at 5 p.m. the next day when I should have a fax machine. He didn't want to give me any information over the phone. At precisely 5 p.m. the telephone rang and I switched on the fax machine. Details of the operation and my flights came juddering through.

I was to be working with Danny, whom I had first met on the six-week course in Wales. Danny was to be in charge of the whole operation and I was to do everything he said, without question. Who was I to question anyone anyway, I thought? I was pleased, as Danny seemed a genuine guy. I knew he was still serving and wondered how he managed to get a week off but I never asked. The other guy, Tommy, I didn't know. We would all meet at the arrivals hall at Belfast International Airport. I had a list of clothes I was to bring. My brief was residential security, while the other two provided driving and protection duties to the principal. It was only going to be a low-risk, three-man operation, but I was elated at being given my first assignment and the chance to actually protect someone, although it didn't quite turn out that way.

The principal was a government minister who was staying with his wife at a rented country residence about an hour's drive from Belfast.

I arrived at the airport nervous but excited. I immediately recognized Danny, he saw me before I saw him as he had started to approach with his hand outstretched. We shook hands warmly.

'Good to see you again,' he said.

'You too, how are you?'

'Fine, as always. Tommy is delayed and will arrive tomorrow morning a few hours before we pick up the principal. We should go to the residence, secure it and get everything prepared.'

Danny chatted about the job as we walked over to Hertz car hire.

'Got your driver's licence?'

'Of course,' I replied, 'Allen has already briefed me.'

We hired two vehicles: an executive vehicle for the principal and one for us. I flung my bags in the boot of the car. We had the address and the directions from the airport and I followed Danny who drove the executive vehicle. I was making mental notes during the journey and refreshing myself on everything we were taught on the course. I was determined not to fuck anything up.

We arrived at a beautiful stately home with large gardens about a mile down a secluded tarmac lane. At the end of the lane on the left there was a big, ornate gate, which was open, and a long gravel drive leading past manicured lawns to the front of the house. We drove slowly down the drive and stopped at the bottom of the steps leading up to the front doors. Further round the drive was a row of garages, outside one of which was parked a Range Rover. I made a mental note of the number plate. I turned off the engine and got out of the car and walked over to Danny. Immediately the doors to the house opened and an immaculately dressed lady in her mid-sixties descended the steps and greeted us warmly.

'I have been expecting you – everything is in order,' she said with a strong upper-class English accent, shaking our hands. I followed them up the stairs and through the main doors. Inside the front entrance was a large and beautifully decorated hall with a wooden staircase leading up to the second floor. On the first curve of the staircase I immediately noticed a line of three figures in coats of arms – mail, breast plates, helmet, visor, leg and arm armour and each holding a long lance.

We stood in the hall while the woman explained a few details. The cleaners came every morning at about ten. The chef with his two assistants would come at 7 a.m. to make breakfast and lunch, depending upon requirements. They would then leave at about 2 p.m. and return at 6 p.m. to make dinner. They would leave at the end of the night once everything had been tidied. However if the principal was on site all day one member of staff would always be on hand, to make tea or sandwiches or anything that may be required.

I mentally took notes, as I knew I was going to be concerned with the residential security and so needed to be aware of the comings and goings of all visitors.

Although, at that time, there was a great deal of sectarian violence in Northern Ireland, the risk to the principal was graded as low, so whilst providing security, we were instructed not to be 'over the top' – the principal wanted a leisurely and relaxing break away from the pressure of his position in London and just wanted us to be there to make sure everything ran smoothly for both him and his wife.

I trailed behind them as we had a brief tour of the house. It was beautiful. On the right of the entrance a door led to a large dining area. In the middle was a beautiful old wooden dining table with four chairs each side and two at each end. The kitchen was attached to the other end of the dining room, separated by a small ante-room which contained shelves and drawers full of silver cutlery and china dinner sets. There was a door at the back of the kitchen leading out to the side of the building behind the staff quarters. The staff would always enter and leave this way and not via the front entrance.

A second door at the far right of the entrance hall led to a wooden-panelled library with row upon row of old-fashioned elegantly bound books. On the walls of the library were portraits of probably the previous owners and mounted heads of deer and stags. There were three soft and comfortable-looking settees, four chairs and two coffee tables on which were placed various glossy magazines. There were various reading lamps positioned around the room.

The first door to left of the entrance led to a small reception area where visitors could wait. From the reception area a door led to the huge magnificently decorated L-shaped lounge with settees, chairs, tables, a wooden ornate writing desk and leather chair, handmade oriental rugs, big velvet drapes and curtains, mirrors and pictures. French doors led from the lounge onto the lawn and gardens at the back of the house.

The old servants' quarters were attached to the side of the

main house, separated from the main garden by a high hedge and a discreet iron gate. This is where we would be staying. Our quarters were small, basic but comfortable. There was a small lounge area with settee and three chairs, TV, video and four small single bedrooms with a basic kitchen. The chef would be making our meals and leaving them in our kitchen.

Once the woman had left and we unpacked our clothes, we started to make a more detailed assessment of the house and gardens. We moved the furniture out of the largest of the bedrooms of the servants' quarters and set up a small control room. We drew a basic plan of the house, detailing all doors and windows, telephone sockets, fire and smoke alarms, all the kitchen furniture including the garbage facilities, ovens and grills – as this was where a potential fire was most likely to start. We detailed the fire extinguishers, three different possible evacuation routes, and allocated a safe room where we could get our principal to quickly should anything disastrous happen.

There were two telephones in our quarters, one we allocated to be the direct line to the principal's personal assistant in London should he need to be contacted, the other to be used by Allen to check that everything was running smoothly and for other calls.

We made a plan of the gardens: the height of the hedges, overhanging trees, the external gates and locks, hinges and the depth of the far exterior fence. We marked the paths and possible external access for both our vehicles and an ambulance should something happen to our principal at the far end of the garden.

We then got into the car and drove back into town, marking the pharmacies, petrol stations, potential road blocks and traffic lights. We drove to the airport again detailing the exact route for the following day. Because we would be picking Tommy up just a few hours before the principal arrived, we had no time to take Tommy back to the residence, so we had to get as much planning and preparation done as possible. We did a complete survey of the airport and the exact place we would meet the principal. We detailed how and where we could bring in the vehicles so that we could easily pick them up without having to walk too far, especially if it was raining. It was already late October and the evenings were getting colder. Allen had said on the phone before I left that I should be well prepared as apparently it rains a lot in Ireland in October. We also had a quick word with the security manager at the airport. It is always good protocol to let them know what you are doing as they are a great asset if anything goes wrong.

From various points along the main route we made two separate routes to and from the hospital. We also made a secondary route to and from the airport just in case there were delays or the primary route was compromised.

We reserved a third vehicle at Hertz car rental to be collected the following day, and found the communications company which Allen had arranged to hire radios from. We hired ten radios and chargers: three of us would each have one, one for the control room, one for each vehicle and three spare. Once we returned to the residence we tested the range, both within the grounds of the garden and along the route.

We finally got to bed at about 2 a.m. but I couldn't sleep. I kept going through everything in my head. Before I knew it the alarm went. It was 6 a.m. and my first day as a bodyguard with a real client. I got up and looked outside; it was pouring with rain. Danny was already up and making a cup of tea.

'Want a brew?'

'Please.'

We sat at the small kitchen table while he issued my orders for the day. Danny was quietly spoken but precise. Everything had to be perfect. He would leave at about 8 a.m., after the chef had paid his first visit with our breakfast. Tommy was due to arrive at Belfast airport at 11.15 a.m. They would then hire the third vehicle; Danny would drive the principal and his wife in the executive vehicle while Tommy would follow. The principal was due to arrive at 2.30 p.m. – they were expected back at the residence at 4 p.m.

My duties for the forthcoming week were to meet the chef at the entrance every morning and escort him to the house. I would then patrol the perimeter of the estate until he was due to leave. I was to escort him off the estate. The front gate and all external doors and gates were to be kept locked and I would have to check them regularly. I would be notified in advance any time the principal wished to leave the residence, and when the principal was returning. I was then to have the gates open and the doors to the house unlocked. Danny and Tommy would take turns driving the client while the other would follow driving the back-up vehicle. There would always be one more vehicle at the residence just in case.

There was no schedule for the client, he was on a short vacation and had nothing planned. His wife may want to go into Belfast and he might like to do some fishing, if weather permitted, but otherwise he would just be relaxing quietly and perhaps writing (his autobiography). However they were expecting guests for dinner and would probably be going out to dinner at some point too. Apart from the residential security duties I would also have to make sure the vehicles were routinely checked and cleaned.

After finishing my cup of tea I put on my waterproof jacket and hat and walked down the drive to the gate. It was almost 7 a.m. and the chef was due to arrive with our breakfast. I stood there for around ten minutes in the driving rain when a car pulled up. I walked to the driver's side of the car.

'Morning,' I said as he wound the window down slightly.

'I have some breakfast and lunch for you guys,' he said. 'You look as though you need it.' He laughed.

'On your own?' I asked.

'Yup, this morning at least, there'll be three of us this evening.'

'Ok.' I unlocked the gate, he drove in and I locked it behind him. I followed the car as he parked by the side of the servants' quarters. He waited for me in the vehicle then got out.

'Give us a hand will you?' he said.

I helped him carry bags of groceries into our small kitchen. He hurriedly prepared a basic breakfast and then went into the main house to start preparing lunch, in case we were hungry later. We never mentioned our movements to the chef or other members of the household. Their duties were to cook, clean and serve and ours was to provide security.

Danny, suited up and looking good, left after breakfast and I was now on my own. I felt very important. The cleaners would come at 10 a.m. so I made a quick tour of the house. I checked the outside doors, made sure the windows were locked and had a quick cup of tea with the chef who was whistling to himself cheerfully in the kitchen.

'I have been here for ten years. We've had all sorts of people staying, Madonna, diplomats, a few foreign business-men, a couple of wealthy Arabs, all sorts. Although I don't actually get to see many of them. I just cook. If there is anything you need to know, just ask.' He seemed a nice guy.

It was quarter to ten and so I put on my waterproofs again and walked back to the gates to wait for the cleaners.

At 15.54 a crackle came over the radio.

'Alpha zero one to base, over.' The first person I was to protect was on his way.

'Base receiving, over,' I replied.

'ETA ten minutes, over.'

'Received. Out.' I unlocked the front door to the house and placed two large umbrellas next to a column. I then walked down the drive. It was still pouring with rain. I unlocked the gates and swung them open and stepped into the middle of the little lane. A few minutes passed and in the distance I saw the headlights of the lead car and then the rear back-up vehicle. I stood still with my right arm stretched horizontal to the ground guiding them through the gates. They drew up, slowed and turned through the gates and up the drive. I closed and locked the gates behind me and let out a big sigh.

I watched as the cars drew up in front of the steps, with the principal's door exactly in line with the entrance to the house. Leaving the engines running, Danny and Tommy jumped out, took the umbrellas, opened the car doors and ushered the principal and his wife under the umbrellas into the house.

And that was that. For one week I was patrolling the grounds in the pouring rain and opening and closing the front gates as the client came and went. I woke up at 6 a.m., let the chef and cleaners in and out, made sure the cars were ready and clean, opened and closed the gate for two sets of visitors. I stood down most evenings 30 minutes after the last light went off in the main house. For three days the client didn't leave the house, and those three days Danny and Tommy spent sleeping and watching videos while I trudged up and down in the pouring rain getting colder and colder, wetter and wetter. I never spoke one word to the clients and only ever saw them sitting in the back of the car as they either left or came back to the residence. But it was my first job and I didn't care.

From that first miserable wet week in Northern Ireland to this present day I have worked as a bodyguard, and then later as a trainer of bodyguards, worldwide, but I would always remember that first turn of the car into the drive with my client and his wife sitting in the back.

At first there was not much work and certainly no money in the Worldwide Federation of Bodyguards and I had to go back to working the doors, but as things developed I was able to spend more time working with and developing the WFB. At first I was just an occasional administrator, dealing with the odd letter and inquiry, but as the WFB became more recognized I had more work. I gained experience working as a bodyguard and started to travel on assignments and then to instruct on bodyguard training courses alongside other instructors. Eventually I ran my own training courses. I became the Director of International Training – a grand title for running about four training courses a year in various countries for both individuals and security companies. Training took me to Israel, Sweden, Austria, Russia, Spain, France, Iceland, Denmark, the Yemen, Tanzania, Nigeria and Malaysia. I enjoyed working as a bodyguard, but loved instructing. That was my strength; I really enjoyed teaching others what I knew and seeing how total strangers would eventually come together and end up working closely as a team. And I am proud when I receive an occasional email from one of my students describing an assignment they are on or a person they have looked after. I have ex-students looking after Arabs in London and celebrities in the USA. I have ex-students that have been to Kosovo and Brazil, Colombia, Bolivia and the states of the former Soviet Union. I proudly saw one former WFB instructor standing behind Milosevich during his war crime trial in the Hague. WFB members are everywhere.

The WFB went on to have eventual representation in over 40 countries. Almost everywhere we would go, either as instructors or on operations, someone in the industry would have heard of the WFB.

In the summer of 1999 Dan Sommer, the head of International Operations for SECURITAS in Iceland attended a WFB basic beginners' course in Wales. He came back on a second course, this time bringing with him a couple of colleagues. Dan loved the world of close protection and had just formed a subsidiary of SECURITAS called Global Executive Outreach which was designed to be the Bodyguarding arm of SECURITAS. At the beginning of the year 2000, Dan Sommer called me and inquired whether we would be interested in selling the WFB. Eventually we agreed and the WFB was sold to SECURITAS in April 2000, twelve years after completing my first bodyguard contract.

The WFB's policy was not just to train students and leave them to their own devices thereafter, but to try to help those that had trained with us to find work. We could proudly boast that about 50 per cent of the students that trained with the WFB would go on to work. For the new officer the first assignment was always the hardest, but once that was added to a CV, coupled with a good training background, students found it easier to find the second and third contract and prospective employers took more notice.

I had a regular annual close protection contract in Stoke-on-Trent. It certainly was not going to be the glamorous first-class lifestyle that many bodyguards envisage. It was a rough place and a rough job. The conditions were bad, the hours were long and the pay miserable. It was one of those contracts that I gave new recruits to test their disposition and stamina and so I contacted a few students that had just completed one of the WFB's basic bodyguard courses in Wales. Would they complain or would they just do the job to the best of their ability?

Altogether I needed a team of eight – two to protect the principal and six to provide residential and other guarding duties. The event was a Pakistani religious festival and attending was one of the highest-ranking religious leaders outside Pakistan – Saint Pir Pandariman. Our task was to protect him and look after the thousands of visitors throughout the festival. Residential security started at around 10 a.m. and finished well after midnight and close protection to Saint Pir Pandariman started at around 2 p.m. and finished at around 11 p.m. Almost all of that time was spent standing next to him, on either side assessing the movements of the worshippers – making sure no-one touched his worship in their frenzy to get close and be blessed.

Food was provided by the hosts: curry. Curry for breakfast,

curry for lunch and curry for dinner. The security team joined the organizers and staff seated on the floor in one of the main rooms not designated for worship. The food served hot and placed in the centre, they ate with their hands in the traditional way.

The accommodation was appalling. The team had to sleep in an almost empty and derelict terraced house opposite the temple. There was no furniture, apart from eight single beds and a couple of electric fires. Even the hot water wasn't working and every morning the team traipsed off to the local leisure centre nearby where they took their showers and got dressed.

For the two responsible for close protection, the task was to meet his worship as he arrived and stand with him for the duration of his visit, while the residential security team would patrol the perimeter, check the car park, check deliveries and meet, greet and search every single visitor.

I called four students from the previous training course. Most were more than happy to work and silently put up with the appalling conditions. Darren didn't complain and has since gone on to find full-time employment in London looking after the estate of a wealthy businessman. Steve didn't complain either and has since looked after many celebrities and artists worldwide including Tim Robbins, Susan Sarandon and Sean Penn. Scott complained about everything and anything, was more concerned about his diet and finding a gym than working effectively and has done nothing more in the world of close protection. But the worst response was when I called Dave. Dave was quite a good student and easily passed the course but when I called him his reply was, 'What, just three hundred pounds! You expect me to work all those hours and live in those conditions for just three hundred pounds, after I paid over a thousand for your course. No thanks, call me when you have something better.' Needless to say I never called him again and, as far as I heard, he is still driving a lorry for a living.

Those that are successful in this business are those willing to put up with a lot of shit for a long time and still have the determination and willpower to succeed. Only then will they truly reap the rewards of the job, travel the world and live in first class accommodation, but it is a very long road for most newcomers to the industry.

Many students also believe that having spent £1000 on an eight-day beginners' course qualifies them to work in any environment protecting anyone. There are a certain number of students that never consider further training. They also end up never doing much in the business and can be a danger to colleagues and the client by pretending they have skills that they don't. Officers should never exaggerate their skills or lie about their experience, but over the years I have met many that have.

On the doors at Tiger Tiger, a nightclub in central Manchester where I was head doorman for a few weeks, I was chatting to a fellow doorman who immediately boasted he was a bodyguard and had just returned from protecting an oil executive in the oilfields just outside Moscow. Now by that time I knew a lot about Russia and in particular Moscow and knew that the nearest oilfields were many thousands of miles away down in the Caspian Sea. When I pointed this out to him he walked off and hid in the corner of the club, after calling me a know-all wanker. Russia seems to be a favourite with those that boast of their experiences; I suppose they don't expect to be working the doors with someone that really does have experience there. I met one girl on another door who boasted she was a bodyguard after leaving an army unit where she was tasked to translate secret Russian intelligence documents into English. Wow, I thought, she must be fluent, so I tried out my Russian to see what she thought of it.

'Strastvooteay kak dila,' I said, which simply means, 'Hello, how are you?'

She looked at me and said, 'Sorry?' so I repeated it. I knew it was perfect because I have said it time and time again in Moscow and everyone understood.

'Strastvooteay kak dila. It means hello, how are you?' I said.

'Oh,' she said dimly, 'of course, I have forgotten most of my Russian, it was many years ago.' She was only 24 . I didn't pursue that conversation – she knew she had been caught out. She never worked that door again.

It is better for someone to say they have no experience but be willing to learn than to bullshit. I can normally tell the bullshitters because they come out with things about the business that just don't make sense. However, even I get caught out sometimes.

We were running another basic course in Wales when I had a call from a bodyguard, already in the business with a lot of experience, but who wanted to join the WFB without having to attend one of our courses. I don't normally take much notice of a CV, as anyone can write their own, but I read it and for some reason invited him to work alongside me for a few days, as we were short of an instructor. Maybe it was because he was originally from my home town of Norwich and currently working the doors in some of the clubs I had worked. I told him to come on the third day and to stay three days. I wanted to see how he operated and asked him to lead the team on a client pickup from Cardiff airport. It was his chance to show me what he was capable of. Could he organize the team, pick up the client and return safely to base? His CV had stated that he had been a team leader on many occasions in Northern Ireland so I was sure he was able to perform this simple one-day exercise. Of course, I had already arranged that things would not go as planned.

A little bit arrogant and obviously nervous, he arrived late afternoon after making the long journey from Norwich to the base. That evening, over dinner, I introduced him to the team. I told them that he would be their team leader the following day for the airport pickup. I think the students were relieved that I didn't pick one of them to run the team, as I had on previous days. Normally every day I picked a team leader to organize the rest of the students. It was their duty to make sure the base was clean, food was prepared and to take charge on exercises and tasks for that day. It was tough for those with little or no experience but was a good way for me to see how people operate under pressure and whether the decisions made by the team leader that day were the best under the circumstances.

Keith was up until late into the night preparing the team and planning a route. Satisfied that everything was in order, he and his team finally got to bed around 2 a.m. They had an early start and a long drive in the morning.

Unfortunately I had to sleep on the sofa in the living room as the place was full with students and there was nowhere for me to sleep. I gave the last remaining bed to a fellow instructor. My colleagues always joked that I could fall asleep almost anywhere and often commented on my snoring as I was found in the most peculiar of places fast asleep. I was also already awake and sitting in the kitchen area having an early brew when Keith appeared.

Good start I thought. Eager, keen, that is what I like.

He was shocked to see me wide-eyed and awake.

'Morning,' I said cheerfully.

'Morning. You are up early. Not tired?'

'Of course not,' I laughed. He didn't know that I would go back to bed for a couple of hours once they had all left.

'All prepared?' I asked. 'It's a simple day, an easy pickup. You won't let me down, will you?'

'Me?' he said a little arrogantly. 'No, I won't let you down.' I never liked arrogance. It can get you killed. I have seen many arrogant people, on the doors and as bodyguards, and generally they end up with their tail between their legs.

'I am sure you won't. Now go and get the others up, you have a long day ahead.'

I had arranged for my friend and ex-bodyguard Pat to arrive at Cardiff Airport and act as our client for a couple of days. Pat was a great guy but left the industry to take on a more lucrative career in computer programming. He was earning around £100,000 a year – far more than he would ever earn as a bodyguard. However he missed the excitement, and jumped at the chance of being our client for a few fun-packed days. During his short time on the circuit he gained the reputation of being a true professional. Exact and meticulous, he worked hard and didn't suffer fools gladly; he would destroy those around him that didn't live up to his high standards. I liked Pat a lot, and away from the industry he was as warm and kind-hearted a person as anyone could wish to meet.

He was no lightweight and at 20 stone I knew he would give the students a hard time. I was looking forward to it.

Pat was due to arrive at the airport at 11.30, and the team had arranged to be there an hour earlier to liaise with airport security and recce the place before their client arrived. Because there were no actual flights from London to Cardiff, Pat in fact caught the train but would make out he had just arrived by walking into the arrivals hall.

It seemed Keith had everything planned – they were suited and booted and ready to leave. The cars, however, were dirty. We had been jumping in and out of them for two days practising embus and debus and no carwash would ever get the cars clean enough for a client to sit in.

'Is there anything you have forgotten?' I asked Keith in front of his team before they set off out the door.

'No, I am prepared. I have done loads of pickups, don't worry, I won't let you down,' he said, again a bit arrogantly.

'And the cars, they are fully prepared, cleaned and checked?'

His face drained. 'Fuck,' he said and rushed outside to see the cars standing in the muddy driveway, splattered and covered in grime and mud.

He thought quickly. 'Ok, we'll stop at the nearest carwash and put them through, a couple of times if necessary.'

'Ok,' I said and could see the look of relief on his face. 'What about the insides?'

Foolishly he instructed everyone to change back into their working clothes and clean the insides of all three cars – they didn't have time to do the outsides. I asked myself there and then how could anyone who was supposed to have had experience leading a team of bodyguards in Northern Ireland forget to prepare the vehicles – one of the most important and critical environments for the client. I immediately realized that he was just another bullshitter.

An hour late they were finally ready to depart but by that time the team was getting pretty pissed off with their new leader. But worse was to come.

They drove to Cardiff in silence. The team leader was in the lead car with Robert in the back, while the rest were in the other two cars. Robert was to observe and assess their performance and detail every mistake, but was not to say a thing during the exercise, only during the debriefing back at base. On the way back Robert would sit in one of the other cars and assess the team while Pat, the client, would assess the team leader.

No-one fucked with Robert and I knew that with him and Pat on the case, every slight mistake would be highlighted and examined in minute detail. I was sure it was going to be a long night's debriefing.

Because they were late leaving the base, and because they had to put all three cars through the carwash twice (at a cost of over £40, which Keith paid from his own pocket), they had no time to recce the airport and just about made it for 11.30. Pat was already standing there waiting, because of course, I had arranged for the 'flight' to arrive early.

Both Pat and Robert were furious but held back their anger. The team managed get Pat into the vehicle with a fairly good formation and then drove away from the airport in good style. However, from there things started to go terribly wrong for poor old Keith and his team.

Pat sent me a text message once he had been picked up. I had Keith's mobile number and about 45 minutes after pickup I called him.

'Base here, Urgent. Primary route compromised, get on to your secondary route. Repeat. Primary route compromised, get onto your secondary route.'

'What secondary route?' came his reply.

'What!' I screamed. I could not believe what I had just heard. 'What do you mean what secondary route?' I shouted, spitting with anger down the phone. 'Do you mean you only have one route back to base?'

'Err . . .'

'You had better get onto a secondary route this minute.'

I slammed down the phone.

Apparently, in the front of the car with a client in the back, he unfolded his map and searched for a secondary route. Finally, about 20 minutes later, he managed to find an alternative route and relay the instructions to the lead car, which didn't have a map. For the rest of the journey Keith had to pass on the route to the lead car with the rear car following blindly. It was becoming a farce.

Pat texted me again, telling me they were finally onto a second route. I texted Pat back telling him to have a heart attack. As Pat was having his attack in the back of the car, I called Keith.

'Where is the fucking hospital?' I screamed.

'I don't know.'

'What do you mean you don't know? Are we just going to let the client have a heart attack in the back of your fucking vehicle?'

'I'll call for an ambulance.'

'You have a fucking car, don't call for a fucking ambulance, get him to a hospital now.'

But of course he didn't know where the hospital was because he was on a route he hadn't planned to be on. Miraculously Pat quickly recovered and instructed that the journey back to base resume.

But the farce didn't end. Two cars had gone through a set of lights just as they were turning red and so the rear vehicle had to stop. But the junction was complex and there was a roundabout shortly after the lights with a few exits and the third vehicle lost the convoy.

The first two cars arrived back to base first and I told them to stand down until the third vehicle arrived. It did so about 30 minutes later. I didn't want to know or hear anything until the debriefing, which I knew would be long and arduous. I instructed the students to eat and be ready for de-brief in 45 minutes.

A few of the students sat in the kitchen drinking tea, while the others went off for showers and to get changed. Keith came down, with his bags packed.

'Where the fuck are you going?' I asked angrily. The other students stood milling around, wondering what was going on.

'I have to go back; I have to work this weekend.'

'What, on the doors?'

'Yeah, I can't get a replacement,' he said, walking out the door. I decided not to try to change his mind. To him the door that weekend was more important than a career in close protection. He knew he was out of his league and had bullshitted both the students and the instructors. He had fucked up, knew it and wanted out. He was no bodyguard.

When I wasn't away on contract, either working or instructing, I would come back to working the doors. It was in my soul, my heart, it was part of me. I loved doing the doors. On the doors I was somebody – I had reputation, respect and I controlled my environment. I would always prefer it to sitting at home watching telly. I could never be away from the doors for long.

For a further three years, as I developed my bodyguarding portfolio, I worked the doors in Norwich. I ended up working a total of ten doors in and around Norwich city centre, each one having its own problems – there were to be many more violent times but also lots of laughs. The doors were changing, because the music and the environment were changing. I started doing the doors at the height of the disco era – there were no drugs, Ecstasy wasn't yet popular, cocaine was available but certainly not to the majority, and most other drugs were solely used by addicts. But during my time on the doors in Norwich things were slowly changing. Ecstasy was becoming more available while disco slowly disappeared and was replaced by house music. I didn't mind. I noticed that with the introduction of drugs into the club environment, violence became less common. Everyone became more chilled out and calmer. Alcohol fuelled violence, drugs suppressed it. Most people on drugs just wanted to fuck and not fight, and this suited me quite well.

The first tabs of Ecstasy were brought to Norwich by a gangster I shall call Eddie C (not his real name). He had arrived in Norwich with his wife and daughter shortly after I completed my bodyguard course with Allen. They had left Glasgow as apparently Eddie was increasingly being targeted by the police. They wanted him off the streets but had problems finding concrete evidence. He was constantly getting pulled, stopped and searched. Eddie once told me the story of when he and his family were going on holiday. With his wife and children in the car, the police closed the motorway, surrounded them, pulled him from his vehicle to the floor, and handcuffed him while they pulled everything to bits. They suspected he was running firearms.

He had served time a few years prior to Norwich, apparently for beating two guys almost to death on the door at a club in central Glasgow, but since then the police had never been able to pin anything on Eddie. No-one ever knew what brought him to Norwich, but he rented a nice little house on the outskirts of the city and set himself up in 'business'.

We got acquainted while training at a new gym that had opened up on Prince of Wales Road. I wouldn't train there often, just occasionally as a break from the dungeon at CEYMS. Eddie and I developed a friendship. He seemed a nice guy but knew a lot of menacing-looking people from out of Norwich that frequently visited him at the gym. He would often be found sitting in the lounge area of the solarium next door, drinking coffee and chatting with his business associates. I wasn't sure if anyone, apart from Eddie and his associates, actually used the solarium for the normal purpose of getting tanned.

Eddie wasn't tall but was in good shape for a 40-year-old. He was a keen bodybuilder and, as well as selling Ecstasy, soon became the biggest steroid dealer in the area. He was as cheap as my other supplier so it was more convenient to buy off him. Eddie looked after himself, bought creams and lotions for his face and even had plastic surgery to lift the wrinkles from his eyes. On his own he wasn't unbeatable but no-one messed with him, as he knew guys harder than most of the hardest men in Norwich.

Apart from Bob's door company, most other doormen were still employed by the pubs and clubs themselves, but that started to change. A guy called Ramsey Khachik, who ran most of the doors in Leicester, was pally with Eddie and started to supply doormen to venues in Norwich, hiring locally or sending lads from Leicester. Ramsey was a hard-looking Asian guy, tall, muscular, intimidating – the guys he brought were also well-built hard-men and there was little most of the doormen in Norwich at that time could do about it.

Bob kept his doors, I kept mine, but many of the other

doors went to the new interlopers. Along with the doors went the sale of Ecstasy. It was brought from Leicester and distributed around the pubs and clubs. I was asked to 'come under their fold', as they eloquently put it, but I always refused and was never intimidated. Eddie became a friend and knew I would not involve myself in any way with his drug underworld. It was not my scene or my style – I was enjoying my life on the doors, and occasionally as a bodyguard, and was astute enough to realize that would all come crashing down should I have taken that other route.

Ramsey and Eddie never interfered with our lives and our doors and we didn't have much to do with them. We were small fry compared to the potential team they could bring to Norwich if they desired but thankfully they left us alone. However they eventually took over many of the other doors in and around Norwich.

CHAPTER SEVEN

The Smoke

Norwich had its fair share of trouble and I had got used to violence over seven years of working the door. I felt that I could handle almost any situation, either diplomatically or aggressively, and, coupled with the few close protection contracts I had also fulfilled, now had a whole range of other interesting experiences under my belt. I felt confident in my abilities and attitude in almost every situation, but I was still a bit nervous about going to London.

I was asked by Mark Ovenden, a manager for whom I worked briefly at Rick's Place nightclub in Norwich, to run his door at a new venue he had just taken over in Ealing, west London.

Apparently Mark had been trying to get hold of me for quite a while but I had never stayed in one place for long enough. Plus I was spending more and more time abroad. He finally found me through Bob, who called me and told me to call Mark. Before the week was up I was on my way to London.

Norwich is a fairly quiet provincial city. London was totally different and I knew I was going to have to start all over again. I would have to prove myself to the other doormen, as well as to the local thugs and gangsters, of whom I was sure there would be many. I was looking forward to it. I was bored with the Norwich nightclub scene and I was getting complacent.

With a couple of bags full of clothes and a box full of books

(Monet and Manet, my two favourite French impressionists, and a few novels by my favourite authors: Graham Greene, Paolo Coelho, Vladimir Nabokov and Gabriel Garcia Marquez – my books went with me everywhere), I arrived at the Broadway Boulevard, a big 1,500-capacity nightclub in the centre of Ealing Broadway. I was to meet Mark there.

The club was due to re-open after an extensive refurbishment. The owner was an incredibly wealthy Irish builder called Shaun Henley. Henley had employed Mark via a headhunting agency, although apparently Mark and Shaun didn't get on too well from the very beginning. Mark was offered and took the job and looked forward to the challenge of opening and running a large venue in the capital.

Mark and I got on very well – I had built up a good friendship with him and his wife Jenny. He understood my loyalty and knew that I would almost certainly be available to work with him anywhere. My brief was to form a small security company to run the contract. My company would invoice the nightclub and Mark would pay me cash at the end of every week. It was a big contract and there was no way I could stand paying the guys every week while I waited for the normal 30-day invoicing period, so we agreed on a weekly cash payment system.

I didn't have grand aspirations to run all the doors in the west of London but, once I had settled, I was hoping to perhaps provide doormen to three or four other venues in the area. I would settle in at the Boulevard and then look at expanding. I had always worked the doors for someone else and thought it was about time I tried my own door company. I wasn't very hungry for contracts in Norwich. I didn't want to go up against Eric and Ramsey and was happy to plod along working for Bob, getting paid cash every week, doing other bits and pieces when I could as well as occasionally working abroad.

When times were bad I even signed on the dole but generally

I was doing fine without the commitment and obligations of running a company. But London would have to be different. I was 29 years old. I knew I couldn't continue with this life.

My first marriage had failed as had a succession of other short-term relationships, none of which lasted more than a few months. I had a life of violence and aggression, of brief relationships and instability. Although I have lots of good attributes and characteristics, generally I was pretty emotionally dysfunctional – I simply could not stay in one place and with one person for any length of time. I hated any form of commitment but, I thought, moving to London might change my outlook. I might find more security and I might eventually accept being loved and loving just one person, without destroying things before they had any chance of developing.

In London I also might have the opportunity to build a successful business. My bodyguarding career was developing and I was sure I could expand things further by being based in London.

I was hoping for a lot.

The problem in London was that I knew no-one. I had no idea how I was going to get a team ready for opening night a week later. Mark's requirements were for 15 doormen Fridays and Saturdays, ten Wednesdays and Thursdays and two doormen in the feeder bar attached to the nightclub the remainder of the week when the nightclub was closed. The bar was open seven nights a week, but just fed the nightclub for four nights.

Mark had already been in London for a few weeks overseeing the refurbishment. He had met Ian (Tinker), who had come into the club one afternoon and inquired about doing the door himself. Mark told Tinker that he already had someone in mind but perhaps we could run the door together. Mark trusted me and Tinker had good contacts for the lads.

Mark arranged a meeting between himself, Tinker and me.

I was big, and certainly one of the biggest and strongest doormen in Norwich, but Tinker was huge; at least 20 stone on a frame three inches shorter than mine. He was wearing probably the only clothes he could find to fit: old tracksuit bottoms, t-shirt and fleece jacket. His skin was extremely bad, probably due to the huge amounts of steroids he must have taken to maintain his immense size and strength. He had a shaven head and earrings – he wasn't a pretty-looking man, but seemed decent enough, and he knew where to find the quantity and quality of lads we needed.

We formed a company, which, after paying the lads' wages, would give both Tinker and me a very good living wage. Of course Tinker would have earned a lot more had he been doing the door without me, and vice versa, but we both would still come out with at least £500 each plus a wage from the nights we worked ourselves. I would work as many as possible – Tinker would just work four nights. This gave him almost £900 per week and myself over a grand. I was content with my wage, and I thought that Tinker was as well.

It took five days for Tinker to get 15 guys together for an afternoon's training and induction. He got most of them from a gym he trained at in Bethnal Green. Some were the biggest guys I had ever seen: Mark Smith, who later went on to be Rhino in *Gladiators*, Pat Rogers (who went on to a brief career as a bodyguard), Sylvester, Stretch – because he was even bigger than Tinker and Rhino – and many others. It was a big team.

Pat and I would work the feeder bar from 8 p.m. until about midnight seven nights a week, then from Wednesday through to Saturday we would finish our shift in the club. Tinker would be head doorman at the nightclub as he knew all the lads quite well and anyway, he only wanted to work the club. I was happy working the bar.

No-one in their right mind would dare to cause trouble at a club whose doormen collectively weighed more than a small planet. But, as in any nightclub anywhere in the world, there were always drunks and idiots, and Ealing Broadway certainly had its share. Ealing had one other nightclub in its centre, but the Boulevard was the biggest and the best and so there was always some kind of trouble on the front door. The club was full four nights a week, so many had to be turned away.

We had lots of small scuffles and fights but it was such a huge door team we rarely had any major problems. However, on one occasion we really did have to work hard for our money.

Tinker and Rhino had turned away a large group of rough-looking lads. After a major stand-off on the front door, with six huge doormen standing ready to battle around 12 much smaller Asian guys, a lot of verbal abuse and confrontation, they slowly backed off and dispersed. We thought it had ended when a scream came over the radio – they had stormed the back doors.

There were two exits close to each other at the back of the nightclub. One of their friends had somehow got in and opened one of the exits. A couple of the doormen on duty inside the venue had managed to get to the exit and were fiercely fighting to stop them getting in. The rest of the Asians had obviously found something heavy and large as the second exit was being rammed from the outside and started to splinter as the whole double exit doors shook and the hinges were slowly giving way. We all rushed to the back exits and started battling. The other back exit finally gave way and in poured about another eight of them. The music stopped, the halogen house lights came on and customers either cowered as far from the scene as possible or left the club altogether.

After what seemed like an eternity we managed to throw out all those we knew had come in the back way. Thankfully none of the doormen suffered injury but a few of the invaders had been battered badly.

The club closed early that night, but we all sat around until dawn drinking and going over the night's events, laughing to ourselves, still high on adrenalin.

The feeder bar upstairs was generally full by 9 p.m., but by 11.30 it would be almost empty. Most customers, not wanting to queue or be turned away from the nightclub, would leave. It made kicking out at the end of the night an easy job for Pat and me.

A friend found me a wonderful apartment the other side of town in the Docklands, in a development still under construction. The open-plan living room and kitchen had beautiful wooden flooring and a glass wall from ceiling to floor, with central sliding doors overlooking the River Thames and Greenwich. There were two apartments per floor, and I lived on the second floor where my neighbour was the Page Three model Samantha Fox. Downstairs there was a small communal multi-gym, swimming pool, sauna and jacuzzi and private underground parking. It was a wonderful place to live, and far enough from work not to have to worry about anyone knocking on my door.

Julian, my best friend with whom I worked at Ritzy and Hy's, came to live with me for a while until he found his own apartment. He had left the doors a few years earlier and became a manager for Pizza Hut. He was given their Oxford Street branch. We had a great time together until he found his own small place near to Tower Bridge. He had just started seeing a beautiful Italian girl who he later married and moved back to Italy. He settled and is still happily married and has two wonderful daughters.

I felt I also wanted to settle. I met Kim, a gorgeous Vietnamese girl at the Boulevard one evening. Kim was slim, delicate and stunningly beautiful. She was orphaned as a child and handed to Canadian soldiers on the penultimate helicopter leaving the roof of the American Embassy as Saigon fell. Her first few years were spent in Thailand at an orphanage. An English couple had been over twice to see her and when they finally managed to complete the adoption papers she was brought to the UK. Her adoptive father was Indian, her adoptive mother English. She also had another adoptive Thai sister. I wondered to myself if there was anything relevant to me marrying women that had been adopted? Or was it sheer coincidence?

She was standing outside the club waiting for a friend when I started chatting to her. I asked her out, she said yes and three months later we were walking up the aisle in a little church in Norwich. When I met her she was only 17 and had lied to me about her age – when we married she had just turned 18 although I had thought she was a lot older. Her beauty intoxicated me. She really was stunning, with delicate, doll-like features and a tight, small body.

She was a child model and at five years old she played alongside Yul Brynner in the West End play *Anna and the King of Siam*. She kept all the countless boxes of toys, catalogues, brochures that she had modelled for.

She was stunning but simply far too young and soon got on my nerves with her behaviour and immature ways. She couldn't cook or clean – I had to do everything and, needless to say, we didn't stay married for long.

In the summer of 1991 I had to go to Thailand. I was contracted to do an initial assessment for a major pop star's Asian tour. It was only one week's work but we decided to stay six. Because her adoptive sister was Thai, the family maintained strong ties with the country and had many friends living there, both Thai and European, so we decided to have a holiday. Her mother, father and sister came with us and we booked a few rooms in a small guesthouse in the centre of Bangkok.

The club was running well, we had a good strong team, there was little trouble and what there was was easily manageable and I didn't see any problems with me taking the time off.

My contract was actually cancelled as the pop star in question decided that Asia and the climate was just too unhealthy for him and probably his pet chimpanzee (yes, it was Wacko himself), but we had all booked the flights and went anyway.

Thailand was an incredible country. The people were warm and friendly and kind, the countryside stunning and the weather wonderful. The only thing I hated were the massive cockroaches that would drop with a clunk in the middle of the night from the ventilation shaft in our room and scuttle noisily across the wooden floor towards our bed.

By sheer coincidence Mark Ovenden was taking a holiday at that same time – we were both due back on or around the same day, although he was only going away for two weeks as opposed to my six. I left the running of the door to Tinker, and Mark left the running of the nightclub to the owner, Shaun Henley. Neither of us had jobs when we got back.

Tinker had always been greedy – he always moaned that he wasn't earning enough money, that he had commitments and obligations that he had trouble fulfilling. I had known Mark for many years, we got on really well, yet Tinker didn't like Mark and he took any opportunity to belittle him in front of the other doormen. Not to his face but behind his back.

When we were away, Tinker sidled up to Shaun Henley and told him about a fictitious arrangement Mark had made with me regarding the door money. Tinker told Shaun that Mark was getting a weekly backhander for getting me the contract. It wasn't true; Mark had asked me to work for him simply because he trusted me to run an excellent door and he knew my capabilities. Doormen are extremely loyal to good managers; it's like a client–bodyguard relationship. In a bizarre way doormen would probably die for their managers if necessary. But Shaun didn't much like Mark and so believed everything Tinker had told him.

While I was away I called Tinker numerous times and left

loads of messages on his answer machine, firstly because I had arranged with Tinker for him to put my salary into my bank account every week so I could access the money while I was away, and secondly I called informing him of the dates and times of my return. With each message I asked him to urgently contact me but he didn't return any of my calls and nothing was paid into my account.

The minute I got back to the UK I called Sylvester. He worked at the Boulevard and I trained with Sly almost every day at the gym in Bethnal Green. He was a good friend. I asked him what was going on and he replied sadly that I should not go to work – Tinker was now running the contract. He told me that Shaun had given the contract directly to Tinker. He also warned me that Tinker had quite a few lads ready to handle me should I turn up at the Boulevard.

Mark was still away but was due back the following day. I wrote a letter to him explaining briefly what was going on and dropped it through his letterbox, asking him to contact me immediately on his return, which he did. I had no money, as Tinker had refused to pay anything to me while I was away, and I now had no job. I was also married to a mad Vietnamese teenager that didn't know how to put a kettle on. Because I had no job, there was no way I could afford to keep up payments on the apartment. Things were not looking good.

I explained everything but there was nothing Mark could do either – he had been put on a month's paid suspension until Shaun Henley decided what to do. Shaun sacked Mark. Mark eventually took Shaun to court for unfair dismissal and about three years later he paid Mark compensation.

But I was fucked. I came back from Thailand to absolutely nothing. I was being paid cash so there was no written contract, which prevented me from doing anything legal. So I decided to do something on my own. I had decided that this greedy shit Tinker was going to be punished. I was going to make him suffer – I would make him beg forgiveness.

I went to see a female friend Susan who had got me the apartment in the Docklands. She had moved back to London after a brief spell living with her boyfriend in Norwich. Susan was the only girl in a family of nine brothers, and all her brothers were criminals. They ran a lot of the East End of London.

They were a notoriously hard family and were into anything and everything, from drugs to car ringing, from prostitution to protection. Susan did her own thing – she led a very comfortable existence, renting a big apartment in another wharf complex close by. She never worked.

Susan had just recently been released from Holloway prison. I had been to see her a few times until she was transferred to an open prison in the Midlands for the remainder of her sentence. She had made an awful lot of money borrowing from the banks but forgetting to pay them back. Because of an unrelated incident she was caught and sentenced to three years.

She was a lovely-looking lady: late thirties, immaculately dressed, well-spoken and never would anyone ever suspect her of being a criminal. She looked as much a criminal as I looked an accountant.

'I need a favour,' I said as we walked through the local Tesco supermarket car park. I explained what I wanted. We never talked about anything sensitive on the phone or at our apartments. Susan regularly had a friend sweep her apartment for listening devices and was always cautious, especially after her recent spell at Her Majesty's Hotel.

A week later she called me. 'Your book is here,' she said.

'Thanks, have you read it?'

'No, but it looks good. Let's meet.'

'Same place?' I asked.

'No, number two,' she said.

'Ok, in about an hour.' I put the phone down and put my coat on. I would get to our number two meeting place 30 minutes or so early, just to check that she wasn't being followed.

I sat in my car in the far corner of the car park where nothing could park behind me and where I could see most vehicles coming and going through the main entrance. Number two meeting place was the Sainsbury's car park on the east side of the Isle of Dogs. The Docklands was a bizarre place. The east side housed many poor black, African and Asian immigrants and the signs are written in Bangladeshi and Urdu. The west side is where the multi-millionaire yuppies lived in renovated modern apartments. The National Front also had its headquarters on the Isle, so it really was a diverse mixture of cultures and classes.

Susan drove in, parked and waited. We both waited to see whether anyone had followed her in. After about ten minutes I got out of my car and walked over to hers and jumped in the passenger side.

'Your toy is in the bag, cleaned and untraceable,' she said. 'What are you going to do, have a fucking war?'

'Yeah, in the centre of London.' I didn't even look into the McDonald's bag which contained my toy, I just rolled up the top of the bag a bit more, kissed Susan on the cheek and said my goodbyes.

I was going to shoot Tinker as he got into his car after work that night. I was going to empty the full magazine into him. I realized I would have to kill him. I couldn't injure him or threaten him, as he knew an awful lot of people and I was certain that he would be knocking on my door with a team bigger than I could handle, and it would then be me in a casket and not him. So I had to kill him, to show him and everyone around him that I was not to be fucked with. What he did to me was done purely to satisfy his greed. He had got me the sack and had made me homeless – I thought I had every right to kill him.

I understood that I would be the prime suspect. People knew I had a major grudge against him, but surely there must be others with such a grudge? Also I decided to kill him after work so it could also be attributed to someone that he might have turned away that evening. I would then disappear for a few weeks, giving me more than enough time to dispose of the weapon. The police might eventually bring me in and question me, but I would have an alibi and plead innocence, and at least I would get my revenge. I had nothing: no job, no money, no home, and a fucked-up wife – I had nothing to lose.

At about a quarter past three in the morning I stood in the High Street, outside the club, waiting for Tinker to leave work. I knew that most evenings we would have cleared the place by about twenty-five past three, and ten minutes after, most of us would be on our way home. I knew where Tinker normally parked his car – there was a small car park opposite the club, which was accessible down a small driveway, dark and almost empty at that time of night. There was also pedestrian access from the car park to Bond Street, then out onto New Broadway. New Broadway runs down the centre of Ealing Broadway and, at that time of night, would be packed with people and cars. I would shoot him as he started his short walk down the small dark drive leading to his car and escape via the rear of the car park, slipping silently into the crowd. I didn't have a silencer so I knew that firing the number of bullets I intended would cause a great deal of commotion, but I would have disappeared by the time the police arrived.

At about twenty to four I heard laughter and voices from the front door of the club. I was standing on the street side behind one of the pillars near the post office. There was CCTV covering almost all of the shopping centre, but not on the street. Tinker couldn't see me standing the other side of the pillar. I heard the front door close behind them and two people talking: Tinker and Sylvester.

'See you tomorrow,' I heard Sylvester say.

'Yea, see you tomorrow,' Tinker replied. I heard Sylvester's footsteps disappear up the road as I watched Tinker cross the street towards the car park and his car. I followed behind him, my sweaty hand gripping the weapon tightly in my coat pocket. The safety catch was off, the magazine was full and I was ready. My heart was racing, I was nervous but prepared. Because of his greed and selfishness he had taken my job, my money and my home and because of my anger and madness I was going to take his life. I followed as he disappeared down the drive. Suddenly a hand grabbed my shoulder.

'He's not worth it,' a voice behind me whispered. I turned round; it was Sylvester. 'Robin, he's not worth it, he is not worth serving time for. Leave it, what goes around comes around, he will have his time.'

I turned towards the sound of his car starting up. It was too late to catch him before he got into his car, but I could shoot him through the windscreen as he came towards me or I could shoot him through the window as he passed.

Or should I just walk away, build a new life, get myself back on my feet, and try again. Maybe I did have more to live for – maybe better things would happen in my life.

I looked at Sylvester once more, hesitated and then nodded. 'You're right,' I said solemnly.

He put his arm around my shoulders and turned me away from the car park entrance. We walked off as Tinker's car emerged. Tinker never knew how close he came to dying.

Eight years later, Pat Rogers was drinking at his local pub near Maidenhead. Seated in the corner was a thin, gaunt, ill-looking man who, initially, Pat didn't recognize.

'Pat,' the man said. Pat turned round. He still didn't recognize him. This man looked so old, so ill.

'It's me, Tinker. Boulevard, remember?'

Apparently, according to Pat, Tinker had just been released from prison where he had served five years. He looked a sad, miserable, lonely old man, sitting on his own in the corner of the pub, with his pint. Maybe it was better that I didn't kill him; maybe he went through hell being alive and in prison.

CHAPTER EIGHT

Paris and Bosnia

I was in a real mess and completely destitute. I had to go on the dole but I hadn't been legally working so there was no record of me earning. I had no P45 and had to make up a story that I was trying to start my own business but ran out of cash before the business had a chance of developing. I wasn't allowed Unemployment Benefit, just Income Support, which amounted to about £70 a week, plus a contribution towards the rent. But the rent in the Docklands was over £200 a week and the DHSS money didn't even cover the shortfall. I had a little money left for food but nothing to live on, let alone to pay the bills and, to cap it all, a few days after leaving the Boulevard the gearbox went on my Ford Sierra so I had no car either.

Mark let me have an old brown wreck that he had parked outside his front door for a few months but didn't use. The engine was good and it ran well, but the bodywork was falling to pieces. He called it the tea bag – because when it rained there were so many holes, water seeped in everywhere and soaked the floor and the back passenger seats. It had no MOT, I wasn't insured and there were just a few weeks left on the tax. But the petrol tank was full and I was just happy to have something to drive for a few weeks until I sorted myself out.

But even that had to go a few weeks after the tax expired and even the scrap metal merchant could not believe I had actually been driving it.

I lost my apartment and for a short time moved to Kim's parents' house. But that didn't work and soon after I split up with Kim – although that was on the cards anyway. From a beautiful and luxurious apartment in the Docklands I moved into a grotty bedsit on the outskirts of London.

I remained on the dole for a few months, trying to find some kind of work and struggling just to survive. Some days I would have no money, nothing at all, and had to wait inside until my next dole cheque arrived. I was desperate. I phoned Allen a few times to try and get another bodyguarding job but his answerphone was continually on, which meant he was still away. I was ready to move back to Norwich, when a call came from Mark.

He had been asked to go to Paris to manage a nightclub on the Champs Elysées. A British company called European Leisure had bought four units – Le Palace and the Privilege Club in Montmarte and Pau Brazil and Le Central on the Champs Elysées. Mark was well known within the nightclub management circuit and had approached European Leisure a few days after leaving the Boulevard. The Operations Manager, David Chipping, was temporarily based in Paris and was struggling to find a manager for Le Central. The French manager was ripping the place off, Dave knew it and needed to stop it, but didn't know how. He asked Mark to spend a week in Paris with a view to running the club, but Mark didn't want to live in Paris so he called me.

'You speak a little French, don't you?' he asked me, phoning from European Leisure's office in Paris.

'I do, why?'

'Well, get on a plane, I have a job for you.'

'I don't have enough money to eat, let alone buy a plane ticket.'

Mark bought the ticket which I collected at the airport and was on my way to Paris.

I had dropped from 18 stone to just over 14. I was pale and

gaunt. I had not eaten properly, had not been to the gym and certainly had no money for drugs. Mark didn't recognize me as I stepped off the plane.

On the way into Paris, Mark explained the situation with European Leisure. They had bought the four units but were having problems managing them. All the units had managers in place but Le Central was a particular problem. The management and staff knew that a British company had just bought the place and so had decided to take as much from the unit as possible. The labour laws in France were strict and it was not that easy to sack someone so my brief was to change everything, making it as hard for them as possible so that they left of their own accord without being sacked. David Chipping could not speak one word of French and shouted at the staff expecting them to understand. But they spoke no English and so it took great effort to get anything done.

There was already a 'head doorman' of sorts. He ran the security at Le Central and at a private African nightclub where he was based. Initially I was asked over in the capacity of Security Consultant, but things turned out a little different.

I would get paid £2,000 a month plus accommodation in an apartment next to the offices and above the Privilege Club. So, if I could only put up with Dave Chipping, I had an opportunity to start again. We met Dave in a Mexican restaurant and bar just across the road from the office. He was playing pool with a tiny balding guy who was introduced to me as 'the accountant'. He had also just arrived from their London office to oversee the transition from being French-owned to British. He would be sharing the apartment with me – apart from the time he accidentally locked himself in the office from Friday evening to Monday morning.

Dave seemed affable, but, according to Mark, I was not to be fooled by first impressions. I never fell out with Dave but I soon learned that he was a hard man to work for as well as rude and did nothing to promote Anglo-French relations.

Dave immediately told Mark that the general manager of Le Central had handed in his notice that morning. I was now asked not only to be the security manager but to be the temporary general manager until the company could find a replacement. I didn't even have an interview, but agreed to the job there and then.

My return flight was booked the next morning. Dave would get the manager of Le Palace to run Le Central for a few nights. I returned to London as planned, packed what few things I had, dropped my books off with Susan, and returned to Paris the next day.

Travelling from Place de la Concorde towards the Arc de Triomphe, Le Central was situated on the right-hand side of the Champs Elysées near the top end at number 102. The club was open from 10 p.m. until 5 a.m. Monday to Saturday. Up until around midnight the pavement was full of gorgeous-looking, stylish Parisians and tourists from almost every nation parading casually up and down. The nightclub office was above the front entrance, with a huge floor-to-ceiling window where I could look down from my desk onto the pavement below. The first day at the club I sat and looked at the traffic and people below and smiled a big fat smile. I was going to like living here and marvelled at my good fortune and the dramatic change in my lifestyle and environment.

Paris was glorious and the women were simply stunning. Even the toilet attendant at Le Central was beautiful, with long curly dark hair and a slim, fit body. She used to stand and talk to me as I was taking a piss, which was a bit disconcerting at first but I soon got used to it. In fact I often used to go for a piss when I really didn't have to!

However, the first few weeks at the nightclub were a nightmare, and the first few nights the worst. I spent the first day in the nightclub office sorting, re-filing, cleaning, checking the books, the liquor stocks, cloakroom and admission receipts. The club had a capacity of 1,000 but most nights, including weekends, the ledger showed admissions of only around 300. From the mess and contradictions in its administration, I knew I was going to have a lot of work to do.

That evening the first members of staff to arrive were the receptionist and his wife. For some reason they worked the reception together. During the day I had taken all the admission tickets and re-filed them, so I knew what numbers the next ticket would start at. I started a new ledger with the first admission ticket number logged as well as the last. I had also taken a clicker from the main office and I was going to stand on the door all night clicking every one in. I introduced myself. They said everyone was expecting me. I think they thought I was going to be another David Chipping and were surprised when I spoke to them in French.

The other staff slowly arrived and I greeted each one on the front door in French so they knew immediately I would understand what was going on and what they were saying. In fact a lot of the time I didn't; I hadn't spoken French since studying it at O level many years ago at school, but was blagging. I greeted the bar staff, the waiters, the cloakroom attendant, the glass collectors, the dancers, and finally, five minutes before opening, the doormen. I thought there was a lot of staff for a venue that only had 300 admissions.

The receptionist, Sebastien, said no-one really came into the venue until after 11 p.m., so I took a walk inside to see what was going on. Most of the staff were milling around talking, but as soon as they saw me walking down the steps they got to work. The club was down a large wide staircase in the basement of the building. The long front bar was separated from the dance floor by the mock wreck of an aeroplane, with seats in front of the fuselage and windows overlooking the dance floor. There were podiums on the floor for the dancers and seats and tables on both sides of the dance floor. At the far end of the club was the DJ console, hidden behind a pane of glass and accessed from a door to the side.

Every drink was 50 francs but most customers bought bottles of spirits which were tagged and held for them in a locked cage. This was where most of the bar staff and waiters made their money; they sold their own bottles of spirits. I noticed that a few were nervous when they saw me standing at the front door that first night. They probably realized that from now on it would be harder for them to get their bottles into the club without me noticing.

That first night, bottles were smashed and trays of glasses dropped. They swore and cursed and apologized, pretending it was an accident, but I knew better. They were demonstrating their anger at their sudden loss of vast extra income.

I returned to the door that first night at about 11 p.m., after clicking a few early admissions. I checked the admission tickets and the number on the tickets did not correspond to the number in my book. The receptionists had their own book of admission tickets. At 100 francs (£10) entrance per person, six nights a week, they had been making a wonderful salary.

When I questioned Sebastien he told me he always took the tickets home with him as he worked every night and sometimes couldn't get access to the office. I told him in future the system was changing and I was to give him the tickets at the start of the night and take them back at the end of the night, and that every customer would now be clicked in.

The nightclub was full that night, with over 1,000 admissions. We made three times more money than normal. Before I arrived it was probably one for the club, one for the manager and one for the staff.

I knew I just could not storm in and immediately change everything. Everyone would have walked out and instead of losing some money we would lose it all. So I slowly started to change things. I knew it was still being ripped off but it was now under more control and fairly minimal. Eventually I ended up getting on quite well with most of the staff, including all of the doormen, and even managed to shag the toilet attendant.

Doormen in France are different from doormen in the UK. They certainly do not look like a typical UK doorman. Most are average build, average height, polite and fairly non-aggressive. There is a completely different attitude to alcohol in France; pubs and clubs are open much longer, which means less binge drinking and so less violence. I never witnessed one fight in all the time I spent in Paris. Le Central was situated in the centre of Paris on one of the most famous streets in the world and most of the customers were tourists and the only problems arose when someone had one too many to drink and needed to be escorted out. There was always a heavy police presence nearby, as a Turkish consulate office was situated a few doors up from the club. The armed police in Paris had a fearsome reputation and dealt with drunks and yobs quickly and aggressively. No-one, particularly tourists, wanted to be carted off to a grimy French police station.

The biggest doorman was Gérard. His family originated from Angola but he grew up in Marseille. He was about 17 stone and well over 6ft, big, black and slightly unapproachable-looking as he stood in front of the door with his arms crossed, eyeing up the ladies as they struggled to get past. However, he was always friendly, laughed a lot and liked to play practical jokes on everyone, me included.

On a couple of consecutive nights a beautiful, tall, elegant black woman came to the club. I noticed her straight away – she was obviously not a tourist as she sounded French and seemed to know all the doormen well, especially Gérard. They would have a chat, laugh a little and stand for a while together downstairs at the end of the bar. I had greeted her both times and thought how lovely she looked: delicate dark features, fit-looking figure and always dressed immaculately in long, flowing, brightly coloured dresses. On the third night she came, greeted everyone as usual with a double kiss, looked at me straight in the eye, smiled and said, 'Bonsoir monsieur,' and walked downstairs where she stood with Gérard. Gérard knew how much I liked the girls and, after a brief conversation with her quickly came over to where I was standing.

'My friend Isabelle would like to meet you,' he said with a smile.

'Ok', I said, I wanted to meet her too. I walked over and said hello, kissed her on the cheek twice in the traditional French way and stood by the bar chatting as best I could in my broken French. She was gorgeous without a doubt, but there was something not quite right, especially when I looked past Isabelle's shoulder to see Gérard standing at the other end of the bar grinning and nodding at me.

'I must leave now,' she said, 'but maybe we can meet a little later, perhaps when you finish work?'

'That will be nice,' I said, thinking how much I would really like to fuck her but I couldn't put my finger on what was wrong.

'Until later then,' she said and kissed me gently on the lips. As she turned to walk away I looked over to Gérard who by this time was almost crying with laughter. He came over, patted me on the back and said, 'Beautiful isn't he?'

'You mean she?' I asked, thinking he had made a grammatical error.

'No, I mean he!' He roared with laughter. I had just been kissed on the lips by one of Paris's top black transsexual prostitutes.

For a while I got to live at the Hilton Hotel. I started seeing Katy, the daughter of the Hilton's European Operations Director. She had an apartment at the hotel, which overlooked the Eiffel Tower. For two months I lived in luxury, with room service, cleaners and excellent food. She was a very pretty girl but at almost 6ft 2ins she towered above me. It wasn't a problem prone, but I felt a bit uncomfortable going out with her and the relationship didn't last long. She wanted to do more than to be flat on her back.

I didn't have too much to do during the day once I had set in place new procedures and paperwork. Grant had helped me set up new accounting and stock control procedures. There was always stuff going missing but it was infinitely better than it was when I first started and we were taking a lot more money. Almost all the admissions and spirits bottles were now being accounted for. Sebastien and his wife left Le Central a few days after I arrived and we employed a new receptionist from the main office. I saw Sebastien driving down the Champs Elysées a couple of weeks later, in his fairly new convertible Mercedes. Not bad for a receptionist.

I had also started weight-training three times a week at a health club close to the apartment and when I wasn't training, or off with some girl or other, I would sit in a little café boat I had found moored alongside the Seine and read. For me there was simply nothing better that to sit in the sun with a good book, a good cup of coffee and looking up periodically to a most splendid view of the Notre Dame. I wanted nothing else.

I had been in Paris for about eight months when a call came from Allen.

It was 10 a.m. – I was in a deep sleep when I was woken by the telephone. I reached over and picked it up.

'Hi Robin, how's Paris?'

Whenever Allen called I knew we were going to work. He rarely called me for a social chat – we would work together and then went our separate ways until another operation brought us back together. Although extremely tired I woke myself a little. I knew it was going to be important. Corrine, a beautiful French girl I had been seeing, was sleeping next to me and murmured a little.

'Ssshhh,' I said to her and stroked her hair gently.

'Great, love it here. Paris is wonderful, so much to do and the French women . . .' I whispered, looking down at Corrine.

Her delicate features looked quite beautiful, even in sleep. 'Why?'

He chuckled 'So you don't want to come to Bosnia with me then?'

'When?'

'Tomorrow.'

'Tomorrow?' I said and sat up. 'Are you serious?'

'Deadly,' he said and laughed. 'I catch the overnight ferry tonight from Calais. I will pick you up in Paris tomorrow afternoon. We will drive to Bosnia, find a decent place to drop off some medicines and food I managed to collect from the shop, and drive back, you can be back to work in less than a week, can you take the time off?'

'I think so. Anything else?'

'Oh yes, you don't get paid, just a humanitarian job.'

'What shop?' I asked.

'See you tomorrow,' he replied and hung up, ignoring the question.

'Who was that?' Corrine asked, opening one eye.

'Just a friend,' I replied. 'Might have to go away for a week.'

'Where?' she asked, sleepily.

'Bosnia,' I replied softly but she didn't really hear me. Nevertheless I had to wake her up – I wouldn't get a fuck for at least another week.

I never saw Corrine again.

I didn't really want to leave Paris. I was having a great time and finally enjoying my life again after the difficulties I suffered after losing my job at the Boulevard. I didn't want to lose what I had struggled to attain, but the lure of Bosnia was just too great.

At the time everyone knew about the conflict in the Balkans but no-one understood much about it. Most people knew that Yugoslavia was a communist state and that after the fall of the

Soviet Union various small states were fighting for their independence. Yugoslavia was never part of the Soviet Union but it was communist and it did originally comprise smaller states that lost their independence when the communists took over.

As a powerful dictator, Tito held Yugoslavia together but when he died it began to fall apart. The Slovenians, Croats, Bosnians, Macedonians and Kosovans all wanted independence from Greater Serbia. With minimal violence and very few deaths Slovenia obtained independence first, but bloody war soon followed in Croatia and Bosnia.

As the conflict progressed, the United Nations became more and more involved. War crimes, atrocities and the plight of the millions of refugees were broadcast on every major news programme and in every newspaper worldwide.

Allen was also very interested in the Bosnian conflict and was saddened and sickened by the plight of refugees forced from their homes as the Serbians 'ethnically cleansed' vast areas of Bosnia. Unbeknown to me, Allen had left the special forces about three months previously and was now running his own health food shop in the centre of Norwich. He had a business partner who ran the business when Allen went away on assignments. Allen wanted to do something humanitarian for Bosnia and so started a small collection of money and food at his shop. Because Norwich is a relatively small city, Allen's collection soon made the local headlines, especially as he was intending to take the aid directly to Bosnia himself. It wasn't long before he had more than enough money and supplies to fill his pickup, which was when he called me in Paris.

Allen managed to find the office of European Leisure and parked directly outside its doors, tooting his horn loudly. I had asked David Chipping for a few days off. At first he refused, but after I assured him I would be back in a week and it was for a good cause, he let me go, arranging for the manager at Le Palace to take over. I packed and sat and dozed in the office foyer for about two hours, with my holdall next to me when the sound of Allen's car horn jolted me awake.

As I walk out of the office I saw Allen's smiling face peering across the passenger seat of his bright red Toyota Hi-Lux. In the back, piled high and covered with a green tarpaulin, were the supplies he had managed to collect. It was good to see him, because I always knew that with Allen I would go somewhere exciting and do something different, and Bosnia during the war was just about as exciting as it got.

'Let's go to Bosnia,' I said casually.

'Yeah, alright then, why not?' We drove off. I never made it back to Paris and ended up staying in Bosnia almost a year.

First we drove to Innsbruck, stopping the night at a first class hotel overlooking the snow-capped mountains. We then drove through Italy and into Croatia.

Allen had somehow managed to get a contact with the Red Cross in Austria, who in turn had regular contact with the Red Cross on the island of Krk. They were struggling to find supplies and medicine for the thousands of refugees streaming on to the island for shelter. Allen had promised them his first consignment of aid. We found Krk and we found the Red Cross office in the centre of the pretty little town. We parked the car and weaved our way through the tiny cobbled streets to where we had been directed was the office – easy to find as it was next to the only church in the town.

The tiny Red Cross office was full of women with crying children and harassed-looking workers sifting through mountains of paperwork. A tired-looking lady came over to us and asked us something in German. Allen asked if she spoke English, which she did. We explained that we had a small van full of supplies that his local community in England had collected. Tears filled her eyes; she could not believe we had driven all the way from England to their tiny island to help.

She walked with us to the car park, where she had also

parked, and we followed her to a small industrial unit on the outskirts of the village and unloaded our goods into an almost empty warehouse. With more tears flowing down her cheeks she thanked us and everyone in Norwich. Allen told her he had another load and would return in about a week.

Although I loved Paris and one side of me wanted to return, the other side had really enjoyed driving to Bosnia and I was eager to return. I had been through bad times, desperation and poverty, loneliness and depression but this paled into insignificance compared to the plight of many millions here in Bosnia and Croatia. These people were really having a bad time and I was honoured to have been able to help. It was exciting to have the opportunity to do something good for a change. I could always return to the nightclubs but I doubt I would ever have another opportunity to work in Bosnia. So when Allen asked me to come back with him, reload and return I readily agreed. I would call Paris once I got back to the UK.

Early next morning Allen and I set off home. We drove almost non-stop to the port, stopping only to re-fuel and for the odd takeaway

While we were in Bosnia, the charity called Feed the Children had read about us in the paper and had contacted Allen at his shop. When we returned we had a message to call a David Grubb, director of the charity, at his office in Reading. Allen called him and the next day drove to London for a meeting at the Institute of Directors. He returned that evening, excited.

'Do you want a job?'

'What do you mean?' I replied.

'Well, we have been asked to set up an office for Feed the Children in Croatia. We will be based over there. They will send supplies to us every week and our job will be to deliver those supplies to places of greatest need. We will be working full-time, they will also pay for our accommodation, food, et cetera. We will need to stay at least six months, as they are planning a major TV appeal in the next few weeks. What do you think?'

I didn't have to think and agreed immediately.

'What about the shop?' I asked.

'Peter will run it, no problem. What about Paris?'

'Fuck Paris.'

So two days later we set off for Bosnia again and settled on the Island of Krk.

We helped set up the biggest appeal of its kind ever run by a British charity. Feed the Children launched a massive TV appeal whereby individuals, schools, nurseries, hospitals, offices, in fact almost everyone packed boxes of food, clothes, medicine and other supplies and sent them free via Red Star Courier to the depot in Reading. They were then sorted by dozens of voluntary workers and sent by articulated lorry to us in Krk. We would then deliver the aid into Bosnia, to where we thought it was most needed. We drove our way around, identifying areas of need and reporting them back to Reading. We sent aid to hospitals, refugee camps, schools and orphanages. We also delivered aid to other charities in Bosnia who were unable to meet their own commitments. At one time we were receiving up to six trucks a week. From an almost empty and barren warehouse, Davorka now had to look for a second, but all the aid went out within just a few days, and got to children, the elderly, the injured, the homeless and the destitute refugees. None of the aid was wasted, apart from the occasional chocolate bar we ate during the journey.

Allen and I returned to the UK for Christmas. We had by then spent six months in Bosnia and needed a break from the horrors of war and the stress of driving all over the country with container upon container of aid. I had a few thousand pounds as I managed to save much of what I had earned, and Allen desperately needed to get back to running his shop as apparently it was losing money.

* * *

I was relaxing on Boxing Day when Robert, a bodyguard friend of mine, called.

'You are a hard man to track down,' he said.

'Yeah, been away for a while.'

'I know. Eager to get back?'

'Not really. Why?'

Robert had been asked to look after a rookie reporter from a Canadian newspaper. It was his first mission into a war zone and so the newspaper had contacted a security company in the UK, which in turn contacted Robert. Although from a military background, Robert knew nothing of Bosnia so asked me to join him, which I agreed to do.

The contract would be for one month only. We would have to find an apartment, which would be paid for. We would take the reporter anywhere he wanted within Croatia and Bosnia but not over to Kosovo or into Serbia.

I knew of a few nice apartments in Krk that the locals would be more than willing to rent to us. There were no tourists in Croatia and most people were desperate for money. So shortly after the New Year I returned to Bosnia.

The contract ended at the beginning of February when we saw the reporter onto the plane at Zagreb airport. We were tired and instead of returning home decided to stay on for a few weeks having a break. We had a bit of money and so we went diving, to Italy shopping and sightseeing, and generally having a lazy time. We were just about to tell the owner we no longer required the apartment when we had a call. This time it was from a specialized and very private security company based in the heart of London. They wanted a small team on the ground that could pick up new recruits from Zagreb airport once or twice a week and take then into Bosnia, to pre-arranged locations where they would be inducted and trained and then sent to the front line fighting for the Croats. We agreed.

We stayed until the summer of 1993, involving ourselves

in various other assignments as and when required, including the extraction and smuggling of a family of refugees from the front line for a Croatian family living in London and the delivering of medicines into a town under bombardment.

We were due to come home a few days after Robert had his head virtually blown off sitting next to me one sunny morning on the motorway from Zagreb to Belgrade.

I had already been to some strange and hostile places in the world but nothing compared with Bosnia and war. I loved the challenge of travelling, of exploring new environments, of experiencing new things but Bosnia during the war affected me deeply. Before the war, violence never really bothered me. I felt I could do almost anything to anyone and not think twice about it. To me, smashing someone's face was the same as crushing a spider between my fingers – it meant nothing. I had no feelings; if someone upset me or showed me disrespect, I would deal with it in a bloody way. The problem was that I often didn't know when to stop. I would go on and on and on until my victim was beaten beyond recognition. My actions were unreasonable and unnecessary.

But in Bosnia I could do more or less what I wanted and no-one really cared. War was war and it was a fact that only the strongest survived. They say men become animals in war, but men have always been animals, it is just that in a war this behaviour multiplies itself a thousand-fold, and seems justified. No-one questions it. In most cases, it is the only way to survive. Only an animal can survive war, only an animal can experience the results of war and stay sane. Any human quickly becomes crazy.

It is not possible for a sane and rational human to kill another human without feeling or remorse. Only an animal can kill without feeling. Only an animal can maim without compassion, can kill and decapitate children and babies without emotion, can rape without sentiment or sensation. War turns humans into animals and animals to madness.

I think I was slightly mad before Bosnia but I was madder after. I had changed. I had experienced the worst violence and atrocities any human could experience. Before Bosnia I loved violence; after Bosnia violence made me sick. Before Bosnia I could handle any violent situation and only feel the slightest apprehension, the smallest amount of pressure, but after Bosnia violent occurrences would make me panicky and anxious. I was never scared about the situations I would find myself in, and I knew I was still able to handle most situations, but what frightened me was that I knew I could so easily and quickly kill and I didn't want to. Killing is not difficult but I knew that after Bosnia, I would forever more be walking on a tightrope, the slightest touch pushing me back into the dark hell that was inside my head.

The first experience of death is the hardest – it robs you of your soul. Seeing someone die, looking into their eyes and seeing their tears of death, watching as they fight for that last breath, as they struggle to survive, to live, to hold their children, to make love to their wives, to kiss their mother. The complete terror and utter sadness in their eyes as their life drains from them, finally destroys whatever was left in you that was human.

After the first kill you are no longer human but an animal. Your eyes become dead, sad, empty. The only way to survive is to separate yourself from reality, turn reality into a movie that you are watching in the cinema with your girlfriend so when the film ends you stand up and leave saying it was all just a movie, a fantasy, that nothing really happened.

I realized this all now had to stop. I had survived Bosnia for a reason whereas others close to me hadn't. There must be a reason why.

I believed I had reached the end of my path, I was destroying myself both emotionally with my relationships and physically with violence, and I was sure I couldn't survive for much longer.

At various times in my life I have been so low, so sad and depressed I could think of nothing else but escaping this world into the next. I had no reason to stay, but I was never taken to that point, I was never allowed to cross that line.

After Robert was killed next to me in Bosnia I realized that there must be some purpose to my survival. It could so easily have been my brains dribbling down Robert's shoulder, my body in the casket being loaded onto the plane for the flight home. But it wasn't me, so why am I still here and what will happen in my life to justify my existence, my survival?

CHAPTER NINE

Back to the Doors

I returned from Bosnia three days after Robert got shot. I had no job, nowhere to live and very little money. I didn't know what I was going to do.

I moved in for a short while with Pat, with whom I had worked in Ealing. He had a house in Maidenhead and I rented a room from him. I signed on the dole and searched the newspapers for a job. I looked at all sorts: selling cars, working for an agency selling advertisements, working in a café as a waiter, but nothing appealed. I couldn't see myself doing any normal job; the only thing I knew was the doors. Pat was also looking for a job and we both had no choice but to go back.

I really wanted out. I didn't want to return to the world of nightclubs, alcohol and drugs. I had spent a year in the open seeing a completely different world and I couldn't stand the thought of standing back on some dingy, dirty club door dealing with all the arsehole drunks whose only desire is to cause hassle and problems. But the only job I could easily get was on the doors and even that wasn't going to be easy this time.

I had lost most of my size during my year away. Using my first dole cheque I ordered a course of steroids and started training in a gym nearby. I didn't know anyone in Maidenhead apart from Pat, and I didn't know any clubs. I had no reputation and looked like shit, but I persevered and Pat and I eventually got a contract to run the security at the nightclub and bar attached to the Coppid Beech Hotel in Bracknell. Pat and I did the door and we brought in a couple of lads we knew from Ealing, Nigel and Nigel. One was a bodybuilder, so we called him Big Nigel, and the other wasn't, so we called him Little Nigel.

Bracknell had its own set of problems, which I initially struggled to cope with. The worst was the gypsies. There was a large caravan site about six miles further down the road towards Wokingham and at the weekend many of them would try their luck in the nearest nightclub – ours. They had no morals, no decency and cared about no-one. They would be abusive and expect us to back down and give in to them just because they were gypsies; they somehow thought that we should fear them. Occasionally some were polite, especially the elders, but most were rude and nasty.

This was my first experience of a gang culture. The head of the group was a guy called Curly. He came to the doors of the club one evening and introduced himself to us politely. He said that if ever we had any problems or trouble with any of his clan we should go to see him and he would deal with it. Curly was around his early fifties, hard-looking, with short hair and on four fingers of each tattooed hand wore huge, solid gold, ornate rings. Behind him stood two other older but even more aggressive-looking individuals who I didn't fancy fighting no matter what the situation was. Gypsies look hard and often lead a very aggressive life. Curly introduced us to them. The hardest-looking one, with a nose broken in so many places it covered most of his face and scars over his eyes and chin, was introduced as last year's bare-knuckle champion. I believed him. They came in for a drink and left shortly after, shaking our hands politely. We never saw them again but every weekend we did see many of his clan and turned almost all of them away.

The youngsters were the most aggressive – they were the ones climbing the status ladder and felt they needed to prove themselves to everyone else around them at every opportunity. And they didn't back down easily either. Sometimes we had a real battle keeping them from entering the club. However we never went to see the head. That would show we had backed down.

Pat and I worked at Bracknell for over a year, as well as occasionally working at other clubs in the area including an awful hard house venue in Henley, the Ritzy in Guildford and Cinderella's in Kingston-upon-Thames.

Mark Ovenden knew Richard Scaley, the managing director of Juliana's Leisure Services, an international nightclub consultancy company based in Ealing that provides managers, security managers, bar managers and bar training as well as hardware systems and refurbishments for new projects worldwide. Most of their contracts are abroad, many in the Middle East, but they do manage a few contracts in the UK, especially within the hotel environment, where managers generally know nothing about nightclub management and prefer to bring in outside help.

I had moved from Bracknell after being offered a job running one of their clubs in Reading. Mark had helped me out again and put my name forward.

The Mill at Sindlesham, Reading, was a nice, basic little club that attracted a middle-of-the-road customer base. The nightclub was attached to the Moat House Hotel, which made it a nice environment to be based in.

The first few months at any club are the best, especially if the task is to clean it up, to change the client base and to get rid of some of the bad elements. These are great times, where anything could happen. The first few months are also the most important – this is the time when respect has to be earned, when the rules are laid down and imposed and when a battle of wits is fought. If you give in during these first few months, if you step back or make bad decisions, then the club will never be as you want it to be, and you will never have the respect that you need.

The club was extremely busy; it was taking more money than ever before. It was open three nights a week, from Thursday until Saturday but there would often be private functions during the week. The functions would generally be booked by students who tended to go way over the top, drink too much and generally arse around. But it was not a violent place, which I was pleased about. However there would generally be somebody to throw out or some form of confrontation on the door.

Earley, a few miles up the road, was one of Europe's biggest council estates and so we would occasionally have a few of the undesirables trying to get in. The Mill was situated in the country and about five miles to the nearest village and so was a fairly expensive taxi drive. After a while most scumbags didn't waste their money trying to get in.

I liked it at The Mill. I liked the place, the staff, the environment, the club itself. I was working three or four nights a week with the occasional day in the office for a fairly good salary, I had a little apartment, a girlfriend and things had become fairly stable but once again I was getting bored. One side of me enjoyed the settled existence and the security of a regular income, but the other side of me still yearned for a challenge. I could never seem to find a balance. I found myself yearning for something different. And boy, did I get it.

I was looking around at other opportunities in the area when Richard Sealey called me.

'Do you fancy a change of scenery?' he asked. He must have been reading my mind and knew what my answer would be.

'Does a bear shit in the woods?' I replied. 'Does a one-legged duck swim in circles? Yes of course. Why, what have you got and where?'

'Manchester,' Richard replied, ignoring my stupid

comments, as always. 'We opened a club there a few months ago and we are having a few problems. We would like you to go and sort things out. Go as a manager but concentrate on the door, which is where we have most of the problems, although to be honest there are many problems.'

I must say that was one of the biggest understatements I had heard for a very long time. They didn't just have problems – the club was totally out of control.

'When do you want me to start?' I asked.

'Tomorrow.'

'What about this place?' I didn't mind just packing up and leaving on a moment's notice, in fact that has been a part of my life for so long I actually didn't know any different. I had few possessions but nothing of value. Even to this very day I only have my books. When I look around even now, at 40 years of age, at what I have that is dear to me – there is nothing apart from a few books.

'Don't worry about that place, it is taken care of,' Richard said. 'Just go home, pack and I will pick you up tomorrow. We will spend a weekend there together, you can assess everything, and we can then have a meeting with the hotel manager Monday morning and take it from there.'

And so I moved to Manchester.

I didn't mind going to Manchester for a variety of reasons. One was that I knew there was a highly regarded institute of Krav Maga with one of the best instructors in the UK based just outside. After studying karate and tae kwon do, I eventually went on to Krav Maga, the Israeli style of self-defence developed by their secret service. Krav Maga was introduced to me by my good friend and professional bodyguard Pele.

I first met Pele in Sweden in 1995. He was Croatian but had moved back to Sweden after the war in Bosnia. His mother was Swedish and she had apparently met his father while on holiday in Croatia. Pele had voluntarily enlisted in the Croatian army when the war started, first as a regular soldier then in the Croatian Special Forces. Pele is probably the hardest man I have ever met. He has evil, ice-cold eyes and is scared of no man. His skills at fighting are efficient, swift and devastatingly vicious. If an opponent was foolish enough to throw a punch, kick, or use some kind of weapon, Pele would quickly turn the attack into a series of devastating counters, leaving his opponent disarmed and disabled. For one hour, every single day of the week, before he does anything else, Pele puts on his tracksuit and practises Krav Maga.

At the end of 1995 I was asked to instruct on a close protection training course in Tomelilla, south Sweden. The course was run by Michael Hjallmarsson, a bodyguard who I worked with a couple of times and who later went to prison for trying to rob a bank with his brother. Apparently his brother knocked himself out as he was hurriedly exiting the bank, woke up in the police cell a few hours later and spilled the beans on where his brother was hiding.

Michael wasn't hard to find. At around 6ft 4 and 19 stone, with a shaven head and a hard-looking face, he stood out. Apparently they had worn masks but he was still easy to identify in the police line-up, especially as he also had a distinctive voice. So he ended up in prison, wrote a book, sold the rights to a Swedish TV company and went on to make more money that he had originally tried to steal from the bank.

Pele joined the training course, as he had just left the army and was looking for a new career. It was during our self-defence instruction that I saw that Pele had infinitely more skill than either Michael or myself and we quickly 'interrogated' him on his style. Pele introduced us to Krav Maga, which I have been studying ever since.

Krav Maga is self-defence and fighting style and is not a martial art. It is particularly relevant to close-quarter street attacks and its objectives are to disarm and disable an assailant immediately and effectively, giving time for evacuation. It is now taught in almost every school in Israel, and is also very popular in the US but it has yet to take a hold in the UK. The techniques are particularly useful for the doorman having to disarm an assailant brandishing a bottle, glass, brick, baton or perhaps a knife or firearm.

I had gone over to Sweden with some steroids for Michael. My bags were not on the connection from Copenhagen to Malmo and so I filled in the appropriate forms and I was told my luggage would be delivered a few hours later as they would come on the next shuttle from Copenhagen. That evening I was enjoying a barbecue outside in the garden with Michael and his family when two police cars drew up outside the house. Out jumped four policemen with a warrant. I was under arrest for smuggling a banned drug into Sweden and held in solitary confinement for three days while the drugs were tested. I was released after agreeing to pay a fine of the equivalent of £2,000, which of course I never paid.

Richard Sealey and I eventually arrived at the hotel, having spent four hours stuck in traffic on the M6. Juliana's Leisure Services had just refurbished and re-opened a club which was again part of a Moat House Hotel in the town of Wilmslow in Cheshire, on the outskirts of Manchester. Apparently Wilmslow and the surrounding areas, including Alderley Edge and Prestbury, have more millionaires per square mile than anywhere else in Great Britain outside Belgravia, London. Television celebrities, footballers, pop stars and top executives all have homes in the area. Looking at the cars you can instantly see that Wilmslow is not a place where money is a problem. While working in personal protection I have driven some of the world's finest cars but I have never possessed a nice new car of my own. I have never had the money and I have always driven an old cheap car, even when I lived in the Docklands. I would always jokingly pride myself on parking my bog-standard, falling-to-bits family saloon next to my neighbour's Porsche or Ferrari.

It didn't bother me. When driving around I like to remain anonymous, and my car would blend in, nothing special and nothing too cheap, but in Wilmslow my old banger brought attention because no-one else drove such a shit car! My little Peugeot stood out a mile.

The nightclub I was to run was called Equivino. Prior to its closure and refurbishment it was a singles-type venue called the Valley Lodge. The Valley Lodge was well known in the area as a standard over-25s watering hole, where almost anyone was guaranteed entrance and almost everyone could pull as long as they didn't mind what they pulled and whether it had two legs or four!

Business at the Valley Lodge had slowed and so, in the hotel's infinite wisdom, instead of spending time and money marketing and promoting the venue back to its original status among the singles and the ugly in the area, they decided to give the club a complete renovation and revamp, a new name and a new style.

They had decided to go from something that had once been extremely successful to something completely unknown. The Valley Lodge was known throughout Cheshire as a typical 1970s- and 80s-style 'discothèque', attracting a loyal but middle-of-the-road customer. Nothing awful yet nothing special and for the same amount of money the group spent on renovation, consultants, marketing and promotions, they could have easily brought the Valley Lodge back from its decline to its original level of success. But it was decided to change everything.

The Valley Lodge manager was sacked and a younger manager was hired to open and run the new venue. Ron had lots of ideas and worked hard but sadly nothing really worked. All the locals knew the venue as the old Valley Lodge but when they tried to get in after it had re-opened, they were turned away. They were now not the kind of customers that the new management at Equivino wanted. So eventually there were only a handful of customers left.

Business was slow. Friday and Saturday nights they were lucky if they reached 40 or 50 customers.

So, because of heavy pressure from the hotel manager and his bosses, Ron decided to bring in an outside promoter by the name of Andy Bassett and a promotion called Peruvia. Andy had been successful with a couple of smaller promotions in the area and wanted to expand. Equivino, Ron and the hotel management were desperate for business. They would have probably tried anything to get customers through the doors.

Andy Bassett wanted a Saturday night – he got it. Andy wanted the club free of charge – he got it. Andy wanted the use of the hotel for pre-club drinks – he got that too. In fact Andy got almost everything he asked for, including free hotel rooms, free drinks and free use of the leisure centre. It seemed that Ron and the hotel manager Liam Walsh were desperate to prove to their bosses that the hundreds and thousands of pounds of the company's money had not been wasted. They agreed to almost everything Andy Bassett asked for.

Peruvia was an instant success. Within just a few weeks of opening it was full to capacity and turning away hundreds of disappointed customers each week. At that time Peruvia was revolutionary. It was an extremely glamorous, over-the-top event, using velvet drapes, abstract images and erotic pictures projected around the club. Andy hired a designer to create a seductive atmosphere. A giant decorated bed was positioned in the middle of the club, and there were exotic dancers on podiums and an uplifting music policy. The flyers to promote the event were specific and well thought out, but word of mouth did more for the reputation of the night than any marketing could have.

People travelled to Peruvia from as far as London, Birmingham and Scotland and every Saturday night the car park would be overflowing with luxury sports and executive vehicles. The car park attendant made an extremely good living reserving space for regular and wealthy customers.

The club was licensed for around 500, but up to 1,000 tried to get in almost every week. So the door was a nightmare to manage. Andy employed a 'picker' whose job was to say yes or no. It was the doorman's job to enforce her decision. Even those getting out of the most luxurious Bentleys and sports cars, dressed in what I considered beautiful and expensive clothing, were turned away. It was a certain style that Andy was looking for. You could get in one week without a problem as long as your face fitted and yet get turned away the following week for wearing exactly the same clothes and looking exactly the same. They said they wanted a certain and specific style but it seemed inconsistent and invariably changed from one week to the next. This was eventually Peruvia's downfall, as people got pissed off with the attitude and uncertainty. Customers eventually stopped coming rather than risk being turned away.

Every Saturday night before the club opened, the hotel bar would be crammed full of nightclub customers. This was a big added bonus to the hotel's liquor revenue, but sometimes had hilarious consequences for the hotel guests. Mostly nightclub customers meeting in the hotel bar were well-behaved and looked wonderful. They were good-looking, well dressed and glamorous, albeit sometimes slightly over the top. Two of the regular dancers also used to drink in the hotel bar before dancing in Peruvia. They were always provocatively dressed. I remember one night they were wearing skimpy tops and cowboy-style chaps with no arse. A couple of elderly ladies staying in the hotel were quite upset after seeing these two girls prancing around the hotel with their arses hanging out. Few hotel guests could actually drink at the hotel bar Saturday nights as it was so packed with Peruvia customers.

I arrived at Peruvia a couple of months after it had first opened, and it was doing very well. It had become extremely popular. However, like many events of this kind, it had some major security issues.

CHAPTER TEN

Gangchester

Peruvia attracted everyone that was anyone; pop stars, celebrities, soap stars, footballers and probably every single gangster in Greater Manchester. Andy was becoming increasingly unhappy, not just because so many people were getting in free, but because the standard of dress was sliding and things were becoming increasingly difficult to control. It wasn't so much that the gang 'heads' dressed badly – they were usually immaculate – but it was all their hangers-on, their 'soldiers', that wore tracksuits, trainers, caps, hoods, and brought bad attitude with them. The doormen found it difficult to turn them away.

A gang head runs the whole show and controls everyone and everything in his territory. Every decision made, every deal done, every life taken, is authorized by the head, and no-one does anything without his say so. Heads are feared, not so much because of what they are personally capable of, although most are extremely hard men themselves, but what they are capable of getting done. If a head wants a person killed, that person will be killed, usually by one of the soldiers on his way up the ranks. Soldiers are the runarounds, the doers, and they take the rap for the head. A soldier does whatever the head tells him to do, and will serve time for their head if necessary. No soldier would dare to contradict the head or rat on him.

Most gangs stay close to their home base, because they are safer within an environment they control. Most areas of

Greater Manchester had a gang – some big, others fairly small. The smaller gangs tended to be the most ruthless, as they have to fight harder to stay in control. Gangs would rarely encroach on another's territory – not without starting a war – but this did occasionally happen. Cheetham Hill, Moss Side, Longsight, Salford and many other areas had their own gang controlled by a head. They controlled the drugs, the doors, the nightclubs and bars, the prostitution, the car thefts, the counterfeiting, the distribution of stolen goods, the armed robberies, the extortion; in fact most organized crime was controlled by that area's gang head. Only by imprisonment or assassination would a head lose authority or his territory, and then there would be a mad scramble among others to seize the vacant terrain.

Peruvia soon become known as *the* Saturday night venue in Manchester and had almost every head from every area visit the club at some point. When a head approached the door at Peruvia and indicated that the ten scruffy scumbags following were with him, the doorman found it virtually impossible to say to the head, 'You are ok but those with you will have to wait outside as they have a bad attitude, are too young and are inappropriately dressed.' It was an impossible situation for the doormen. The head just waved them through, shook the doorman's hand and no more could be said.

Also, having most of the major gangs at a nightclub that was part of the Moat House Hotel chain meant that the hotel was occasionally receiving bad publicity and getting a bad reputation. Many complaints were made by customers of the hotel.

The nightclub also had a major liquor stock problem. So, because of my strong security background, my experience on the doors and a little managerial know-how, I was sent to see if there was anything I could do.

It wasn't until I had spent a couple of days there looking

at everything that I realized what an uphill and virtually impossible task it was going to be. 'My suggestion,' I said to Richard at the end of our brief assessment period, 'is to close the night down, keep it closed for a few weeks and then re-open, going back to the old Valley Lodge days.' I was honest and this is what I thought we should do. The gangs, the atmosphere, the tension and the police made running an event like this more difficult than can be justified and with a potential for more violence than can be accepted.

Violence didn't bother me but it bothered others, the hotel management more than anything. Violence at the club would affect the hotel: the families, the elderly and the innocent. I thought it was wrong to have a night such as Peruvia associated with a hotel chain such as the Moat House.

'I tell you what,' came Richard's reply, 'let's give it another few weeks, let's see what we can do and what changes we can make without upsetting too many people and causing too many more problems and if we feel it is an impossible task then we shall close and go back to what it was.'

I agreed. I like a challenge in my life and a challenge this was going to be.

Although my task was to primarily concentrate on security and the door, I actually went in as manager, to work closely with the hotel's food and beverage manager in an attempt to curb the vast discrepancies in stock.

I started work on the Tuesday and spent the first week acclimatizing myself to the club and its administration systems, as well as to the hotel environment. We had a liquor stock check, which showed a huge deficiency. I checked the bottle bins at the end of the first Saturday night and found that there were more empty bottles of champagne in them than had been rung in the till. There were also more brands than the hotel had actually ordered. Someone was making a good living selling champagne that they were probably buying at the local off-licence in the town centre and selling for cash in the nightclub.

I explained my predicament to the managers of three off-licences in the immediate vicinity and found out exactly who was buying champagne, in what quantities and what brands. Every Saturday afternoon the same person would turn up at the off-licence with a shopping list and buy at least 20 bottles of different brands, often a lot more. I later found out that the gang heads had their preferred brands and were placing specific orders from a member of staff. I laughed to myself when I read in a local newspaper that the off-licence in question sold more champagne in that village than at any other one of their outlets nationwide. I knew why.

We had some major problems to sort out and we had to do it quickly, not least because the police were very unhappy with the type of customer Peruvia was attracting. Cheshire Police simply did not want Manchester gangs coming into their district – they wanted them to stay in Manchester where they belonged. The Serious Crime Squad were also extremely concerned with the gang and drug element.

An ultimatum by the police and the hotel management was given – either it gets sorted out or the night gets closed down.

During my first week as manager of Equvino nightclub and Peruvia, I had to attend a meeting with the hotel general manager and three officers from the Manchester Serious Crime Squad. They were going to work closely with us in monitoring the situation at Peruvia. They were specifically interested in the gangs and the gang leaders. They also wanted assurances that it was not going to get any further out of control. I had no choice but to agree to co-operate fully with them at all times, otherwise the police would certainly force us to close the club and it would remain closed.

The conversation with the police went something like this:

'In order to stay open and continue trading, and for us to feel happy with the situation, there are various suggestions we should like you to consider implementing,' they said.

'Ok,' we said.

'We would like you to install a full CCTV system through-out the club and on the front door,' they said.

'Ok,' we said.

'We would like copies of the tapes every Monday morning,' they said.

'Ok,' we said.

'We would like to have plain-clothes officers in the club as and when we feel the need,' they said.

'Ok,' we said.

'We should like to also film those coming into the club by our own independent officers and equipment,' they said.

'Ok,' we said.

Of course we didn't *have* to do anything they suggested but we didn't have a choice.

The first thing the hotel did was to spend £5,000 installing a CCTV system throughout the club, with particular emphasis on the VIP lounge area, where most of the gangs would congregate. It was illogical, but while outside on the streets the gangs were bitter enemies and fought savagely over territory and business, inside the club one gang head could sit and talk with another over a bottle of champagne. The soldiers were their bodyguards and kept close.

The first weekend the gangs were unaware of the new system and it made for some extremely interesting viewing. I rarely went down to the VIP area; it was not a nice environment. It was at the back of the club near the toilets and the back bar. In the toilets and outside the fire exit on the back staircase were where most of the drugs were dealt and the back bar was where most of the illegal champagne was sold. The first night's video showed cocaine being snorted off the glass tables in the VIP lounge, someone shagging in the corner, someone showing someone else a knife they had concealed in their jacket and one of my management team running backwards and forwards with bottle upon bottle of champagne. I counted at least 15 bottles, but the till only showed that five bottles were sold that night.

After that first week the gangs got wind of the CCTV system and covered the cameras with masking tape. It was impossible to go into the VIP area and take down the tape: I tried it once but no sooner had I returned to the front door than the tape was back up. I gave up after the second attempt.

Another condition was for the police to have access to the videotape. Every Monday morning they would come and take the recording of the previous Saturday night. The police were also interested in standing on the front door filming as the gangs came and went. They did try it one evening but word spread quickly and no gang member appeared that night. The same happened a second week so that idea didn't last long and they reverted back to taking the in-house video. It was a shame they couldn't have continued filming overtly for a few extra weeks, as there were no gangs at all at the club and the atmosphere inside was much calmer and nicer.

The other major problem I had to quickly sort out was the liquor stock. It didn't take a genius to guess who was selling the illicit champers, as firstly she was seen on the first night's recording flogging bottles in the VIP area and secondly there were not many members of staff with access to the tills, the stock cupboard and the club out of opening hours. Of course she would eventually be sacked, but the problem we had was getting rid of her. This would cause uproar with the gangs, as they had got used to cheap champagne. We didn't want them all deciding to help themselves to house champagne free because they couldn't get their own preferred brand cheap. Actually I thought it quite sad that the staff member was being controlled and manipulated by the gangs and was being forced to act in this way. She was not only stealing from her employer but the gangs were forcing her to steal for no other reason than to save money and have cheaper drink.

I sympathized a little – it must have been hard for her, especially being a woman in such a difficult environment. She probably just didn't have the strength to stand up and say no. It was hard enough for most men and on many occasions impossible for even the doormen to say no to the gangs.

It was certain we would have to sack her, but I decided not to inform the police. She would have enough problems finding another job and supporting her family without the added pressure of criminal proceedings. But first we had to stop her selling anything but our own champagne. We had to find a compromise with the gangs and effectively implement some sort of alternative. So I initially decided to sell our own champagne to the gangs at 50 per cent of our normal selling price. This was slightly above what they had been used to paying privately, but not so expensive as to cause uproar. I called the woman into my office and presented her with the evidence and I told her that I knew exactly what was happening. I didn't blame her directly but just presented the facts as I had them, and explained that this could no longer continue and that the nightclub had to present an alternative to the gangs. Her job, I said, was to explain to the gangs that the hotel manager had caught her selling champagne. He had simply had enough of the place and was determined to close unless they accepted this deal. It was still good for them, as they were still getting their champagne cheap, the club would remain open, and they saved face.

For the first couple of weeks I had gang heads OJ, JD and G storm over to me annoyed with the change, demanding that they be given back their 'right' to free or very cheap champagne. They came up to me, surrounded by their soldiers, telling me that I should toe the line and show them respect.

'You're not respecting me, are you?' they would ask menacingly.

'Of course I am,' I would say but it was not my call. I just blamed everything onto the hotel manager.

'Yeah, but you are the manager, aren't you, so you can do this for me, he doesn't have to know.' They would then offer me a little bribe, telling me I would be well looked after. It was hard talking to these guys, they have a way about them that makes you nervous – it is their way of controlling you.

If you say to them that you don't respect them, they will probably kill you there and then and a soldier would plead guilty and do the time. Heads rarely got caught. If you say you respect them, then you have to give them what they want. If you back down, you are controlled. But they also will not back down, so you have to find a compromise, so that everyone saves face.

So I compromised and agreed for the hotel to buy in their preferred brand. But I made it quite clear that either they accept these changes and paid a little extra, or the club would close. It was simple. The hotel manager really had had enough. For a few months it was touch and go as to whether we should close or not. In fact there would be weekends when the threats against us were so real we did actually have to close. But it had not come to that yet.

So the bar was slowly getting sorted out. I say slowly because the person that had been involved was so used to the extra income she had generated for herself she couldn't actually stop and we eventually caught her again. We then sacked her immediately.

The next problem was the door. And that was a big problem. It has to be said that when I arrived, the team working the door were mostly good, decent and conscientious guys but completely out of their league. In fact I doubt there was an independent door team in Manchester that, at that time, could effectively have controlled and run that door. Having worked the doors for years I knew that the only way this door could be controlled was by another well-known major local gang. I tried to explain my reasons to the hotel manager but he was adamant that, for the time being, he wanted to continue using his own in-house door security. I thought it was a mistake, though I understood his point of view – he didn't want the hotel, and the recognized Moat House Group, to have its security run by a Manchester gang. He could see that it might be bad for the hotel's reputation and thought that it might compromise the hotel – he was concerned that a gang might not be content with providing security for the nightclub but might want a bigger slice of the cake or perhaps extort money from the hotel or steal from it. So it was decided to stay with in-house security for the time being.

The priority was a strong head doorman. We did have a head doorman but he simply wasn't strong enough – he backed down too quickly, didn't have many leadership qualities and wasn't respected by many of those coming into the club. Though a nice guy, he was heading one of the hardest doors in Manchester and simply wasn't up to it.

One of the doormen suggested a friend of a friend, Ray McKenna – a hard-man in Liverpool who had fallen foul of a few guys over there and was looking to head a door somewhere out of town where he wasn't known. It didn't really bother me that he had fallen out with someone – that is bound to happen on any door anywhere – and it didn't bother me that he was from Liverpool. I thought that Liverpool was just too far from Manchester to worry about any comeback. In a way I thought it might be good that he didn't actually know the Manchester faces; he could treat everyone the same and try to impose some sort of restrictions as to who would and wouldn't get in.

I arranged for Ray to meet me at the club on Friday morning. Stocky, well-built, late-twenties, he seemed hard enough in his attitude and his approach to the door. He knew what he was talking about and seemed to have had quite a bit of experience at some of the more notorious clubs in Liverpool. He looked as though he could at least provide better control and leadership and that was all I was concerned about. The gangs were on the verge of running the venue.

I knew a lot about the business but one thing I didn't know

was how much many Mancunians hated Liverpudlians, and vice versa. Wilmslow was not Manchester and I genuinely thought that having a Scouse doorman in a sleepy town in Cheshire would be fine. The last thing I needed were more problems.

Having Ray would not have been a problem had we not attracted most of the Manchester gangs but they fiercely resented his presence and simply did not tolerate being told what to do by a doorman from Liverpool. After the first weekend we could clearly see Ray was going to have some big problems. I spoke to Ray after his first night and we both decided to give it a few weeks and see if things would settle down.

Ray was struggling without the backup of a good strong team and, after the second week of being on his own and of not really trusting his fellow doormen, he asked me to hire his friend and partner Alex.

Alex Penarski, nicknamed 'Bronson' because he looked like the actor Charlie Bronson, was a hard and menacing looking man, mid-thirties, well-built, a boxer and champion bare-knuckle fighter. I had a good feeling that between the two of them they could finally start to get this door sorted out.

The other doormen certainly had a lot of respect for these two. With the backing of Alex and Ray, the other doormen became more attentive to their job, stricter with the customers and with the dress code and a little stronger on the door with the gangs and with free admissions. They still let a few people pass through without paying but things had become a lot tighter and more controlled. Any problems and Alex or Ray were immediately called for support. However, unbeknown to me, having Ray on the door was actually having severe consequences. Almost all of the gangs were getting pissed off.

One afternoon the Serious Crime Squad arrived wanting to speak to me urgently. With the hotel manager, we sat down in the hotel lounge.

'We have some bad news,' one of the officers said. 'We have certain information regarding a possible contract put out on both you . . .' he looked at me, '. . . and your head doorman Ray McKenna.'

'What sort of contract?' I asked. I was fully aware of contracts – I was a bodyguard and laughed silently to myself, thinking that I might soon need one.

'We have information from more than one source that some of the gangs are pretty pissed off, firstly with a Liverpool doorman running a club in Manchester, and secondly with yourself for employing him. Word is out that things have changed here and they don't like it.'

'Who has put the contract out?' I didn't feel scared, just annoyed that these gangs were trying to run the club and trying to control me.

'We can't tell you that,' he replied but went on to say their intelligence was real, active and accurate and we were to either close the club with immediate effect or change the head doorman. The gangs had had enough, they wanted the club back under their control, they wanted to be able to come and go as they pleased, to bring into the club whomever they wanted and to drink whatever they wanted. I was becoming a nuisance and was in the way, especially as I had the audacity and gall to bring a Liverpool doorman to run a club in their territory. After talking with the police for quite a while we all decided it was too late to change the doorman or to close, as closing would probably cause us even more problems. So the SCS promised us that there would be a strong police presence that coming Saturday night, with an armed response unit placed permanently in the car park. That would hopefully deter any planned activity. We assured the police that we would definitely change the security for the following weekend.

As promised, there were two vans full of police on standby in the car park, and two armed response units patrolling the immediate vicinity. The night passed without incident. In fact word got out that something was going on and not one gang member turned up to Peruvia that evening. At the end of the night I sat down with Ray and told him about the conversation we had earlier in the week with the SCS.

'Sorry Ray, we have to let you go. There is more at stake than just the nightclub – it is part of the hotel and that has to be a priority. If things continue as they are, the hotel will just close the club down. They have had enough as well. I am sorry Ray.'

It was a shame, as he was genuinely a good guy and hardworking – he really did want the place clean and running well. He also had won the respect of the other doormen and treated them all with respect in return. He was just in the wrong place at the wrong time.

'Don't worry, I understand.' He was ok but, like me, was pissed off that the gangs were running the show and not us. It was awful that we couldn't employ who we wanted because of the gangs. It was Ray that Manchester had a problem with, not Alex. Alex could have stayed but he was loyal to his friend and colleague and left Equivino at the same time.

We now had a week to find a company that could provide us with strong, suitable and effective security or we were going to close. It was urgent. The manager still did not like the idea of using a local gang to control the other local gangs, so we decided to look at an out of town security company.

I was considering contacting Chris and Carl Bailey in Nottingham. They were a major force in their own area and also probably had many local contacts which they could use. They had the security contract for Luminar Leisure at most of their Chicago Rock Cafes around the UK, as well as providing security to many other leisure companies and independent operators.

I knew the managing director of Luminar and was sure that they could sort this place out quickly and effectively. I wanted to bring them in but the hotel manager still preferred to try a more corporate image in line with the Moat House Hotel's identity. He wanted me to find a more 'respectable' company. I argued that we didn't need 'respectable', it was too late for 'respectable' and if we were to continue trading we needed a really hard team, a team that no-one would fuck with and I knew the Baileys were such a team.

Chris, Carl and Richard Bailey ran most of the doors in Nottingham and surrounding villages. Their company was called Doorcare. Chris and Carl ran it while their younger brother Richard managed their nightclub in Mansfield. Chris and Carl were big, heavy, hard-looking guys – their company was the biggest in the area and they controlled a lot of Nottingham and were connected with many hard men in other major cities around the UK. I was sure that not only could they supply a good team to work the door but they were also well enough connected to be able to sort things out behind the scenes if necessary.

I put my suggestions forward but I was ordered to look at an alternative.

I looked in the latest issue of *Night*, a trade magazine for nightclub owners and operators. The only advert listed for security services was by a company called Capes and Cullington. I knew Paul Cullington, as I had met him a few years earlier in Corby. His company provided security for a unit I briefly worked at. I doubted he would remember me but I knew that they were a large and very well-established national company who provided security to licensed premises throughout Great Britain. At the time they were probably one of the biggest door security companies in the UK and they were the first to push for a standard national doorman's licence.

At that time, many door companies were run by criminals and gangsters. Licensing had been introduced and the door scene was slowly changing but most doormen were still hard, uneducated, aggressive mobsters managed by a central gang, which was in turn managed by a head. It was unheard of for one gang to put doormen into a club within the territory of another gang. The only exceptions were companies like Capes and Cullington, who were not gang-based and operated nationally. By not having any gang affiliations they could sometimes operate within the territory of a gang, although it was still hard work and there were still places, such as areas of Liverpool and Manchester, where even the 'nationals' couldn't operate. Although these companies worked under the heading of 'national', most actually ended up subcontracting to a local firm or employing local doormen.

At that time there were only a few so-called national door companies; two of the biggest were Prosec and Capes and Cullington.

Geoff Capes was the managing director of Capes and Cullington. An ex-policeman, Britain's Strongest Man and an Olympic shot putter, he was a minor TV celebrity and could still be frequently seen on game shows and quizzes. Although I wasn't sure that such a company could control this door, I called them in for a meeting. The hotel manager finally seemed happy – he liked their credentials and their corporate image, and the size of their company gave him added confidence.

The following day at 10 a.m., two 6ft 4ins, 18-stone, immaculately dressed giants walked into the hotel reception and asked for me. One was the area manager and the other was to be the head doorman should they be given the contract. Although monsters in terms of size and I am sure quite handy in their own right, they didn't look like hard-men, more like businessmen. They had an air of professionalism and confidence but tinged with arrogance. I didn't want arrogance – I knew that this attitude would get them in a lot of trouble. The area manager was an ex-policemen and the head doorman had been working the doors for about ten years and was currently heading the door at a club in Birmingham.

I showed them round the venue. We spoke for a while about some of the problems we were having, and what our objectives were, what we would like improved regarding the door and what was going to happen should we be unable to sort everything out. We spoke at length about the Manchester gang scene. They listened and said they understood the situation but it didn't seem to bother them. I told them about the contract out on the current head doorman and the reasons why we had to let him go and why now we had to change the whole team but they didn't seem to care. They just wanted the contract and assured us all would be well.

They told me that they had many clubs throughout Great Britain, which they would draw their best guys from to sort this place out. They also advised me that, in the interests of safety and for the security of the door team and me, everyone would have to be searched, including every gang member. They assured me that from then onwards there would be far fewer free admissions, that heads could have two or three guests only and that everyone else would have to pay. They also assured us they could have a good team here by Saturday and stressed that none of the doormen would be from Manchester. They would then remain totally unbiased and totally unaware of who was who. Also, by using an out of town team, there could not be any personal comeback on individual doormen – they couldn't easily be followed home or traced. They would buy all the door staff new uniforms and there would be radio contact between every member of the team.

I knew this was too good to be true but I gave them the benefit of the doubt; after all, they were a well-established national company with a large and impressive portfolio of clients so they should have enough experience and expertise to handle most situations and environments. Shouldn't they? I was looking forward to Saturday evening.

The sad thing was that I had to let the other doormen go.

They were all good guys and had all put up with a lot of aggravation, threats and coercion and now they would be jobless. But most were only working one night a week and I felt sure they would all quickly find other clubs to work in. I called them all up one by one and explained the situation. I told them that if we didn't sort things out at the club quickly it would close anyway. Most understood but of course a couple were pissed off. Peruvia was certainly a nightmare to work but the atmosphere was sometimes great and most of the guys enjoyed working there, it was always interesting. They wouldn't miss the aggravation but would definitely miss the night. Unlike most nightclubs that got rid of their staff, I didn't ban them from coming into the venue for a night out. I felt they had put up with so much shit that depriving them of a night out at one of the best venues at that time in Manchester would have been too harsh and unfair.

As requested, the new Capes and Cullington door team turned up an hour before opening for a comprehensive briefing and tour of both the club and the hotel. We needed two lads in the hotel for the first hour and a half, as that was where most of the customers congregated before the club opened. In our casual and friendly chat before the official briefing I learnt that many of the lads lived in Doncaster. I wondered why they had all come so far until I learned that Capes and Cullington had subcontracted the contract to JKM Security, run by a guy called Jon Maddocks (who was later to become quite a good friend). They had all arrived immaculately dressed in new suits, bought not by Capes and Cullington but by JKM Security. They also brought with them metal detectors and most wore bulletproof vests. They were expecting the worst.

Capes and Cullington had not explained everything in detail to Jon so he wasn't sure of the exact situation, but he was told that everyone had to be searched. There were more drugs in the unit than pigeon shit in Trafalgar Square. It was interesting to watch the amount of customers that turned back to their cars once they saw that searching was taking place.

Everyone would now have to pay, except those given the ok by Andy Bassett, who assured us he would be spending every evening on the front door and would personally walk them through by himself. It was agreed that for the next few weeks Andy would have to stay by the door and vet everyone coming in. In theory this was a good idea; in practice it soon became a nightmare. Andy was never polite, diplomatic or subtle. He would look at customers in such a way he would actually offend many without even opening his mouth. He would look at those that arrived inappropriately dressed in the same way you would look at your shoe after treading in dogshit. There were times that he would look up and down at people and actually laugh in their faces. And yet he never understood why he had the amount of problems that he had.

I personally believed that if he treated people with more respect, no matter who they were and what they were dressed like, and turned them away politely, he would never have had as much trouble as he did. Maybe he was too young to understand. But because he was such a target on the night, he couldn't stay on the door for long or enjoy the evening in the club but would spend most Saturday nights cooped up in his hotel room with a few friends drinking champagne. He came down occasionally to take the door money, accuse everyone of stealing, moan about who we were letting in, shout at his staff for not doing their job properly and then disappear back up to his room. Take away Peruvia and the environment and Andy was another nice guy. I met him a few times a few years later and he was decent, quiet and normal, but not then.

It was evident from the first night that the door was too much even for Capes and Cullington (trading as JKM). Jon was a good guy but again out of his depth regarding the gang situation and trying to get everyone searched was impossible.

No head was going to be searched and it was virtually impossible to turn away the soldiers. Telling the head that his soldiers were too young and inappropriately dressed was seen as a mark of disrespect.

Needless to say, Andy soon disappeared from the front door, leaving us to cope and make our own decisions as to who could and could not come in.

It was a farce. A head would turn up with five or six scruffy scumbags in dirty jeans, training shoes, baseball caps and be allowed in whereas someone getting out of a Porsche, expensively dressed, would be turned away. Trying to explain that they were not suitable when a group of scumbags had gone in directly in front was impossible and embarrassing. We had no justification, we just had to ignore their outrage and walk away.

I never sat and drank with the heads, but as the manager of one of the biggest nights in Manchester I had got to know most of them fairly well. Well enough to shake their hands and to pass a few words on the door. The heads generally did not want to cause any trouble, they just wanted to enjoy the evening, look at the gorgeous women, drink cheap champagne, take drugs, and talk business with other heads. The atmosphere at the back and in the VIP area was sometimes very tense, but there was never real inter-gang trouble. If there had been it would have been a bloodbath.

There were times when it seemed the whole of the club was one big gang. On some occasions, especially after a major boxing or football match, it seemed that every head had descended upon Peruvia. I didn't remember the names of all the heads of all the gangs but some of those I met included JD and Giro from Moss Side, OJ from Cheetham Hill, various main men from Salford and many others. Peruvia was so popular it even occasionally brought out some of the older heads from the Quality Street Gang. The Quality Street was one of the first true organized crime syndicates and grew to be a major force in Manchester in the late 1960s and early 1970s. One evening, a Bentley convertible pulled up and out climbed three elderly, well-dressed, respectable-looking men. The doormen backed away.

'Fuck, they're Quality Street,' I heard one of them say quietly.

They nodded to us and walked straight in and spent the remainder of the evening sitting at the back of the VIP lounge drinking champagne and chatting to groups of gorgeous, scantily clad women.

It was a difficult situation for me. I was asked to come and sort things out, using my experience on the doors and in security to implement new practices for the long-term benefit of both the nightclub and the hotel. Yet I was continually being tied down and hampered by what the hotel manager wanted and would accept, as well as by the whims of Andy Bassett. I knew what to do – I knew what would work and what wouldn't but no-one seemed to listen. I was asked to run something I wasn't allowed to run and was trying to change something that no-one seemed to want to change. The rhetoric was there, I was always being told that I wasn't doing enough, that the place was in big trouble, un-controllable, and yet when I told them what would have to be done they didn't listen and continued to tell me I would have to find alternatives to my suggestions. There were no alternatives. I could see things coming to a head; something was waiting to happen which would shut the night once and for all and force Peruvia to move.

We ran for about two more weeks with Capes and Cullington on the door when we decided to close down. Things could not be controlled any longer, no matter how hard we tried. Jon Maddocks and his team simply could not stop the gangs coming in, there were just too many of them. It had got to the stage that many of the regular customers had now stopped coming because of the tension and the atmosphere. There were too many soldiers wandering menacingly around the venue, looking totally out of place amongst the well-dressed and glamorous.

I knew that the only way to control everything was to get Manchester men to run the door, and unless I could persuade the hotel manager to take on board my suggestion, the club would remain closed. I didn't mind, I would go back to the doors somewhere, possibly in Manchester, as I quite liked the place. I could do some more bodyguarding contracts – to be honest I didn't actually care what would happen.

CHAPTER ELEVEN

Sorting the Door

I had chatted to Mickey Francis on a couple of occasions in the club. Nothing much, just a polite 'hello' but I knew he was a pretty big man in Manchester and that he ran a door company called Loc-19. They had clubs and pubs in the centre of town and I knew that Mickey more or less ran things the way he wanted. But he was always civil and polite to me.

On that second Saturday before we were due to close I was talking to Mickey briefly on the door. I was telling him that we had decided to close Peruvia because of the problems we were having with the other gangs and the demands of both the hotel manager and Andy Bassett were just impossible to implement effectively. I had had enough, the hotel had had enough and we could not see any other alternative but to close. Mickey said he might have a solution. He suggested a meeting first thing the following Monday morning. As far as I believed there was no solution, we had tried almost everything and the hotel manager would not let me bring in a local door team so as far as I was concerned we were closing and that was that. And actually I was looking forward to it. Peruvia was a great night, it was successful and it did attract all the faces and names, the gorgeous women and the extravagance of one of the most unique nights of its kind at that time in Manchester. But there were just too many problems and I was looking forward to a change. Nevertheless I agreed to meet Mickey and his partner Steve Bryan. I left a message for Liam Walsh and Andy Bassett to be at the hotel on Monday morning for a last-ditch attempt to save the club.

At 11 a.m. Monday morning Mickey and Steve came into the hotel and asked for me at the reception. The poor receptionist must have had a fit as she came running up to me in my office saying that two nasty, frightening-looking men were asking for me at the reception and should she call the police? Most of the staff in the hotel were aware of the problems we were having in the nightclub as hotel gossip is like wildfire and everyone knows everything about everyone and most knew that Peruvia attracted not only the local celebrities but also the local gangs.

'No,' I said, 'don't worry, I am expecting them, tell them I will be there in a minute and order them a coffee, thanks.'

I called the hotel manager's office and he told me he was on his way. But Andy Basset had still not arrived. Maybe he had also fallen out with Mickey, as he had with almost every other head in Manchester.

I have worked on the doors with some rough people and in some rough places. I have been involved with all sorts of people and in all sorts of situations but walking into the hotel that morning and seeing Mickey and Steve sitting there frightened me. They would frighten even the most hardened criminal. From just the way they looked I could see that they were able to sort out almost any situation they found themselves in, one way or another. Looking at them I could see why Loc-19 was a major force on the doors in Manchester and employed some of the hardest doormen.

The police had not yet started clamping down the doors in Manchester and it was still the old style of doormanship. It was still possible to get away with almost anything – fights and intimidation were common and arrests rare. Even if an arrest was made, the victim would usually drop charges once they were visited by a few of the doorman's colleagues. This was the environment in which I served my apprenticeship and I understood it well, but things were slowly changing. Bouncer licensing had been introduced at various levels in most local councils and boroughs and the police were becoming more aware of the criminality of some doormen and had started to clamp down hard. But it was taking time and there were still a great many doormen practising the old style of hitting first and asking questions later.

In a way this method worked; there was a lot more respect back then than there is now. Doormen now have to stand and take verbal abuse, being spat at, even having to take the first punch before being allowed to defend themselves – if it isn't too late. But back then if someone called a doorman a wanker he would be kicked out of the club and taken round the back to be taught a lesson – a lesson of respect, for us as well as for others. Some people need to be shown that they should show respect to those around them and the only way for some people to be taught is to give them a good hiding. I have always believed in this philosophy and always will. In some cases there is no other way.

I wanted to get someone to run our door who all the gangsters knew. Although gangs competed with each other over many things, they would rarely fight solely over a door. When they did there was usually something else that acted as a catalyst for the disagreement. Of course drugs played an important role, as running the door frequently meant running the drugs for the club and that was extremely profitable, but the door for the door's sake was rarely a reason for a gang war. I knew also that if there was an incident, Mickey would generally be able to sort things out before it ever reached the club doors – telephone calls would be made, meetings would be set up and everything would be settled before things got out of hand and went too far.

I decided that the next weekend we would stay closed as planned, citing technical problems as the reason for the club's closure but would reopen the following week with Mickey and his crew fronting the door. This would give Mickey time to make the necessary calls, speaking to everyone he needed to speak to and to put the word out that Loc-19 were now running the door at Peruvia.

It worked well, or as well as we could have possibly hoped for considering the circumstances. Mickey could not stop or search the gang heads, that still remained impossible, but their soldiers did not turn up en masse and when they did they were dressed correctly. Only a couple of the more important soldiers were allowed in with their heads and they rarely caused trouble.

Andy Bassett was still not happy – he never was – but things had quietened down. There were no more threats, and staff and customers in both the club and hotel felt a lot more comfortable. Loc-19 were doing a good job, as I had predicted. We were still open and still trading, which would have been unheard of a few weeks earlier.

But business was changing, and fewer people came to Peruvia. Many of the customers were fed up with the uncertainty of getting in, the music policy had changed and other clubs had followed the style that was once uniquely Peruvia and were working hard attracting Andy's customers. Many of Andy's promotional team left and ran many of these new events. Very few of his staff were actually loyal to Andy and there were now equally as good alternative nights in and around Manchester.

There was one time at Peruvia when Mickey's connections really did save my skin. It was the Sunday evening before a bank holiday. A promoter had approached us wanting to run the night and we agreed. We had nothing to lose, as we would normally have been closed on that particular Sunday anyway. And, as usual, the hotel had not given us any money to promote our own night so we agreed to let an outside promoter run the evening. We predicted that it wasn't going to be busy and so arranged for just three doormen to work, plus I was going to be around in case they needed an extra man as backup. We didn't expect there to be many customers, let alone any gangs. We were to open at 9 p.m. and had a normal Sunday hotel entertainment licence, which meant we had to close at midnight. An easy night, I thought.

At 8 p.m. I was sitting in the office pottering around getting the end of the week's figures and paperwork completed, when a call came through from hotel reception. 'Robin,' said the receptionist, 'would you come to the hotel immediately?'

'Is there a problem?'

'No, just come through straight away, there are some people that need to see you urgently.'

She sounded concerned and I thought that something was going off in the reception area and that she couldn't tell me on the phone. But I couldn't believe that something was actually happening in the hotel on a slow and quiet Sunday evening. Then I thought, with what had been going on recently anything was possible, so I rushed through the restaurant to reception. There I saw two men waiting who looked official and very obviously looked like police. Everything I had done in the past rushed through my mind – my steroid dealing, my petty crime in Norwich, even my outstanding fine from when I was arrested and imprisoned in Sweden a few years previously.

The men asked for a private word in my office. I had got to know the Serious Crime Squad officers quite well, as every Monday or Tuesday they turned up for the video of the previous Saturday night at Peruvia. We would generally have a coffee and chat for a few minutes – the SCS never seemed to be in much of a hurry to go anywhere. They would also occasionally pop in during the week, mainly for a coffee. If there was anything pertaining to Peruvia I was sure it would have been them standing in the hotel reception and not these two strangers, and especially not on a Sunday evening; I knew that the SCS never worked on a Sunday!

They stood in my cramped office and flashed me their badges – they were customs officers. 'We have intelligence that a wanted suspect will be at your venue later this evening,' one of them said. 'He will be coming directly from the airport and we will be arresting him in your venue once he has met those he is due to meet.'

Fine, I thought, there was not much I was able to do. He then radioed through to his colleagues and two more customs officers appeared almost immediately at my office door.

'Can we look round?' the same officer asked.

'Of course. I'll show you round.'

There were two doors to my office, one through to the hotel restaurant and into the hotel lobby, and the other door to stairs leading down to the front door of the nightclub. Inside the club were two emergency exits, one at the back that led to the rear outside car park and the other halfway through the club, which joined the hotel exit at the back of the kitchens. These were noted by the officers as possible escape routes should the person who they were hoping to arrest make a run for it.

After they had looked briefly around and assessed the surroundings I was told that from 9 p.m. four officers would wait in my office. There would also be an armed response team in the car park and two officers in the club itself. Once they had positively identified the suspect he would be arrested and taken off the premises.

What could I say? I just nodded and left them to it; I did not want to get involved. They showed me a photo of the person they were going to arrest and asked if I knew him or if he was a regular.

I looked at the picture but didn't recognize him. We had so many gangs and friends of gangs and known criminals at Peruvia that I couldn't know them all.

That evening I busied myself getting the club ready for opening – checking the floats, the bars and the sound system.

I didn't really want to go into the office; it was only small and was fairly crowded with the four that were waiting in there already. Our three doormen turned up for work and nervously asked who the guys in the office were. They looked uneasy – I am sure that they had not led perfect lives themselves, but I assured them that it was none of our staff they were looking for and not to worry. They were looking for a customer and they should try to ignore whatever was going to happen.

We opened on time. At about 9.30 one of the undercover officers came in, paid the entrance fee like a regular customer and stood at the front end of the bar nearest to the door. A little while later the second undercover officer arrived, paid, bought a drink and stood the other side of the bar, watching both the entrance and the exit. To me they looked obviously out of place, but no-one else seemed to think so.

I could only presume drugs was the reason for the operation and I knew that it was quite big, as there were six officers on the ground plus probably a few more outside, as well as the armed response unit and probably some normal police officers somewhere as well.

The club was slowly filling up. It wasn't busy but there was a constant stream of customers through the door. At about 11 p.m. all hell broke loose. The moment the two officers inside the club seized two men standing at the bar, the four from the office came bounding down the stairs. Two other officers also came running in from outside the front door. They pinned the two arrested men to the ground, handcuffed them, read them their rights, pulled them to their feet and swiftly dragged them away. That, as they say, was that.

Everyone was talking, asking questions, speculating, curious as to what had just happened and why. One of the top Moss Side heads came over.

'What was that about?' he asked.

'No idea,' I replied, trying to look as shocked as I could. 'Did you know him?'

He didn't reply, he just shook his head and wandered off.

Tuesday evening, I was half watching the local news while on the phone chatting to a girlfriend. I wasn't really concentrating on the TV but caught the presenter speaking about one of Manchester's biggest drugs hauls outside a nightclub late Sunday evening. They didn't mention the venue but I was certain it was the arrest they had made on Sunday.

On Wednesday afternoon the Serious Crime Squad paid me another visit. It wasn't to pick up the video as they had already collected it first thing Monday morning, taking away all evidence of the arrest as well as details of who else was in the club and the images of the customs officers involved. They didn't want to leave anything that a gang member might possibly get hold of.

This time they had something more important to tell me. The Manchester drug underworld was blaming me for the arrest of one of their key players. They thought I had given information that had resulted in the arrest. The underworld was accusing me of assisting in setting up the operation. How they came to that conclusion I have no idea, as I genuinely had nothing to do with it. And I certainly had no power to stop customs officers doing whatever they wanted. But word on the street was that I was involved and I would soon be visited and severely dealt with.

I called Mickey Francis, as he knew everyone in Manchester, and he had also heard that I was involved. He came over to the hotel the next day and I explained everything to him in detail.

Three days later he called and said everything had been sorted out. I was no longer blamed, they understood that it would have been impossible for me to warn anyone and there was nothing I could have done to stop the arrest, even if I had known the suspect. To this day I still don't know the name of the person arrested or the quantity of the seizure.

There were always celebrities, pop stars and football players at Peruvia. I remember seeing a couple of the Spice Girls and chatting briefly to Errol, the lead singer of Hot Chocolate. Many Manchester United and Manchester City footballers were regulars as were most of the stars from *Coronation Street* and *Hollyoaks*.

One evening I was at the bar, relaxed and drinking my usual large Southern Comfort with ice while watching what was going on around me when there was suddenly a commotion – shouting and pushing – next to me. I looked round in time to see Davina, from the soap *Hollyoaks*, rushing off holding a bloodied nose. She and her then boyfriend, the soccer star Ryan Giggs, had apparently had an argument and she received a punch on the nose, though I didn't see the punch, I just heard swearing and shouting and saw Davina with blood on her face and hands rushing up the stairs and out of the club. He followed shortly after, ushered by his brother and the rest of his hangers-on. Someone in his group and very close to him must have telephoned the press the minute it happened, as it was on the news and in every national paper the following day. There was intense media frenzy for a few days and almost every tabloid newspaper in the country called asking me what had happened and whether I had seen or heard anything. Of course, being the manager of the club, I said nothing. I have always been very discreet and confidential about customers, whether in a nightclub or working as a bodyguard. I was even offered £5,000 by one tabloid newspaper for the CCTV video footage from inside the club, but the incident was out of the range of the camera and the only thing that was recorded was Davina leaving the club via the main entrance with a few friends and Ryan leaving shortly after.

I had been at Peruvia for almost nine months. Christmas was on its way and I was feeling bored and fed up. I had not been abroad on any contracts for quite a while. My last job had been back in July when I briefly went to Tanzania to look after the teenage daughter of one of the directors of a tobacco company. I was missing the excitement of going into strange places. I was having it easy in Wilmslow, things had quietened down and there was little trouble. I needed a change and Peruvia was no longer challenging. It was boring and I hated boredom.

I handed in my notice the day after I had a big bust-up with the hotel general manager.

He had asked me to find a new promoter for New Year's Eve. Andy had a written contract with the hotel to promote and run the club every Saturday night. Liam had closely looked through the contract and saw that there was no provision for any other night except Saturdays. New Year's Eve fell on a Tuesday. He was constantly moaning about Andy Bassett, and was getting fed up with Peruvia. He told me he wanted to find someone else to promote New Year's Eve. He stressed that I was to make sure I had a clear-cut signed contract with the new promoter which would safeguard the night. I knew that once Andy found out he didn't have New Year's Eve he would go mad. I wasn't wrong. New Year's Eve would be a big earner and I was sure he would already be planning that evening. He would have no idea that he wasn't having the night until after I had signed the contract with another promoter.

I did what Liam Walsh told me. I had found a new promoter, a guy called Beeley. He was a regular at Peruvia but also ran his own nights in and around Manchester. After negotiating an acceptable fee, he committed himself to promoting New Year's Eve and signed the contract. He felt confident that he could easily fill the club, especially as his proposed entrance fee was going to be half of what Peruvia would have charged. However, as New Year's Eve approached, Andy started talking to me about his plans for the evening. He presumed it was going to be his night, so he wasn't a happy bunny when I told him that Liam Walsh had instructed me to find another promoter. I then told him that I had given the night to Beeley.

As expected, Andy went crazy and stormed to the hotel manger, who came storming back to me. 'What the hell are you playing at?' he demanded angrily. We were standing in the lobby of the hotel.

'What do you mean?' I replied, confused.

'Andy has just told me he hasn't got New Year's Eve.'

'You know he hasn't,' I replied, 'I have done exactly what you told me to.'

'I didn't tell you to do anything,' he said.

'Yes you did,' I was getting annoyed, 'you sat there in the restaurant and told me to find another promoter for New Year's Eve. You said you didn't want Andy to run the night and that I should find someone else and to get a contract signed, which I have done.'

'I did no such thing.' The manager of the hotel was shouting at me in front of Andy, hotel customers and the reception staff.

'Yes you did.' I was trying to control myself, but it was getting difficult and I was getting very annoyed.

'Are you calling me a liar?' he shouted, his face dark red with anger. 'I did not tell you anything of the sort, now cancel this other promoter and tear up the contract, it is invalid!' He stormed off to his office.

I realized there was no use arguing. He was denying everything that he had asked me to do just a few short weeks ago. But what could I do? I was not going to be talked at in this way, or lied to. He had always been a difficult man to work for. So the next day I handed in my notice. I worked out the remainder of my month in solitude in my office, only doing what was absolutely necessary and counted down the days until I could happily leave.

Shortly before leaving Peruvia I met Thelma. She worked at the hotel in the restaurant. She was married and had a daughter but was living a miserable life – she was terribly unhappy and desperately wanted to leave her husband. Soon after we started seeing each other, while her husband was getting drunk at his local pub, she packed her bags one evening and walked out on her marriage.

I bought a small house in Wilmslow and Thelma and her daughter came to live with me. A few months later she fell pregnant. I have never, nor, I expect, will ever feel joy like that again. I was going to be a father and I was so incredibly excited. Time could not pass quickly enough. I would rush home just to hold Thelma and feel the movement of my child inside her. I would put my ear to Thelma's belly and listen to my child's heartbeat.

Holding my delicate little daughter in my arms in the maternity clinic while Thelma slept was the most magnificent moment of my life. It was a magical time, smelling that sweet smell of a newborn baby. I didn't want to do anything or go anywhere – I just wanted to spend all my time with my daughter. I doubted I had ever loved anything or anyone in my life. I had walked in and out of relationships, time and again – they all meant nothing. I had no attachments, I could tell them I loved them one minute and walk out on them the next. But everything changed. For the first time in my life I felt love, total and absolute. I knew in my heart what it was like to love. Lying awake in the middle of the night listening to her delicate breathing, standing over her cot in amazement, I couldn't believe that I had been blessed with these glorious emotions and wonderful feelings. My daughter gave me purpose. She was perfect in every way.

Of course, like everything in my life, I would eventually lose her and Thelma – I would fuck things up again and again until Thelma simply had enough. We would eventually separate but at that glorious moment in my life I could think of nothing but my wonderful little daughter and the magnificent love I had for her.

I heard that Peruvia closed a few months after I left. To escape the Manchester gangs, Andy Bassett moved his promotion to Birmingham where I heard that things were equally difficult for him and eventually he closed the night altogether.

After Peruvia I vowed I would not go back into nightclub management again. It was too much of a commitment, it took too much of my time and I wanted the freedom to do what I wanted and to go where I pleased, when it pleased me. As a club manager the salary was good, there were perks and tips, there was job security, accommodation was generally provided free, I could eat and drink free and I thought it was better than doing the doors but I preferred to do what I knew best and what I liked doing the most – bodyguarding, bodyguard training and the doors. The problem was that I had no money and so I spent the next few months concentrating on working for the WFB. I hadn't done a lot for the WFB while at Peruvia because I didn't have the time or the facilities. It seemed a good time to run a training course.

The best thing about running a course is not the hard work, the late nights or the situations I put the students in. It is simply seeing a group of unfamiliar anxious individuals slowly transform into a united confident team. I love the first meeting, seeing the eyes of the students as they tensely wait for me to enter the room, hearing them shuffle in their chairs nervously. I love to look at their faces and try to predict their outcome – would they pass or fail – but never could. Generally those that I think will pass don't, and those I think won't, confidently pass with flying colours.

The WFB's basic training course is hard. It is eight long days of both theoretical and practical work and self-defence. It is incredibly stressful and both physically and mentally demanding. The day runs from 6 a.m. until well past midnight, with the occasional night exercise thrown in for good measure. There is so much information that the first few days are just a blur without meaning or sense, but as the week progresses everything slowly comes together and by the end of the week most students have the ability to set up and run their own low-risk close protection assignment. They evolve from isolated individuals to a compact and professional bodyguard team.

Courses were never very profitable for the WFB. We charged less than most training companies, and generally had fewer students. We had an ideological view that we were all in the same business and should look after each other. The WFB didn't want to be just another bodyguard company making money from students and then having nothing more to do with them. The WFB wanted to be part of their life, part of their development. I am still in contact with many old WFB students, unlike many other training companies that just take their money, train them and never say another word. However, having the philosophy we had meant not only that we didn't make money, we frequently lost it – not just on the training but on the memberships and other bodyguard-related businesses I tried to set up.

I published *Close Protection* magazine but after just five issues had to close down after losing a personal investment of around £4,000. I also published an *International Directory of Close Protection*, listing over 1,000 companies and organizations worldwide that provided close protection. This was specifically aimed at helping new bodyguards find work but I also lost quite a bit of money on that project and spent much of the next year in poverty recovering from my bad investments. I was never commercially motivated, but ended up sacrificing much of my money as well as my family's lifestyle on my ideology.

CHAPTER TWELVE

The Mirage, Wigan

About six months after leaving Equivino and Peruvia I had a call from Daniel, who was the new manager of the Moat House Hotel in Standish, near Wigan. Daniel had worked at the Moat House in Wilmslow as operations manager. He was a great guy. He would often come for a chat in my office – we would sit for hours talking about anything and everything. He enjoyed being involved with the club and loved the crowd of customers it attracted. Daniel was second to Liam Walsh, so he couldn't really influence Liam's decisions relating to the nightclub, but Daniel was on my side a lot more than Liam was. Daniel would often listen to my arguments and would frequently agree with me about things Liam did not. Sadly Daniel didn't spend many evenings at the club, but it was always a pleasure to have him.

Most hotel managers believe that they can apply the principles of hotel management to nightclubs. Nightclubs are different beasts altogether. It is not hard to manage a nightclub, it is quite straightforward; what takes skill is the promotion and marketing. This requires a specific mindset, a great deal of flexibility and a special attitude which hotel managers don't seem to have. This is why many hotels with a nightclub attached prefer to bring in the skills of outside consultants such as Juliana's rather than manage the units themselves.

Daniel was very flexible. He did not get too involved in the day-to-day running of the club but preferred to sit and observe rather than to dictate and argue. He had just been promoted to general manager at the Moat House in Standish. It was his first hotel in the role of general manger and, as in Wilmslow, attached to the hotel was a nightclub, this one called The Mirage.

The differences between The Mirage and Equivino were immeasurable. They were at completely different ends of the nightclub spectrum – where Peruvia attracted the most glitzy and attractive in Manchester, The Mirage was lucky to get someone through the door that was vaguely good-looking. Where the dress code in Peruvia was smart, extreme and over the top, The Mirage, well – you could get in wearing almost anything. Customers travelled for miles and miles to go to Peruvia whereas The Mirage was just a local club and anyone not recognized as being a local would look immediately out of place. The Mirage was a basic down-to-earth, rough and tumble, run-down, tatty club for local Standish people.

Actually, before I started on the door there, I was asked to manage the club. I was invited to spend a weekend at the hotel assessing the unit and suggesting promotions and marketing ideas in order to attract customers from further afield than just Standish. I enjoyed the weekend but it made me even more resolute that I would never go back into full-time nightclub management.

As usual I was poor but now I had a family to support. I needed the money desperately but management just wasn't me. I could no longer go through all the shit that managers go through, of having a boss breathing down my neck every day, the stress of trying to increase revenue while not having the support and structure to facilitate it. So I worked the door.

Mick Lyons ran the doors at most of the nightclubs and bars in and around Wigan. I had never met the guy but he had a formidable reputation. It was difficult to have a pub or club in Wigan without employing Mick Lyons. The police and licensing didn't allow him to work the doors himself so he employed some very hard men to run things for him.

Wigan is a hard place. A typically working-class town where a huge amount of alcohol and a good fight seemed to be the basis of a good night out – women included.

Before Daniel arrived The Mirage had big problems. For whatever reason, Mick Lyons had just lost the door to another company. A few weeks later, a big crew turned up at the club and put most of the doormen into intensive care. Two guys went through the front doors on their own but once inside immediately opened the back fire exits where at least ten other big, hard, balaclava'd men, armed with baseball bats and coshes, were waiting. The four doormen working that night bravely defended themselves but simply didn't have a chance. They were all seriously beaten up and put into hospital – some were in intensive care for weeks.

Most of the attackers were eventually arrested, held on remand and finally imprisoned. But a lot of nervousness remained on the door at The Mirage – there was always the feeling that someone would do the same thing again in a takeover bid, so Daniel called me and asked if I knew of some good lads that could work the door. They could not be local lads because, as a condition of the licence, both the police and the licensing authority had stipulated that only a team from outside the local area would be allowed to work.

I called Jon Maddocks, with whom I had developed a friendship in the short time he worked at Peruvia. He was a good lad, tough, hard-working, extremely conscientious and very well known in Doncaster. He would stand up to almost anyone and he wasn't frightened to use his fists.

I knew he still had his security company and was sure he could bring a few good lads with him from Doncaster to run the door at Standish. I would also work it with him. I didn't want to run it – I didn't want the hassle of looking around for good guys, paying wages from my money while I invoiced the hotel, registering them with the local council, providing uniforms etc., so I called Jon.

After a successful meeting, Jon was awarded the contract. The club required six doormen, and four came with Jon from Doncaster, the sixth being myself driving from Wilmslow. For me it was a 70-mile, one-hour round trip, double that for Jon and the lads, but we didn't mind. It was a good team and, although The Mirage was completely different to Peruvia, it was a good although sometimes difficult venue to work – there was trouble almost every night.

Jon was head doorman. It was his company, and although he had other doors to look after, one of the conditions that Daniel set for Jon being awarded the contract was that he worked the door himself until things looked more settled and everyone felt more at ease. Then there was 'Big Steve', a giant of a man at 6ft 5ins and 22 stone. An older guy, not easily frightened and if he decided you were to go, then you went, simple. In contrast to Steve's immense size there was Little Clive who, although only about 5ft 4ins and slightly built, had the balls of a gorilla with a face to match. Clive didn't really care who he came up against, he would have a go at almost anyone. Many times I witnessed him throw out guys twice his size. The problem with Clive was that even though he was small he would try and handle every situation and there were many times when we had to pick him up off the floor from underneath everyone. It became quite farcical – if there was a fight and we couldn't see Clive we would look on the floor or under those fighting and, lo and behold, there he would be. He just didn't have the power and strength to stand his ground against those a lot bigger and stronger.

But it was always funny and he never suffered any serious injuries. I would have him behind me in a confrontation any time – you could never take away the fact that he would back you up to the very end. To our utter amazement he eventually married a beautiful girl. We all struggled to understand what she saw in him – he had a shaven head, crooked teeth and piercings everywhere – but maybe he had something else that was disproportionate to his size!

There was also Big Jeff, a pig farmer by trade who tended to exaggerate and boast but who had a lot of front and wouldn't back down either – he wouldn't hesitate in having a go, even if it was just to show off. Once Jon witnessed pig farmer Jeff wipe blood down his shirt in an effort to exaggerate an incident inside the club, making out it was worse than it was.

Pig Farmer was a 17 stone plus, stocky, shaven-headed doorman who continually talked about the size of his dick. No-one ever actually knew how big it was, nor did anyone care, but almost every night he worked he insisted on telling us how big it was. At least he was proud of it, I suppose.

The Mirage was quite an aggressive club, but nothing we couldn't handle as a team. The average age of the customer was young, around 18 to 21, so most were babies and hadn't yet developed good fighting skills. It was generally a matter of quickly overpowering them and getting them to the door as swiftly as we could. Most confrontations were just immature, alcohol-induced brawls and rarely excessively violent. There were never any real serious injuries, only bruises, black eyes, an occasional broken nose or cut lip and an occasional glassing or two. If we had permanently banned everyone fighting we would have had no customers at all. It seemed that everyone liked to involve themselves in some form of confrontation, for them it was part of having a good night out. We barred anyone fighting for a month after which they would be allowed back in, as long as the violence wasn't directed to us. Then of course they were barred for good.

Working at Standish was like going back 15 years to the Ritzy, where most situations could be sorted out quickly, aggressively and without worrying too much about the consequences or about being arrested. Occasionally the police were called after we had perhaps thrown someone out a little too aggressively, but things rarely came back on us once we gave the police our slightly biased side of the story. This was Standish and the police knew what it was like. Most cases were dropped before they got to the police station, let alone to court.

One time there was a frantic call from the DJ – nothing unusual for a Friday night. Jon and I rushed in to a big fight that had started in the club. People were being smacked and punched left, right and centre. Some were rolling around on the floor while others were trying to pull opponents apart and trying to calm things down. Jon and I looked at each other and shrugged as we wondered who to go for first. It was a bit of a mess. In the semi-darkness and the flashing lights I saw someone bent over smacking the daylights out of someone else. I thought I should stop this one first and rushed over. As I grabbed the guy on top I immediately realized I had my hands full. He was crouched over and was difficult to get hold of but I knew I had to try and stop him hitting whoever he was hitting. I grabbed his head but he was powerful and strong and easily shrugged me off to resume his pummelling. I knew he was going to be a problem so I quickly got him in a tight headlock and pulled him off by cutting his airway. If he had struggled any further I was going to put him to sleep. I pulled him off and looked down to see who it was – it was Pig Farmer's head I had in my arms. He looked up at me, almost blue with asphyxiation. I let him go and we both started to laugh. We just couldn't stop – in the midst of the battle we were rolling around the floor laughing. People must have thought we were crazy.

We had a new guy join the team at Standish, who proved yet again that size and tough looks don't always go with ability. Having a shaven-headed 6ft 4ins bodybuilder working the doors sometimes does act as a good deterrent. I would certainly think twice about having a go with someone twice my size and looking like Tim did. However it is not always the case that someone that looks hard is hard.

I have always had the philosophy that everyone, from the smallest to the mightiest, from the ugliest to the most handsome, can take me out. Having this philosophy has meant that I have respect for everyone. I have never presumed that just because someone is small he has no ability and just because he is big he has every ability. It is not the case. It is important to respect everyone, for there is always someone better.

Tim joined us on a Friday, traditionally the worst night for trouble. In Standish it seemed that men went out in groups on Fridays and with their wives or girlfriends on Saturdays. Consequently there always seemed to be so many more problems on a Friday night than there were on a Saturday. Friday night was fight night at The Mirage.

Tim certainly looked the part and as soon as he arrived he started boasting – trying to impress us with his previous exploits on the door and making out that he was a hard-man. I wasn't really listening, I had heard it all many times before and the proof would be in the next mad dash into the club. We would then see what he was like.

Most newcomers to the doors tend to go over the top on their first call to battle. It was a normal show of strength – a way of proving to the others in the team that they were reliable and trustworthy. I did it at the Ritzy. Almost everyone starting the door for the first time wants to prove themselves and so it is generally expected that new guys rush in and battle hard.

Halfway through the night a frantic call came over the radio from Little Clive in the club – it was going off big time. On the door were myself, Jon, Big Steve and Tim the new guy. The manager was on the till and waved us all in while he closed the door, not letting anyone else in until we had dealt with whatever was going off inside. As we all ran into the club we could see it was another monster brawl. People were kicking and punching everywhere, it seemed as though everyone was bored that night and they all wanted to have a pop at someone, anyone. Girls were running out screaming and terrified while others were trying to separate those fighting.

We ran in, blindly grabbed whoever we saw fighting and dragged them to the nearest exit, or separated them, leaving them to their friends to deal with. We were all working individually as there was just too much going on for us to work as a team, we just went wherever we could independently, smacking, punching, kneeing, elbowing and grabbing. We were so high on adrenalin we really didn't think about anything and really didn't care – we were like animals reacting on instinct alone. Bottles were flying and glasses were smashing. The DJ had turned the music off and the lights up and the noise was akin to a pack of vultures fighting with each other as they tore at a carcass.

It was hard work but great fun – we really didn't give a fuck. Thankfully, amid all this mayhem there were no serious injuries. One woman had been glassed, a couple of customers had busted noses, lots of bruises and cut lips, but nothing too bad considering what a mess everything was. We had our fair share of injuries, each of us was bleeding from somewhere, although we didn't stop to assess our wounds until the last person was chucked out and we all met in the foyer. We were all together, exhausted, bleeding, shaking from the adrenalin and laughing a little. Jon looked at us all then suddenly, a look of horror crept over his face.

'Fuck, where's Tim?'

We looked at each other, confirming we were all there apart from him.

'I didn't see him,' Clive panted.

'I hadn't seen him either,' Pig Farmer confirmed. 'In fact I don't remember him being with us at all.'

'Where the fuck is he?' I asked. I wasn't sure whether I was angry because I hadn't seen him either, confused because I just hadn't noticed him, or really pissed off that he hadn't been with us.

There was a disabled toilet on the left between the foyer and the actual entrance doors to the nightclub. It was easier and safer for us to use this toilet than the public toilets. Just as we decided to rush back into the club to look for Tim, we heard the toilet door unlock and slowly open. Out came Tim, looking down at his mobile phone as though he had just been making a call.

He looked up at us standing in front of him. 'What the fuck happened?' he asked noticing our battered and worn-out faces.

'What do you mean what the fuck happened?' I shouted. 'Where were you?'

'I had to have a crap just as it went off, then my missus called.' I couldn't believe what he was saying to us.

'Didn't you hear the shouts on the radio? Didn't you hear the fucking music had been turned off?' I shouted close to his face, spraying him with bloodied saliva from my cut lip. Jon and Clive could see my face reddening.

'No,' he replied nervously and looked at his radio. 'Must have turned it off earlier. What happened anyway?'

I grabbed him hard by the neck. I squeezed tighter and tighter and could feel his windpipe crushing between my fingers. He was going blue, he was going to die and I was going to kill him. I looked into his eyes; I saw the tears of fear and despair. I squeezed harder, I was going to kill him and I didn't think anything of it, I didn't give a fuck. He would never let anyone down again. With both hands he tried to prise my fingers from his neck but he wasn't strong enough. I squeezed and squeezed and he started to go limp. Suddenly Jon and Clive grabbed me and pulled me off. Tim collapsed to the floor, barely conscious and fighting for breath.

I paused, confused. My mind was blank. I had no feeling.

'If I ever see your ugly face again I will kill you.' I turned away. Just as I started to walk off I turned round and kicked him full in the mouth, smashing his teeth and lips and knocking him unconscious.

I expect various things from any team I work with. I don't expect anyone to be the best fighter in the world, but to work the doors as part of a team, every member of the team must show dedication and commitment, a lot of front and a load of bollocks. But more important than anything, never, ever to give in or to back down. He did the unspeakable and he would have died for it. Thankfully Jon and Clive not only saved his life but mine. I was no longer in a war and I didn't fancy serving life in prison.

Tim never worked the doors again, and never came to The Mirage for a pint with me either.

Driving home that night I was scared that I could have so easily stepped over the line, stepped back into the world of horror, of death. I was fighting for my survival, my sanity. In my rage I could have killed without emotion or feeling. I had been struggling with myself for years and, although I still lived and worked in a violent world I had always managed to stop and control myself. This time I had lost it and could have easily gone too far.

There were lots of incidents at The Mirage, and something seemed to happen every evening. It was busy for us – there was always something to do and someone to throw out but I enjoyed it. It was a basic, down-to-earth nightclub, the kind of club I used to enjoy working in yet without the excessive violence.

On their nights off doormen that go to other clubs generally fall into two categories: those that have an attitude and those that don't. Those with an attitude saunter up to a door with an 'I am harder than you' way about them. They seem to mock other doormen, regarding them as of no use – shouldn't be working the doors. They often walk to the front of any queue expecting to be let straight in. Some don't even ask, they just stroll in with a stupid way of walking that really pisses me off.

One such guy came into The Mirage one night. Big, nasty-looking guy, thinking he was hard. There wasn't a queue so he came straight in and flashed his doorman's badge.

'Doorman,' he said and started to walk straight through.

'So?' I asked, stopping him.

'Doormen get in free, don't they?'

'Sometimes – it depends if they ask or if they have attitude.' I didn't like the look of him but wanted to assess his reply. 'Which one are you?'

'Is it alright then?' he replied with a bit less attitude.

I nodded, let him through and thought, what an arsehole.

He stood drinking alone at the bar. He looked suspicious so at first we kept checking the exits in case he was a decoy or going to let others in, but he just stood on his own. He was a dick but seemed a harmless dick.

The evening was uneventful until 30 minutes before closing when I noticed Mr Arsehole Doorman at the bar getting into an argument. He was getting louder and more aggressive. He looked an arsehole but up until that time he was a harmless-looking arsehole, but an arsehole is always an arsehole and shit always comes out from it and this was going to be no exception. It seemed as though he was trying to prove himself to others around him and of course to us. I went over to see what was happening.

'It's alright,' he said to me as I approached, obviously not remembering me as the person that stopped him when he first came in. 'I am a doorman in town.'

'I know you are and I'll decide what is alright and what isn't, and I don't give a fuck whether you are a doorman or not, you don't cause trouble in a venue I am working. Now sort it out outside, ok?'

'Don't be like that,' he replied. 'It's this arsehole,' pointing to somebody standing directly opposite. 'He's causing all the problems.'

Now the other guy looked quite normal, not hard or menacing but average and a bit too smartly dressed for The Mirage; shirt and jacket, longer than average hair, quite good-looking – nothing out of the ordinary.

'It's a private matter,' the other guy said to me quietly.

'Well take your private matter outside,' I said and ushered them both towards the exit. Arsehole Doorman decided to put on his 'I am hard' act and started to threaten this other guy.

'Come on then you cunt,' he said, 'let's sort this out once and for all. I've had enough of you and your fucking family. I am going to wipe the floor with you, you wanker.'

I ushered them through the front doors and out into the cold. Arsehole even had the audacity to tell me he wouldn't be long and would be back as soon as he had sorted this 'cunt' out. I was looking forward to seeing what was going to happen, as this doorman was bragging a little too much. This other guy was cool – he was taking everything calmly and didn't seem worried in the slightest. I would have been planning my moves by now and would definitely have been getting a little nervous, as Mr Doorman did look the part.

I left them to it and closed the door behind them. I wasn't going to get involved outside. We would rarely go out, but I was keen to see the outcome so I watched through the small rectangular window in the centre of the door. Mr Doorman was pointing and shouting at Mr Normal, pushing him on his chest. Suddenly, from nowhere, Mr Normal came in with a beautiful uppercut, and put Mr Doorman straight on his back. I smiled. Now this was getting interesting.

He then stood back slightly, letting Mr Doorman get up. As soon as he was back on his feet, wham, a right hook put him straight back down. Mr Doorman was now on his hands and knees crawling away from Mr Normal, who stood silently over him. When Mr Normal had let Mr Doorman crawl far enough away, he turned and came back to the door, which I opened.

'Is it alright if I finish my pint?' he asked. I nodded and he walked straight through, without uttering another word. I looked back outside to see Mr Doorman still on all fours. The moral? Respect everyone and never presume you are harder or tougher than anyone else, because everyone meets their match one day. We never saw Mr Doorman at The Mirage again.

On the other side of the coin there are excellent and very professional doormen without egos the size of the Twin Towers (and we all know what happened to them). These are the ones that wait in the queue, that are polite to other doormen and offer to buy them a drink, that don't belittle or look down at other doormen. These are the ones that know what it is really like running a door, dealing with wankers every single night, and wouldn't ever want to be classified in that category themselves. I have seen an equal amount of both types and in my experience it is the modest ones that are the real hard-men, that never have to prove a thing. These are the guys I truly respect.

I have never been able to resist a pretty face and although I had a steady girlfriend and a wonderful baby daughter I started seeing a cute 23-year-old blonde who had just started working on the door at The Mirage as a female searcher. She was a lot younger than me and still lived with her parents and so the only place we could screw was in my car after work. I didn't tell her that I was still with my girlfriend – instead I said that I had just split up and was staying with a friend, which was why I couldn't bring anyone home. She believed me. I saw her for a few months, shagging in the car or in the fields or in the nightclub car park, sneaking home at four or five in the morning, rushing up to shower before jumping into bed.

Of course I was eventually caught, and that was the start of the separation between myself and Thelma. Thelma had found a letter that Liz had written to me. She must have suspected something as she had gone through all the drawers in my office. One afternoon I came back from being out with Liz and Thelma was sat in the living room with the letter on her lap. It was the start of our separation and my eventual admission into a psychiatric hospital.

I was becoming more and more unhappy. I was leading an awful life, was no longer interested in intimacy, we didn't talk much and I disagreed with some of the fundamental ways in which my daughter was being influenced. Thelma already had a daughter from a previous marriage and as she grew older I disliked her more and more. She had learning difficulties and I had little patience. I wanted to leave Thelma but I hadn't the strength to leave my daughter, the only person that I felt adoration and complete love for. I dreaded the thought of my daughter growing up without me and without my influence.

I was also struggling to support my family financially. I certainly couldn't support my family and myself separately. So I was stuck and slowly slipping back into a dark depression. It took two more years before we finally separated, and those were perhaps the worst years of my life. I left the doors again, and pursued other interests.

CHAPTER THIRTEEN

Loaf

I had just finished training at my regular gym in Altrincham. I was training hard again and enjoying the gym. The facilities there were good and the gym was large enough to be able to do what I want without having to wait for equipment or get involved talking to anyone. I just liked to train hard and get out. I was looking good, 17 stone and quite ripped. I was taking gear again, 300mg of Viromone every three days and 10 Dianabol a day. Not much but I was making good gains. I no longer wanted to take a lot of gear; I didn't want to be much bigger than 17 stone as I found that it slowed me and made me less supple. Getting into better shape was a priority. I would take Dianabol for six weeks and then go straight onto a more anabolic oral such as Anavar or Primobolon. I would then stay on that for six to eight weeks then go back onto Dianabol. In this way the Dianabol got me a few extra pounds of lean muscle and the Anavar would help me keep it while dieting. I would stay on Viromone permanently, 6ml every three days. It was good stuff, although worked out quite expensive and was a pain to inject. It didn't hold much water, the side effects were negligible and it was fairly safe.

I was training every two days. I had found that to stay fairly ripped as well as maintain a good level of fitness, super-setting the exercises – going directly from one exercise to another without a break – worked best. Day one I would superset chest, back and shoulders. Day two I would rest.

Day three I would train my legs first, then superset bicep and triceps. Day four rest, then back to day one. I would train abs every day. For most people this training routine would be too hard, but it worked well for me – it kept my bodyfat low and my fitness level high. I never did any more than six to eight exercises per body part and I could no longer lift heavy, but I now wanted shape more than size. Some guys go into the gym and do 12, 14 or 16 sets just for chest, but for me this is far too much. I have found that by cutting my training right down, but training to the maximum, I can make just as good gains with less time in the gym and less gear.

I had already had a few weeks off the doors after returning from a trip to Russia. I had managed to secure a fairly long-term contract with an American banker, based in the UK. He would travel to Moscow two or three times a year for up to two weeks at a time and would require that I escort him throughout the duration of each trip. Banking laws in Russia were still archaic but were changing slowly and it was becoming easier for foreign banks to open up representative offices. He was the Director of Eastern European Operations for a major American bank and was planning to open representation in Moscow. Things take a lot of time in Russia, but I was told after the first trip that I would accompany him on all future trips until the office was up and running. I was pleased to have long-term employment, although it would only be for about five or six weeks a year.

A few years previously, while I was running training courses in Sweden, Michael and I made contact with a Russian security company called Centurion VI. They sent six guards to us for training and since then I had kept in regular contact. A month prior to my first job with the banker I had faxed them advising them of my requirements. They were to meet us at the airport and provide an armed driver and bodyguard throughout the duration of my client's stay.

Centurion VI had an excellent base in central Moscow,

complete with their own training camp, shooting range, armoury and fleet of executive vehicles. They could also provide police escorts.

My client and I generally stayed at the Radisson hotel in the west of Moscow. He usually had a tight schedule – he didn't much like Moscow, especially in the winter and so he rarely had time for relaxation. He came, met who he had to meet and left.

He almost always arrived in the lobby at 8 a.m. after his breakfast, which he took in his room. We would then sit for a few minutes confirming the schedule and appointments for that day and any changes that he had made. Some meetings would last all day and I would wait outside the boardroom or in the office foyer, reading or doing a crossword. Other days were hectic, rushing from one meeting to another and I would continually have to monitor and check those around him.

I had now been in the business for quite a while and knew many people in the industry. Most of my contracts had originally come from Allen, but I slowly developed my own portfolio of clients who would call or email me about a month before they were going on a trip and I would plan and organize their entire security operation.

I would never do any more than three or four contracts a year, as well as perhaps a couple of training courses. It was never enough to give up working the doors, and certainly not enough to get rich. Most bodyguards have other jobs. But it was a good life, although at times a struggle. Full-time bodyguarding contracts are rare in the UK. Apart from a very few celebrities, most people don't require full-time protection. Thankfully we live in a relatively stable and secure environment. Only when clients had to travel into areas of greater risk did they need protection.

My clients soon included a banker, the chairman of a record company, the managing director of a fabric production company and the owner of a chain of electrical shops – all with business interests abroad. I was also working hard during the day developing the WFB, as it was due to be sold and I had to make it look as good as possible. It had developed quite considerably and had a large database of members worldwide as well as a good reputation for training. I spent the days working in a small bedroom I had converted in my office. Since Standish I hadn't been on the doors – just chilling out and enjoying my weekends off. However, the money I had earned in Russia was running low and I needed to work again.

As I was leaving the gym I noticed a sign on the wall which read 'Doorman Required'. Over the previous few months I had started to think about giving up bodyguarding altogether. I had started to miss my daughter terribly while away, and even more whenever I had an opportunity to speak to her on the phone. I had vague ideas that maybe I could find a regular yet decent full-time door to work, which would give me just enough money to live on while I looked around at other business opportunities. I loved my life as a bodyguard. For a single man it was great but I had a daughter who I adored. I had been married twice and lost count of the other relationships I had had, but I was now almost 40 and my life really had to change. My daughter was my world and my joy and I simply hated the thought of her growing up without me. Yet it was real and tangible that if I continued to push the lifestyle I was leading, one day her daddy would be shot and killed somewhere and her only memories of me would be in photos and on video.

There are many door companies operating in Manchester. Some only have contracts at one or two clubs while others have many units and are large, well-established, legitimate security companies. Most are always on the lookout for good doormen.

The company advertising on the noticeboard at the gym in Altrincham was called North West Security, later changing their name to the National Security Network.

I quickly jotted the number down. Once home I gave them a call and spoke to a guy called Neil, whose nickname I was later to learn was 'One Punch' as he rarely needed more than that to knock out any opponent. Neil confirmed they were indeed looking for doormen and requested that I come for an interview at their office in Adlington, near Bolton. I must admit, apart from my first job at the Ritzy in Norwich, I had never ever been to an interview for a job working the doors. I had always gone from club to club on a referral or a recommendation. Usually there was a particular job to do at a specific pub or club and I was chosen because of my reputation and ability.

That morning I woke up late feeling lazy. I didn't really want to drive all the way to Adlington. I was making excuses not to go but time passed and I didn't have anything planned for that morning so reluctantly I popped on a shirt and some trousers, jumped into my clapped-out old Peugeot and drove the 40 miles to Adlington.

I found what I presumed was the office but there were no signs for the company or the services they provided, just a windowless building with a single door and buzzer. I didn't want anyone to see what crap I was driving. If I happened to mention I was in security in Moscow how would I justify driving such a clapped-out old banger? So pride took hold of me and I parked up the road and walked down to the office and rang the buzzer.

I was greeted on the door by Neil, a 17-stone, shaven-head, hard-looking monster that I couldn't imagine anyone in their right mind wanting to upset. He was the personnel manager for North West and vetted everyone that applied for a job on the doors. Although quite menacing to look at, he was pleasant and we chatted for over an hour – a little about my job, about the style of self-defence I studied and of course about the history of my work on the doors. It was quite relaxed – he was interesting to talk to as he too had some great tales to tell about his life on the doors.

As we were talking, an even bigger guy walked in and nodded to me as he passed, disappearing up the stairs. I recognized him but couldn't think where from. It was only as I was leaving that I remembered that he occasionally came for a quick drink at The Mirage in Standish. He wouldn't be in often, and it was usually last thing at night just as we were closing. His name was Tony Hill and was one of the directors of the company. Tony was in his late twenties, good-looking and a big man at around 19 stone on a 6ft 2ins frame. Tony Hill and his boss, managing director Tony Ratcliff, built the company from virtually nothing to around 400 staff in over 40 venues throughout the north west. Before he joined North West, Tony Hill was an area manager of a mobile phone company so they were not members of any gang or organized crime group. They were just good businessmen who were in the right place at the right time and worked very hard.

When Mickey Francis and his partner Steve Bryan were put in prison for storming Applejacks nightclub, their firm, Loc-19, was one of the biggest in Manchester. But both the directors went to jail, leaving no-one running the company with the strength, leadership and reputation they had. This left a gaping hole on the doors in Manchester with gangs and rival companies fiercely competing for the business. Loc-19 lost many of the doors they had while Tony and Tony exploited the situation. They could offer licensees a service that other door companies were struggling to provide. Over the course of time they had developed a good relationship with the Manchester Police as well as the council's licensing committee. They made good friends with Kevin Bray, the head of the Manchester Door Safe training programme, which was responsible for training door security staff. They promised pubs and clubs throughout Greater Manchester a more professional attitude to the doors as well as back-up of literally hundreds of guys working in the centre of town but unconnected to gangs. Tony Ratcliff and Tony Hill already had a few venues but went on to take and keep many of the contracts Loc-19 once had.

National Security were always tendering for new contracts and so were on the lookout for new staff. From the 18-year-old student to the 40-year-old veteran there would be a unit to suit anyone and it was the second category that I neatly fell into. Neil had told me he might have a nice, fairly new venue in the centre of Manchester which he thought I would enjoy working at.

He called me the following day and offered me Loaf, at Deansgate Locks – a new strip of bars and nightclubs built along the canal in central Manchester. Loaf was a nice venue, recently opened and attracting the good-looking and better-off Manchester crowd. It was a bit like Peruvia, drawing pop stars and celebrities, footballers, soap stars, models and of course, the gangs. It was open until 2 a.m. Thursday, Friday and Saturday nights. I was to be there at 10 p.m. on Friday for my first night. When I arrived I was to introduce myself to the head doorman Assini, a big Samoan from New Zealand.

Assini had been working for North West for quite a while. Like most New Zealanders, he played rugby and was hoping for sponsorship to play in the US. Assini and his equally big female cousins had been working the doors in and around Manchester for quite a number of years and had all developed a good reputation.

It is always interesting approaching a new door. You can almost hear the team think, 'What is he like?' 'Is he a handy?' 'Is he hard?' Everyone does it, it is natural in this aggressive and fierce environment: everyone sizes everyone else up. It is a bit like going into a bodybuilding gym for the first time – everyone looks, wonders how strong you are, how big you are, how hard you train, what gear you take; like a wild dog being accepted by a new pack. There is always a little hostility towards a new doorman, some mild confrontation, a sizing up and a battle of egos. It doesn't last long, but I believe it's necessary for newcomers to become accepted as part of a team. If he can give what is given and match what is on show, then the new member becomes accepted. If a doorman is not accepted on the first few nights it is doubtful he ever will be.

I have worked with hundreds of doormen and I can tell almost immediately whether one will be good at the job or not and whether or not he will have the character and strength to be accepted by the team. Every doorman wants to feel that, in case of any confrontation, all the team are working together and backing each other up. Not being there when a major incident occurs is the worst crime anyone could commit on the doors.

I don't care if they are not the best fighters in the world, I don't care if they are not the hardest-looking or the biggest or strongest, I just care that they don't lose their bottle and are willing to back me up. I think it is foolish for someone to work the door with little or no self-defence or fighting experience. I have spoken to many doormen, young and old, that have had no experience at all. It is so important to be able to defend yourself yet there are those that have not had the faintest idea about evicting someone quickly and efficiently and without injury to either themselves or other customers. Many doormen rely too much on the skills of the other doormen and that is wrong. No-one should work the doors without having experience in unarmed combat. But there are many that are just on the doors for some extra money, to chat up women or simply for something to do on a Saturday night. I was one of those people many years ago when I started at Ritzy, but after my first fight I realized how naive and stupid I was, that having that attitude could have got me or my team into a great deal of trouble.

Many inexperienced newcomers remain lucky for months or sometimes even years and never get into trouble. Or they have the backing of a good team and never have to work for their money. They become complacent, thinking it will never happen to them.

However, most doormen in that category don't remain doing the doors for long. After their first major confrontation they realize that this job really isn't that easy and they are out of their league. For anyone that thinks doing the doors is an easy job, it isn't; for most people it is virtually impossible.

The doormen at Loaf had nothing to worry about as I had probably seen more violence in a year then most of them would ever see in their lifetime. But I still had to go through the stages of being accepted. I quickly settled in, they seemed a good team although as time passed most of the regular doormen either left the job completely or moved to other units.

I got on very well with Assini. He was very interested in my life away from the doors as a bodyguard. He said it was something he had frequently thought about doing but he never actually got round to attending a training course. He would make a good bodyguard. He was an interesting guy, modest, quiet and hardly ever used violence to settle difficult situations. I had got to know some of the Maoris very well in New Zealand. I shared a house with one and trained at his social club on the high street in Hastings, a town near to where I lived in Hawkes Bay. Most Samoans and Polynesians look ferocious and I can see why people feel intimidated by them, but it was just their appearance. Mostly I found them to be nice, quiet, peace-loving, gentle people. But they were all well-built, even the women. Their diet was mainly fish and seafood with plenty of fresh fruit and vegetables. They were a monster race – the Polynesians are the biggest in the world, and even the women are big and strong. I went out with a Maori woman and I can tell you from experience.

The wonderful thing about Assini was that he always preferred the diplomatic approach. He was fundamentally a tactful man, although he looked quite the opposite.

All the door team at Loaf were good guys (and one girl). I was new to the central Manchester doors and so didn't interfere with their systems or procedures, I just got on with my job of looking after the security inside the venue, leaving the others to run the front door. Inside was not that difficult and often quite boring, but when it did go off it was big time.

Loaf attracted a fairly decent, glamorous yet very snobbish and pretentious crowd who were generally full of themselves and stuck up their own arses.

Because of the profile it had in Manchester, it also attracted many of the people I knew from my Peruvia days. On my second night, Mickey Francis, Steve Bryan and crew came in. I was standing at the bottom of the stairs at the entrance to the canal bar – so named because it overlooked the canal at Deansgate Locks. I was at a vantage point where I could keep an eye on the dance floor as well as on the doorman standing at the far end. The stairwell divided the canal bar and the dance floor.

I immediately recognized Mickey and Steve and his team lumbering down the stairs. It was a big team. Mickey and Steve are not small guys and the people they were with were equally big, if not bigger. There wouldn't be many doors in Manchester that could stop them coming in – if they were so inclined. Mickey didn't see me at first; it had been a few years since I had last seen him at Peruvia and he would not have expected me to be working the door.

I let them get settled in the far corner of the canal bar, near where the other doorman had been standing. I could see the look of worry on the doorman's face as Mickey and his team approached. He quickly moved off to find a less obvious and safer place to stand. I was sure Mickey and his crew would never cause trouble but to be a sole doorman standing among that lot would never be a good idea. Once they had settled I decided to walk over and say hello.

Mickey seemed genuinely pleased to see me and it was good to see him and Steve again too. They had done a good job running the doors at Peruvia and in the end I had got to know them quite well. We chatted for a while, he told me about getting arrested and serving time and what plans he now had with his new security company, North Cheshire Security Services. He was building up his portfolio of doors but this time staying well away from central Manchester. Instead he was concentrating on the suburbs as well as in Chester. He had joined forces with Lesley Aimes. Lesley used to work the door for Mickey at Peruvia and her husband had a contract for a few doors in Wilmslow, which she inherited after he went to jail for grievous bodily harm. Long gone were the days of Loc-19. North Cheshire Security aimed to offer an excellent standard of service to both the licensee and the customer.

Why was I a manager at Peruvia but now working the doors? Mickey asked. I explained in more detail that before managing Peruvia I had also worked the doors for many years and had recently been working as a bodyguard in Russia.

Mickey and Steve hadn't changed much in the four or so years since I had last seen them. They were still fearsome but I got on well with them as people, a side many didn't see. I was introduced to various friends of Mickey's including a young guy called Tommy. He was another hard-looking, well-built individual with a fearsome reputation.

I was told about one specific night when Tommy and a friend were drinking at the Venus Bar, a late night watering hole. It had closed and everyone had left apart from Tommy and his friend, who were quite happy to take their time. They were asked to drink up and leave on numerous occasions, but ignored the doormen's requests and sat indifferently with their feet on the table sipping champagne. The ten doormen that worked the venue that night surrounded Tommy and his friend, but not one dared to make the first move and throw them out. When he was ready – and only when he was ready – did Tommy get up and leave.

I chatted to Tommy for quite a while. It turned out he had a product that he wanted to launch in Russia. I had a few interested contacts and arranged to meet him later to discuss a possible business partnership. Sadly nothing came of it, as importing products into the Russian Federation can be a logistical nightmare but it was worth a meeting and it just might have made us both very wealthy.

In a way meeting up with these guys again settled me in at Loaf quicker than I had originally anticipated. The other doormen could see that I had some pretty heavy connections. I settled nicely at Loaf as other doormen came and went. I hadn't actually intended to stay as long as I did but soon found myself working five or six nights a week. I still had the occasional week or two off working abroad either body-guarding or training. I helped set up a training camp for the new owners of the WFB and had arranged three courses during that year, but the majority of the time I spent at Loaf.

The longer I worked at Loaf the more people I met from Peruvia days. I knew most of the 'heads' in Manchester and so was frequently asked to head the door, but I wasn't interested. I didn't mind aggravation but I didn't want responsibility. I was trying to change. I was getting older and I needed a new life, but staying away from violence on the doors wasn't always possible and sometimes I would still be taken to the edge.

Assini left to manage his own club and JT came in as head doorman. I teamed up with a new doorman called Jamel. Jamel was Tunisian; 5ft 8ins, strong, stocky, shaven-head, well educated and with black belts in various martial arts, but was above all a really nice guy. We trusted each other and worked well together. He would call me if he needed backup on the front door and I would do the same inside. He would eventually go on to head the door after JT left.

Tereska, a tough little female doorwoman, also worked with me at Loaf. She had been at Loaf from the beginning and knew just about everyone. Tereska was a bodybuilder and looked awesome, especially just prior to competition. With 17-inch-plus arms, an incredible v-shape back, a tiny waist and arse, and huge silicone breasts, she had a look that was quite unique. On the face of it, she was a hard tough girl that stood no nonsense, but as I got to know her I found that within she was rather insecure and timid. I liked Tereska a lot and we became good friends. She signed up for a bodyguard training course which we were due to run in Iceland in October.

I had been to Iceland a couple of months earlier to set up a training camp and run the first course. The facilities were great. The camp was situated about an hour's drive from the capital, Reykjavik. Isolated and barren, the building was once used by Iceland's Mormon community. It comprised a big house with a basement and three upper floors with about 20 rooms per floor. In the basement was a large dining area and industrial kitchen, on the ground floor, classrooms, a smaller kitchen and two lounge areas. Next to the building was a sports hall and outdoor swimming pool. There was a huge area of private land surrounding the building and access to it was via a two-mile gravel road leading from the main road.

The landscape was barren volcanic rock, with no trees and very little vegetation. The wind blew relentlessly in off the sea. Even in August it was cold and occasionally the rain turned to sleet. In October the weather was even worse – the Icelandic winter was on its way.

The building was in good condition and very warm, but the bedrooms were small and the only furniture was a single bed and wardrobe. It was pouring down with rain when we arrived and I could see the look on Tereska's face as we drove down the bleak, isolated track and pulled up outside the house. She just wanted to turn around and go home.

'Don't worry,' I said to her jokingly, 'it gets worse.'

There were four other students all due to arrive the following morning. They were Icelandic and all apart from one spoke good English. There would be three instructors, me, Dan Sommer who was the new owner of the WFB, and Carlos, who protected the American Ambassador at the American Embassy in Reykjavik.

Carlos was one of the minority of Christians living in the Lebanon. He had served in the Red Berets – the Lebanese Special Forces unit – for five years and then worked as a bodyguard to Lebanon's Christian leader. However, Christians were continually being targeted and persecuted and, with pressure from his wife and daughter, he eventually left Lebanon. Originally Iceland was a stopping-off point to the US but Carlos ended up staying.

Carlos typically pushed his students to their limit. For the first few days I would often find Tereska sitting outside in the cold and wet with tears in her eyes, wishing she was anywhere other than Iceland. But as time passed she started to actually enjoy the course and by the end of the week she didn't want to go home. She passed.

We also had a contract to protect Miss Iceland during Iceland's movie premier of John Travolta's new film *Swordfish*. It was a long day for Tereska, especially as it was halfway through the course and she was at her most tired. The day started early in the morning and continued well into the night as Miss Iceland decided to go nightclubbing after the party. In reality Miss Iceland had a deranged stalker who bombarded her with sick and depraved mail and threatened to chop her into pieces if she didn't marry him, so there was a real and present threat and Tereska was essentially working on her first real assignment. She did well.

They say the Icelandic people like to party and that was certainly true of that particular night. I was both appalled and

amazed at Reykjavik's town centre at 3 a.m. It seemed everyone was drunk, fighting, screwing, vomiting, shouting and
swearing. Manchester paled into insignificance – I have never
experienced anything like it.

We both returned exhausted but had a great week and
Tereska had become a certified bodyguard.

There was a lot of bad attitude and arrogance on the door at
Loaf, and I hated it. I actually call this a syndrome, an illness.
When being stopped on a door or being evicted from a club,
those that say, 'Do you know who I am?' have definitely been
struck down with some awful affliction. These people are
simple, stupid, ignorant, dense and brainless.

Lets face it, those that really are someone in Manchester
would never have a need to tell anyone on any door that they
are who they are. Almost everyone knows who they are, and
even those new guys fresh to the doors quickly learn.

I have never known door bosses like Mickey Francis and
Steve Bryan, or any of the gang heads I knew, go up to a door
and say 'Do you know who I am?' Hard men never need to
prove they are hard. It is the small-timers that do. Whenever
this phrase is said to me I simply reply, 'Yes, I do know who
you are, you are a wanker, now fuck off.' Sadly many of these
morons really do believe they are somebody, that they are
dangerous, a 'shooter' as someone once said to me.

'I am a head shooter in Manchester,' he said when I
stopped him on the door at Loaf one night. 'I'll get a fucking
Uzi and shoot you.' He tapped me on my chest.

I replied, 'And I'll shove your fucking Uzi up your arse,
now piss off.'

I saw him standing at a bus stop in Moss Side a couple of
weeks later. The head shooter in Manchester catching a bus
to work!

Two big black guys came to the door at Loaf one evening.
They were not well dressed at all: sneakers, trainers, tracksuits

and baseball caps. There were two of them so I stepped forward and into the middle of the doorway. It is vitally important to assess situations quickly as things can very easily get out of control. It is imperative to be able to control the environment to our advantage. This is even more important should a doorman be on his own and critical when confronting multiple opponents. If I had kept to one side of the doorway one of them might have quite easily got round me. It is vital to keep all possible opponents to the front as, once one gets behind, controlling them becomes so much harder.

Whenever there are two or three attackers it is always good to plan moves in advance. It is not that hard to counter multiple attackers if you have a plan, as they invariably do not. Although they may seem to have an advantage because there are two or three of them, you actually have an advantage because you know what you are going to do and how you are going to do it. Most groups are not skilled individual fighters, as most skilled fighters don't fight in groups – why should they? It is only those that think they are hard but don't have any training or skills that need backup. I have never know any truly skilled fighter operate as part of a group. They deal with situations one on one.

I instantly noticed these two approaching the club. They looked out of place and were shabbily dressed.

'Sorry lads, not tonight,' I said. 'Revolution next door is a bit more casual with their dress code. You should be fine there.' I always try to give those I turn away an alternative venue – it shows them that I am a little sympathetic (though actually I don't give a fuck). It can sometimes make things a little easier. I was trying to be as diplomatic and as friendly as I could. It was early in the week and fairly quiet and my colleague had popped to the staff room for a plate of chips. We didn't normally bother with radios during the week – I was on the door on my own and didn't fancy getting into a big argument or a confrontation with these two.

'We don't wanna go next door, we are coming in 'ere,' the taller of the two said aggressively. I could immediately see he had an attitude, and he looked down at me with a sneer as though I was dirt on his shoe.

'Sorry, not tonight,' I replied, shaking my head. I could instantly see this becoming a problem and was hoping my colleague would return to the door before things developed any further. I could see that these two scrotes were not going to be bothered about me on my own, but they might think twice if there were two of us.

'I am not going to argue with you but you are too casually dressed. The manager has a strict dress code – even during the week. In isn't my fault lads but I'm afraid you can't come in, but you are more than welcome any other night when you are not so casual.'

The one with the attitude and doing all the talking was the taller of the two, but they were both taller and broader than I was. The one with the mouth had a shaven head, the other had shoulder-length dreadlocks. Typical big guys with attitude. As far as they were concerned they were coming in and I was just a little inconvenience.

'And you are going to stop us?' baldy said, tapping me on the chest.

I was working out my strategy. Should they decide to take it further – and it looked as though they were going to – I wanted to be ahead of them, to strike and shock and strike again before they got the upper hand. If I was to let them take the first strike then it might be too late for me, as they were both big guys and, from the look on their faces, had been in fights in the past. I was quickly assessing which to go for first and how to then attack the other.

I was still on my own – the other doorman was probably still sitting in the staff room with his feet up enjoying his coffee and plate of hot chips. Bastard, I jokingly thought. Yet I don't actually care how many opponents I have in front of me. I am really not at all bothered, not by the numbers or what they look like. As long as I have a plan of action.

'Listen,' he said tapping my chest with his hand, 'do you know who I am? You don't know who you are dealing with.' He tapped my chest again. 'We're meeting someone and you ain't going to stop us.' That was an old story we hear about a hundred times a night. He tapped my chest again which was really annoying me.

'Listen,' I said, 'I am on my own here and I really don't want any trouble.' I still decided to take the diplomatic approach. 'But I really don't give a fuck who you are, you are not coming in . . . and if you touch me again I shall break your fucking arm.' I raised both hands to my shoulder level in an open gesture. Whenever about to go into action I always raise my hands with my palms open and facing my opponent as though I am backing off, defending myself. My stance throws them into confusion – they think I am backing off and drop their guard a little, and then I strike hard and without warning.

He looked confused for a few seconds, and then he laughed and tapped my chest again. In an instant I grabbed his fingers and wrenched them apart, hearing the bones crack loudly and the middle of his two fingers tear. As he moved forward in pain I headbutted him hard, feeling his nose break against my forehead. Leaving him to fall to the ground I turned to face my other opponent, bringing my arms to head height as defence in case he was attempting a punch to my face. But he had backed away. I stepped back and assessed everything quickly. Mr Mouth was on the floor with two broken fingers and a broken nose, and his mate had backed off; he didn't want to have a go. I stepped into the club and closed the doors; I had done what was needed and I now had to leave it. I wanted to finish the other one off, and perhaps do a little more damage to the scrote on the ground, but it would have been unnecessary – after all, I was trying to be less aggressive.

He slowly got up and stared at me standing behind the

glass doors. His face was covered with blood from his broken nose, and he was grabbing his obviously broken fingers. They must have been so painful, and they were plainly pointing in totally the wrong directions.

His friend had now found some courage and started to shout, 'You are fucking dead, you are fucking dead.' I was still full of adrenalin, it was racing around my body and I was ready to have another go, to finish them off. I opened the doors and moved towards them shouting, 'Come on then, let's do it!' I was high but still in control. 'Come on then, let's finish it now, the both of you,' I yelled. I didn't really know why I was saying it. I walked towards them but they kept backing away shouting, 'You don't know who you are dealing with,' and, 'You're dead.'

By that time, my colleague had returned and was standing with the assistant manager behind me. The manager had seen what was happening on the CCTV, noticed that I was on my own and rushed from his office to the staff room. They had missed all the action. Needless to say I am still alive to tell the tale here and have not been shot or beaten up by these two or any one else that has issued threats against me over the past 20 years. But I keep thinking one day it might happen, one day some coked-up lunatic will shoot me simply because he had been turned away from a nightclub.

None of this would have happened had these guys not had such a bad attitude. They were rude, disrespectful and unreasonable and tried to show me they were hard, but it ended with one having a broken nose and two badly broken fingers and the other too scared to have a go.

My philosophy in working on the door is to respect everyone – from the smallest to the largest, the black and the white, the drunk and the sober. If it comes to the crunch I will fight most people. I will never allow myself to be crushed and defeated, to be overcome and beaten and I know I will do almost anything to prevent this from happening. However I am under no illusion that there are a great many people out there who are better and more able than I am. I don't know what these people look like and one of them might just be the next person I turn away from the door.

If you don't respect everyone you will meet your match one day, and in the person that you least expect it to happen with. One of our jobs in Croatia during the conflict was to pick up Western European mercenaries from Zagreb airport. We would then take them into the conflict zone for an initial assessment, some basic training and induction before handing them over to the Croats or Bosnians, who would send them onto the front line – to whichever unit was most needy. We almost always found that the mouthy ones, the ones that boasted of what they had done and where they had been, the ones that felt they had to tell everybody everything and continually bragged about what they were going to do to the Serbs, were the ones we would be taking back to the airport the following week broken men. Those that were full of shit would quite literally be full of their own shit the first time they were shot at on the front line. They were the ones that would shit themselves or puke at the sight of their first dead body or would break down and cry as their colleagues were blown to bits during their first mortar attack. But it was the quiet and thoughtful ones, the ones that were humble and modest, who sat quietly reading or doing the crossword, that would stay on the front line for months and months. They were the real soldiers, the real hard men and masters of their craft.

And that is exactly how I have found things on the door.

We had two radio calls at Loaf – one was 'green man', which meant that something might be going to happen and the other was 'red man', which meant that something was happening. A 'green man' might be a heated argument between a couple of people, someone too drunk needed escorting out or someone being rude to the bar staff. A 'green man' usually meant that other doormen in the vicinity would attend and act as a deterrent. A call of 'red man' meant it was actually kicking off big time and that everyone should immediately attend. Because no-one knew what was happening until they arrived on the scene, a 'red man' usually meant that every doorman in the building would race to the location, leaving just one on the door whose responsibility was to stop everybody coming into the unit until the disturbance was assessed and dealt with. When the radios worked (and they frequently didn't) the red and green man call system worked well.

One Saturday evening a 'red man' was called to the dance floor. I arrived at the same time as most of the other doormen. They streamed down the stairs and from the canal bar onto the dance floor. It was like a scene from the Keystone Cops, as they all skidded to a halt in a line when they saw who was involved.

Steve Bryan of Loc-19 had just punched an Asian lad in the face. Having to throw Steve out would have been too much for most of the doormen working at Loaf at that time – Steve is a hard man and an experienced fighter and very well known in Manchester. He hardly ever causes problems, preferring to stay away from the spotlight. He just gets on and does what he does, but piss him off and you have major problems.

While the other doormen were standing around, unsure of what to do, JT, the head doorman, asked Steve what happened. Steve said he had returned from the dance floor to see the guy with his hand in his girlfriend's handbag. I can imagine the lad had no idea whose bag it was and what the consequences were going to be. Steve respectfully apologized to the doormen for causing trouble and said he would leave directly. He put on his jacket and turned to walk out, but after two steps turned and smacked the guy, hard, once more for good measure. He then left without saying another word.

The Asian guy was unconscious, sprawled out on the floor.

His friends were unsure whether to pick him up or quickly leave the venue themselves. I hope he learned a lesson and stopped stealing from handbags. I would have given anything to see the terrified look on that poor guy's face as 19-stone Steve Bryan came bounding towards him.

The heads generally don't cause problems, but when they do they can be a real handful. In fact most of the time, when the heads in Manchester are kicking off or have stormed a door the police are called. It would be just too unreasonable to expect most doormen in Manchester to deal with them. Many heads are hard-men in their own right but most are not impossible to defeat. The problem is the retribution that would follow should they be defeated one-to-one. If a head was beaten one on one, and not follow it up shortly thereafter, he would quickly lose all credibility both within his own environment as well as with the other heads. They all have awesome responsibility and a great deal of stress maintaining their reputation and credibility. Once, rumour circulated that a head I knew had lost a one-to-one fight in central Manchester. A week later the person that had supposedly defeated him was found shot dead and floating face down in the canal.

Gang heads sometimes do kick off, of course. I was standing near the cigarette machine at the bottom of the stairs one Saturday night in Loaf. It was the area between the dance floor and the canal bar and a good spot to stand as both could be viewed easily, as well as keeping a good eye on the other doormen positioned in and patrolling each of these areas.

In a venue such as Loaf, it was always important to have regular sight of other doormen, especially as we tended to work alone rather than in pairs. Loaf was not a kids' venue, which meant violence would be harder to handle. Throwing a 30-year-old man out is much more difficult than throwing out an 18-year-old kid. And with the radios, the noise in Loaf made it sometimes virtually impossible to hear the doormen calling each other.

This particular Saturday evening, the Manchester hardcase called Tommy who I had met previously, and his mate Brian, were with a few others milling about near to where I was standing. The place was packed and their usual spot at the end of the canal bar was difficult to get to and very crowded so they stood near the toilets and cigarette machine.

Suddenly Tommy and his friend Brian started shouting at each other. Apparently Brian, high on cocaine, wanted to take a piss in the corner of the dance floor and Tommy stopped him. Brian took offence. Brian was rolling up his sleeves – he had massive tattooed forearms and huge clenched fists. He seemed intent on doing damage to Tommy and was ready to battle, while Tommy was trying to subdue him and back away. It seemed that Tommy wasn't really interested and was trying to calm Brian down, but Brian was having none of it.

The rest of their crew just looked on laughing. They weren't bothered – I think they were more interested in seeing who would win.

There was no way I could stop them fighting on my own – I needed backup. There were no other doormen in the vicinity so I called 'red man'. But I made the mistake of saying, 'red man, red man, Tommy and his crew are kicking off near the canal bar'. No-one came. I called again, foolishly saying the same thing and again no-one came – not one doorman came to my assistance. Normally when any 'red man' is called the entire team descends immediately but on this occasion I was on my own with some of the hardest men in Manchester. Everybody was frightened for their lives. I didn't know what to do. I just stood and waited. Why should I even try to stop them? There was no reason, I couldn't throw them out, and I couldn't fight them. I would just leave them to it and hope it would end quickly. Maybe it was a good thing that nobody responded to my call as having other doormen storming in might have made things a lot worse. I don't think any number of doormen would be much of a deterrent should those guys have decided to kick off.

Thankfully things calmed down. Brian stormed off upstairs and out of the venue and Tommy came over and apologized. The next weekend they were in drinking together as normal, best of buddies.

Loaf was a good venue and tightly run. The manageress was great with all her staff, not just the doormen but everyone that worked with her. She had respect for everyone and in return everyone respected her. She had loyal staff that worked hard and that would often do more than was required. Some managers seem to think they are gods as they walk around their venue with a high-and-mighty manner, dictating, ordering and treating their staff as mere servants. They don't see that they are one of thousands of nightclub managers, running just one bar in one city in one country. They are pretty insignificant in the grand scale of things, but many don't seem to understand this.

I have been fortunate enough to have met and talked to directors and managers of multinational companies, politicians and diplomats and genuinely influential and significant people. Many of these legitimately important people have far fewer feelings of self-importance than most nightclub managers. If managers treated staff well, staff would work hard and remain loyal. With happy staff comes happy customers, happy customers means more customer loyalty and more loyalty means better business and that is what every manager needs. The opposite is also true should a manager treat his staff badly. When revenue falls, managers blame the environment. Or the time of year. Or the day of the week. Or their uncle's sister's herpes – anything and anyone apart from themselves.

Jan was eventually offered an area manager's position with another leisure company and a new manager took over. He had a typical high-and-mighty attitude and almost immediately pissed everyone off. Things at Loaf started to change. It had been very busy most nights of the week. All the staff worked hard and had been very loyal to Jan. However things quickly started to deteriorate.

The new manager seemed to hate most of the doormen. He was abrupt and decided to change all the operational procedures that had been used since the venue opened – procedures that worked well. We were not a bad bunch of doormen – we were polite, responsible and generally professional. We were not thugs and we ran a high-profile venue in the centre of Manchester with little trouble. But he wanted to impose his ideas. Soon the close-knit team began to fall apart. Many doormen asked to be transferred to other venues; in fact most of the staff that had been with Jan since Loaf's opening quickly left.

Instead of sitting with us all and discussing his ideas, the manager demanded that we immediately change. He told us what to do instead of asking advice and wanted to change everything, probably to justify his new role. He started to make things difficult for a few of the doormen. Doormen can be an unpredictable, fickle and strange bunch of characters. However, most are extremely loyal to their manager and quickly carry out any instructions concerning the security and safety of the venue. However, no-one cared to do anything for this guy. Instead of getting involved in the unit, of feeling part of it, most doormen now just came to work, did their job, and went home. He eventually got rid of most of the doormen that had been there since the beginning. They were all good workers and knew all the faces, heads and regular customers.

We were frequently shorted-staffed – there was always plenty of work in Manchester so why work for this guy? And of course, because the staff were not happy the standard of service dropped and slowly customers began drinking elsewhere. Business slowed.

The weekends remained busy, but the other nights were

noticeably quieter. Thursdays, which used to be almost full, slowed from its peak of 700 people to around 100. Fridays were not as busy as they used to be either, although they remained fairly consistent but at a level a lot lower than before. Saturday was always a good night, but almost every venue in Manchester is full on a Saturday.

One Wednesday evening, during the Commonwealth Games, we were instructed to stop customers coming in at 10 p.m. Not because it was busy but simply because there were no staff. This was during one of the busiest times of the year, with many foreign visitors. One of the best-known venues had to close because no staff turned up for work. I am sure head office never found out, as the manager was back to work the next day.

Having been there for about a year it was also time for me to leave. I decided to move on to another venue but I still worked the occasional weekday evening, when it was fairly quiet and the manager left us alone.

CHAPTER FOURTEEN

The Cheshire Set

'We have a nice little venue for you to work, and not far from where you live,' Tony Hill told me on the phone as soon as I returned to the UK.

After leaving Loaf, I went to Moscow. Initially I went for another week's contract with my banker, but ended up staying for almost two months. Coincidentally my client called at roughly the same time as I left Loaf and so I immediately agreed to the job. I love Moscow. It is vibrant, interesting, challenging, crime-ridden, corrupt, crazy, sleazy and sad but the women are the most beautiful in the world. I had wanted to live there but my priorities changed when my daughter came along and so sadly I never got to fulfil my dream – just short trips on contract with a few days extra for relaxation. But this time instead of returning home after the operation I had met a gorgeous Russian woman and stayed a few weeks with her. However the money ran out and I had to return.

As soon as I got home I telephoned National Security, telling them I was back and available. As usual I had no money and needed to work and it would have to be back on the doors.

'We want you to work The Rectory,' Tony added.

I lived in Wilmslow so I knew The Rectory. The same door team had been there for quite a number of years – they even used to come into Peruvia on their nights off or once The Rectory had closed. I had been drinking there a few times, so

I knew it was quite a nice venue for the older crowd and without too many problems. As I was getting older I felt more comfortable drinking at venues such as The Rectory rather than places in Manchester city centre. And I was dreading going back to Loaf, especially with the manager being as he was.

'Ok, what is the deal?' I asked Tony.

Tony had just taken over the door and he said they needed a strong team, but why such a team at a venue like The Rectory? Almost anyone could work there – it just didn't seem like a challenging door. There were rarely problems inside the club, only on the door itself. Wilmslow, although a well-to-do area of Cheshire and an affluent suburb of Greater Manchester, was only 15 minutes' drive from Moss Side, and even less from Wythenshawe, two notorious trouble spots. This meant that Wilmslow attracted more than its fair share of opportunist crime: robbery, theft, burglary, as well as attracting quite a number of scrotes from the town centre at the weekend. It was a strange mixture of the Cheshire yuppies mixing with the city scrotes, which occasionally caused problems. But The Rectory, although directly in the centre of the town and fairly high profile, had a reputation for being an older person's venue with a strict dress code and entry regulations.

'It used to be someone else's door,' Tony replied, 'and they are a bit pissed off that we have it.'

Doors are gained and lost all the time – no-one likes it. A door lost to a rival company in Manchester can sometimes cause problems but the doormen themselves rarely have anything to do with getting the contract. Just because they happen to be sent to work on a door that another company previously had, there is no reason why they should get a beating just for going to work. It is unfair. But losing a contract to another company can become personal. It is not simply a loss of revenue but an infringement on territory and a battering of egos.

It wasn't the fact that the previous door team at The Rectory were doing a bad job. They had all been there a long time and were generally good lads who did their job well. But the problem was political, partly down to the fact that the area manager wanted Tony Hill's National Security Network to be their preferred security supplier to all of their venues around the UK. So the previous door firm, whose boss I knew, were told they no longer had the door at The Rectory – and they were pissed off.

'So you want me to work there because you know that I know them and you don't think they will cause us trouble while I am there?' I asked.

'Well, in a nutshell that's about right. We know you are connected and it might benefit the venue if you worked there, plus it is a nice place and near to your house,' Tony replied.

I knew that me being there wouldn't have made the slightest difference to the other firm. However, I was sure that they wouldn't just turn up and give us all a battering. If they were planning to cause us problems I was sure their boss would call first. I didn't need the money that badly to start going against him and his team and I certainly wasn't interested in any door war. I was too old for all that; I didn't want to be fighting or wearing my bulletproof vest and being constantly on my guard. Not for a measly £50 a night. I just wanted a quiet life, to do my job and to go home safely at the end of the night.

The Rectory was a nice venue and I wanted to work it. I lived just ten minutes away and it closed at 1 a.m. – which meant no more late nights. They didn't have a dance floor, the music was more mainstream and it attracted a decent client base. I had had my time in high-risk venues.

I felt sure I could diplomatically overcome any problems with the previous security firm and, after thinking about it for a week, decided to take the door. However, out of respect I called the boss in his office and asked what he thought about the situation and about me working there. He was certainly extremely pissed off that Tony Hill had taken the door. At first he strongly recommended that I didn't work there, so I missed that first weekend. But he called me the following week and had calmed down a bit. He had hoped to take back the door should Tony not provide a good service and he realized that by causing trouble he would never have a chance of taking back the door. Plus he had most of the other doors in Wilmslow and causing trouble at The Rectory might have brought him unwanted attention from the police and the licensing department at Macclesfield council.

So he told me that no, he didn't mind me working there and promised that it would not be him nor any of his team that would ever cause us problems. And, true to their word, none of the previous team ever caused any problems.

However we did have big problems with Anthony K. He was a hard-man; a hood and a thug who had made some money and had recently moved to Wilmslow. I suppose, in some twisted way, he thought he could fit in with the Cheshire set. He had decided that The Rectory was going to be his place, where he could do what he wanted, act as he pleased and cause whatever trouble he desired and that no-one would dare to lift a finger against him.

I met him the first Thursday night I worked. It wasn't busy and I was on my own, standing just inside the front door as it was getting cold and I didn't have a decent outside jacket.

Anthony walked in with his brother and a couple of pretty girls. At around 17 stone Anthony K is a big guy – a bodybuilder, not tall but broad, the usual shaved head and quite menacing to look at. He obviously took steroids, which would have made him quite strong as well. According to rumour, he was also once a semi-professional boxer. He looked the part, with scars on his head and a face that had seen some battles.

He came into The Rectory at around 11 p.m. He stopped briefly on the door, said hello, shook my hand and said he recognized me from the gym I trained at in Altrincham, but I didn't recognize him. I knew he would be a problem that first night as he was immediately sarcastic and rude. He had attitude, and lots of it. I could see he was marking his territory, fronting me and showing me that he was not to be messed with, that he was the law. It was the same old story, narrow-minded ignorant scrotes trying to prove themselves. I would have had so much more respect for the guy if he were polite and civil, if he took a little time out to have a chat, to perhaps offer a drink. But no, he decided to walk in to The Rectory with his high and mighty attitude and now that the previous firm was no longer running the door Anthony believed The Rectory was going to be his.

Holding up his girlfriend's coat, he whistled to me from the bar and beckoned for me to come over and take it. Of course I ignored him, thinking what would be the best way to deal with him. Why some people have this pathetic attitude I will never understand.

After that first encounter, I knew AK was going to be a problem. As Tony said, we definitely did need a good strong team on the door – anyone weak AK would quite simply walk over. Once he was allowed to do what he wanted inside the venue it wouldn't be long before he would be taxing the bar – drinking without paying – and running drugs. This is typically how many gangsters get their slimy fingers into venues. I could see that he was determined to cause us problems and was certain I would be battling with him in the near future. And what a battle that would be – I was under no illusion that he would be a hard man to fight and I would have to pool all my resources and destroy him as quickly as I could. I had hoped that The Rectory was going to be a quiet, calm place, but it was looking like it was to be just the opposite. So much for my retirement plans.

On the following night I learnt I was to be working with a guy named Dave Power. Dave used to work with me at Loaf, but unfortunately he and I fell out in a big way when I got him the sack. Since then we had hated each other. However we respected each other enough not take our hatred out in a violent way, although I am sure we both were wondering whether we might one day resort to some sort of physical confrontation.

You can imagine both our faces as we turned up to work at The Rectory on Friday night. We realized we would either have to sort out our differences there and then or one of us would swiftly move on. The office wisely didn't tell me I was working with Dave, and didn't tell Dave he was working with me.

He had got to work first. He was standing at the bar chatting to the staff when I walked in. My heart sank and I immediately thought, oh no. He must have thought the same as he turned round and saw me enter the front doors dressed in my working blacks.

'Dave,' I said thinking, now what? I stood at the bar next to him and ordered a coffee.

'Robin,' he replied. 'Shall we talk?'

I nodded, left my coffee on the bar and walked outside with Dave to settle things. I was ready for a battle. It would have looked awful – two of the venue's doormen fighting outside – but our dislike for each other was intense. One part of me was preparing to fight while the other part of me couldn't believe we would actually end up fighting – we should just try to get this weekend over and either Dave or I would call the office first thing Monday morning requesting another venue to work for the following week.

'I think it was wrong of you to grass me up to the manageress,' he said to me angrily as soon as we got outside.

Dave had been verbally quite abusive to a female friend of mine on the door of Loaf. She came up to me crying and distressed and told me what Dave had said. The manageress of Loaf was standing nearby, noticed this girl crying and came over to ask what was going on. I told her what had happened and Dave got the sack. I suppose in hindsight I should have sorted it out myself and I expect I would have done had the manageress not been nearby and heard what had gone on. But he got the sack and I hadn't seen him since, not to talk to anyway, although I would catch sight of him when he would occasionally pop into Loaf to collect wages and he would give me a threatening scowl.

'Well you shouldn't have been rude to my friend,' I replied casually. I wasn't angry, just prepared to resolve our differences mentally first, with words, but physically if necessary.

After about 15 minutes of mild argument we did eventually sort out our differences in a mature and sensible way. We let bygones be bygones. I told him exactly what I thought. He told me what he thought. We agreed to disagree.

As time passed we actually became good friends and worked on the door extremely well together. We ended up being a good, strong team, working the door efficiently. He even kindly offered me a bed at his home while I was going through yet more problems with Thelma. And, if it wasn't for Dave's intervention and diplomacy we would have had a severe battering a few weeks later when AK and his team eventually arrived in force.

The Rectory was in the centre of Wilmslow and generally attracted an independently well-off 25 to 35 age group, as well as a fair amount of youngsters arriving in daddy's Porsche or BMW, a handful of students and a mixture of customers from other backgrounds. The customers were predominantly white, the dress code was fairly smart but casual – jeans were ok as long as they were smart but trainers were rarely accepted. We ran a relaxed door.

The Rectory also attracted a high number of well-dressed, obviously wealthy, and very beautiful women. It was hard to know where to look sometimes. There wasn't as much pretentiousness in The Rectory as there was at Loaf and after a while I had got to know almost all the good-looking girls.

The standard of dress was no real reason to stop Anthony K coming in. He had money, drove a BMW M5 and was normally well dressed. But I didn't like his attitude and didn't want him in. I intended to make this clear to him on his next visit. I planned to tell him that he was welcome if he dispensed with the bad attitude and respected the staff, otherwise we would have no choice but to bar him. However, barring him would be a problem, and I was sure we would end up fighting. I had been in the business too long to expect anything else from these sorts of scumbags. They like to menace and threaten and rule their territory with fear. I knew it would soon become personal between AK and me, which I didn't really want.

He looked menacing. He had a reputation. I didn't really want to fight him. I knew that if it looked as though I was losing, I would have to resort to some of the nastier tactics I had learnt in some of the worst environments around the world, and I didn't really want to go down that road again. I was struggling with myself. What frightened me most was not brawling but going too far. I was still frightened that I would actually kill someone. For eight years since Bosnia I lived with the fear constantly inside me – the fear that some day I would snap, lose all self-control and end up for the rest of my life looking through the bars of a jail.

It is not hard to kill someone. I saw it time and again in Bosnia – one quick shot with a pistol to the temple or into the heart, one quick twist of the neck, one hard punch into the top of the spinal column at the base of the neck. Killing is easy and the fear of killing haunts me, that one day I won't stop until it is too late and I have taken an innocent life. Although AK certainly wasn't innocent and I am sure no-one would actually give a flying fuck if he were killed.

It was a Saturday night. We hadn't seen AK's mob for a couple of weeks. It was about 11 p.m., the place was full and we already had a long queue and were working on a 'one in, one out' policy.

There is a long drive leading up to the entrance of The Rectory and, standing on the front step of the front doors, it was possible to look down the drive and see everyone walking towards the club. Although in the winter when it was dark it was hard to make out faces, it still gave us a little time to assess those approaching before they got too close. Even in winter we could generally see if they were decent or not. You can tell a scumbag a mile away, they have a walk and a posture that is quite distinctive. And of course by the way they dress. I think there is a definitely scrote style, like a sort of 'club for scrotes' where you can easily identify other like-minded scrotes from the way they are dressed.

Standing on the front door that evening I could see Anthony K walking down the driveway with his brother Buba and another even bigger bodybuilder with about ten other scumbag kids, all no more than 18 or 19 years old, and all looking scruffy in t-shirts, hooded tops, trainers and tracksuit bottoms. This wasn't looking too good – there were 13 of them, far more than David and I could handle on our own.

Dave was standing behind me, and we both knew we were going to have a big problem. Anthony and his scrotey-looking crew walked past the queue and straight up to the front of the door. They didn't even pause to stop and acknowledge me; they just started to barge straight past. There were just too many of them but I tried to block their path, and Dave stood directly behind me.

'Are you all together?' I asked Anthony fairly casually. I was nervous, and there was just Dave and me on the front door with one other doorman inside – but he wasn't to be seen. No matter how good we were, we were totally outnumbered.

'Yeah, they are alright, they are with me,' he replied and started to usher them all in.

'Sorry,' I said abruptly, holding out my arm, 'you three are fine of course, but your friends are all too casual and a bit too young, sorry, they can't come in.' Now was the crunch – we were going to see his attitude, his true colours. I was waiting.

'No, you don't understand,' he said aggressively. He was looking at me straight in the eyes and his face was close to my face, he wanted to have a go, just waiting for the first excuse. There were still many normal customers waiting in the queue, all watching what was happening.

'I said they are all ok, they are with me.' Then he motioned them – 'In you go lads.'

It was getting tense. They had surrounded me, all ready to prove themselves to Anthony K, and he was ready to show them that he was a head, this was his place and he could do what he wanted.

'Sorry,' I said loudly, 'they are not coming in.' I was standing my ground. It was suicidal but I was prepared to take it as far as I could.

'Don't fucking disrespect me,' he shouted close to my face. 'I run this fucking place, what I say goes – do you hear?' I could see his fist clench – he was raging and ready to strike. The others closed in around me and I could see that many others also had clenched fists. They were storming the door and there was little I could do. I was worried – it would have been a massacre. Even if we fought like troopers there were just too many of them.

Dave was standing directly behind me. I wasn't watching him but he was unusually quiet, which is a rare thing for Dave. Dave has never been shy with words and certainly seldom thinks before opening his mouth. But on this night he was as quiet as a mouse. While I stood my ground and blocked the entrance he quickly beckoned Anthony to one side. Anthony glared at me and wandered over to Dave.

The queue was ignored for a while – there was just too much commotion on the door to worry about the decent customers. They would have to wait and could be witnesses if everything went pear-shaped and it kicked off.

Dave took AK to one side while these knobheads and scumbags surrounded me. They were all watching me, moving their heads nervously from side to side, waiting for the nod from AK. I would have been more than happy to fight them all one on one, even two or three at a time, but there were far too many, and they knew it. They wanted to show their boss what they could do; they were eager to prove themselves. Individually they were nothing, but as a group they were killers.

I was scared. I didn't think I would be going home to my daughter that evening, I didn't think I would be seeing her again. Once they got going there would be no stopping them. I would battle for as long as I could but it wouldn't take long for them all to overpower me, to have me on the ground and that would have been that, there would have been little I could do. I really wasn't bothered about myself, I just thought of my lovely little daughter and didn't want her to wake up on Sunday morning without her daddy.

I wasn't listening to what Dave was saying, I was too preoccupied with the crowd around me and there was too much commotion to concentrate, but he looked at me, nodded and waved AK and all his scruffy arsehole scumbags through the door.

I was really annoyed but I completely understood that there was simply nothing we could have done. When you are so outnumbered it is wise to back down and work out a secondary plan. Mark came to the door just as all the scumbags had gone in. We discussed calling the police but we had 500 other well-dressed, decent customers and getting the police to remove just 12 scumbags might have been a bit of a problem. Nevertheless, we had decided that we would call the police if any of them turned violent towards either us or our customers. It would have been the only way to get rid of them without a massive fight, and we didn't want that in the middle of The

Rectory. Like all scumbags a couple of them got out of hand. One ended up vomiting over the bar and into the ice tray and another proudly showed his arse to a group of respectable-looking females.

I was seething all evening and vowed to take revenge. I wanted to batter them all senseless. I wanted to cut off their ears. They had no place in this venue, no right to be here and no right to walk past us on the door. They took the piss and it annoyed the fuck out of me. I was proud and I was thinking, illogically, that I would have preferred a battle than to have these scrotes in my club.

Like Tinker in London a few years previously, that evening I decided I was going to kill Anthony K and this time I would definitely go through with it. He wasn't an innocent, a one-night drunk going just a little too far, but a criminal that had respect for no-one and nothing. He deserved to die. I could think of a dozen ways in which I could kill him without any comeback on myself. I was sure there were many people that also wanted him dead. He deserved all that was coming to him.

Throughout the evening my mind was preoccupied. I should let him think that he had one over me and then later fuck him in style and with pain. On his way out at the end of the night he passed me and said, 'Everything's cool,' and shook my hand.

'Sorry about that,' I replied solemnly while thinking, you are going to die you fucking scumbag bastard. I was still a bit nervous and the adrenalin was still rushing around my body. For a brief few seconds I considered taking him out there and then, shoving my fingers deep into his eyes, biting off his nose and ears and ripping his bollocks off. But he had many of his scrotes with him and there were too many other witnesses. But I had decided that the very next time I saw him I would take his eyes out and feed them to him.

Although I was quite exhausted due to the tension of the

evening, I didn't sleep much that night. I was angry, pissed off and had every intention of getting my own back. I lay in bed planning what I was going to do. I knew where he lived and what car he drove – it wasn't going to be difficult.

The next day both Dave Power and I made calls to every gang head we knew in Manchester and asked them if they knew Anthony K. I explained the trouble he had caused and what he had said to us. Most heads had heard of him, and all that knew him said they would have words. Every single head that Dave and I knew supported us and everyone said that we weren't to worry, that I shouldn't do anything rash and to leave it to them. They would help sort things out for us. And even those that didn't know AK put the word out on the streets that he had caused problems at The Rectory and it wasn't to be tolerated.

Mark, the manager, also phoned the Serious Crime Squad. They assured him that they would provide full police support. They also didn't want his intimidation in their sleepy, affluent Wilmslow.

The following weekend we were expecting them to turn up and I wanted to be the one that was going to tell AK he was not coming in. This time I wasn't going to back down, no matter how many of them, no matter how violent it got. We also had a police armed response unit sitting in the car park standing by. If AK had farted in the wrong direction he would have been nicked.

I thought about tooling up, bringing with me a cosh, baton, some knuckledusters, but decided that because there was also going to be a strong police presence it might not be a good idea to been seen battling AK's crew with a variety of weapons. I didn't want to be nicked as well.

Dave and I arrived at work nervous. Tony Hill also came to help out. Everyone that goes into battle is nervous – those that have told me that they don't have any fear are either idiots or full of shit. Everyone should be scared. It is good to be scared, it makes you fight harder and be stronger. We were all scared but we were prepared.

But he didn't turn up. Not that week, nor the week after. I never knew what was said or by whom, as both Dave and myself spoke to so many people. But I am thankful to those who said they would 'sort it out'. They obviously did as neither he nor his brother, nor any of the scrotes came back, not for about 12 months.

I was chatting to one of the doormen at another club in Wilmslow. He worked on the door at Waverley's, which was open until 2 a.m., an hour later than The Rectory. I normally stop for a quick chat to the guys on the door, as I have to pass Waverley's on my way home. They told me that they had also been having problems with AK's crew. They had been at their venue the weekend before causing trouble – biting and headbutting customers and being abusive to women. As long as they don't come back to The Rectory, I thought, and cause me any more problems, but of course they did, much later.

Maybe I should have taken Anthony K out permanently. I had vowed to do it but again I didn't go through with it. Am I being soft or sensible? Should I have killed both Tinker in London and Anthony K in Wilmslow or was it best to leave them to their own fate?

I suppose I saw The Rectory as my retirement venue. I had certainly done my fair share of brawling and more than my fair share of shagging, but I was then 40 and wanted to settle down a bit. For a long time I had wanted to move off the doors and on to a more settled and less violent lifestyle. The shagging bit was still ok, I didn't mind that but I didn't want to brawl and fight any more. I knew that the only way to change my life, to move away from my constant violent thoughts and feelings was to leave the doors once and for all, to look for an alternative job and an alternative life, before it was too late.

Most people see doormen as dim-witted thugs. Sure some are, but many have other jobs and do the doors part-time to earn extra money. I have met and got to know so many good doormen and most of them have been bright, intelligent and civilized people. Take away the façade and most are quite decent people.

On the doors, I have also noticed that money generally affects people in two ways. Those that have worked really hard and have moved themselves from poverty and hardship to wealth and comfort are those people that are the most approachable, the most down to earth, the kindest, most respectful and friendly. They are almost always the ones that greet you on the door and thank you for opening it for them. They sometimes stop and have a quick chat, offer to buy you a drink and drink up quickly at the end of the evening. They are generally the nicest.

Those that have been given money or have inherited it are the worst. They don't appreciate money or people and have little respect for either. They would walk into The Rectory like snobs with a baton stuck up their arses. They are the ones that expect you to open the door. They are the ones hanging around at the end of the night and the ones that just ignore you when you ask them to drink up. They are the ones that are rude and obnoxious. However when you are obnoxious back to them they are the first to complain to the manager or call the police. We had both as customers at The Rectory as well as many beautiful women.

It was fairly early one Friday evening, the club wasn't busy and the car park was quiet. I was standing on the step and leaning on the wall of the entrance. I was facing the car park when a black Porsche drove through the front gates, down the driveway and parked just opposite the front entrance. Both doors swung open and two beautiful, long, tanned legs swung simultaneously out from each side and out climbed two gorgeous girls, both mid-twenties, both extremely slim with long blonde hair and both extremely pretty.

'Hi,' the driver waved and called as she closed the door.

'Good evening ladies,' I replied in my normal slick way. 'How are you this evening?' They were regulars – I had seen them a few times before and knew them slightly.

'Fine, you?' she asked as she approached the front door.

'Fine. You look lovely this evening,' I said as they walked past.

'Thank you,' she looked at me and smiled. I turned to follow them as they went into the venue. As I turned I put out my right arm to lean back on the wall, but the wall wasn't there. Some fucker had clearly moved it and I stumbled sideways and fell flat on my face. Red with embarrassment I picked myself up, brushed down my trousers and discreetly looked around. Thankfully there was no-one in the car park.

Christmas and New Year can be a lonely time for some doormen. Firstly it is virtually impossible to get time off because it is by far the busiest time of the year. This means that we have to work and can't be with our family and friends or attend Christmas and New Year celebrations and parties. Secondly everyone, without exception, has too much to drink and we have to deal with it.

On New Year's Eve, when the chimes of Big Ben sound and everyone shouts 'Happy New Year', doormen stand alone outside waiting for some drunkard reveller to go too far, or stop some lonely drunk arsehole from coming in. We stand alone and alert. We can't really celebrate, as we know that the next 30 or so minutes is the most critical time of the night. Old grievances emerge and new ones are born. Rarely are there problems before the stroke of midnight – everyone is preoccupied with partying and celebrating and having a good time – but after midnight everything changes.

Of course, many people have to work over Christmas and

New Year. But doormen are almost always alone and vigilant – we remain prepared.

I cannot ever remember having a Christmas and New Year away from the doors. I have been on the doors for nearly 20 years and I think every one of those Christmases I have spent working. The Rectory, Loaf, Standish, Peruvia, every year I have stood alone at midnight on New Year's Eve and wondered whether I would be doing the same the following year. And every year I hoped I wouldn't.

It was New Year's Eve and Dave threw someone out. I don't know what for, I didn't ask, Dave just told me that he was not to be allowed back in.

'No problem,' I said. I was on my own on the door. I didn't mind. It was cold but my bottle of champagne was keeping me company. I was drinking it from the bottle and steadily getting drunk.

But this person was not going to leave quietly. It was just past midnight, everyone was partying inside, the noise was deafening and he was standing alone on the front door. There were no taxis and there was nowhere for him to go. He started arguing.

'Come on, let me back in, my mates are there, come on,' he pleaded.

'Listen buddy,' I said, 'I don't know what happened and I don't know what you did to get thrown out but I just know you have been thrown out and so you can't come back in, ok?'

'But I didn't do anything,' came his reply. Everyone who gets thrown out says the same thing. They actually think that you might listen to them and believe what they are saying. I am sure some people really expect you to then say, 'Oh really, there must have been some mistake. In you go then!'

I was being fairly laid back – after all it was New Year's Eve – and was enjoying my champagne on the window sill round the corner. The last thing I wanted was to get into any trouble.

'I don't know what happened because I wasn't there,'

I replied diplomatically, 'so I can't comment, but you must have done something. The doorman wouldn't have just come up to you for no reason and thrown you out, would he? You have done something, you have been asked to leave and you can't come back in. I am not going to argue with you any more so you will have to go and finish your evening somewhere else, ok?'

I thought I was being quite tactful, respectful and polite. It would certainly not be a good start to 2002 if I were fighting at just past the stroke of midnight.

His voice suddenly changed. 'Go and get the manager,' he demanded.

'What?' I asked, again keeping my cool. 'He is busy, now for the last time you are not coming back in so go away.'

'Go and get the manager,' he shouted, 'now!'

'Now you are making me pissed off, and that is not a good idea, believe me, not tonight, now fuck off.'

'You are just a fucking stupid doorman, I have been thrown out for no fucking reason and I want to see the manager, now go and get him, NOW.'

I hate being called stupid. Doorman I am, fucking I do sometimes when I get lucky, but stupid I am not.

'Last time, move away or I will put you on your back.'

'Fuck o—.' He didn't have chance to finish the 'off'. I had slammed him hard in the neck with a flat hand and put him straight on his back.

'Next time it will be worse,' I threatened. But he got up, fists clenched and, as he drew his arm back slightly I stepped forward and did exactly the same thing with a flat hand into his neck, putting him down on his back again.

'I am telling you, don't make it worse for yourself. Go home. Next time I will rip your head off.'

I was angry but perhaps also a little drunk as I was halfway through my bottle and wanted to get back to it quickly. I would never usually drink on the door, but New Year's Eve was an exception and I was hoping to wake up the following morning with another pig next to me, as I had a few years before in Norwich.

Dave had come back out just in time to see the guy land on his back. He walked over to him and said, 'If I were you mate, save face, don't damage your pride any more, and move on before this guy,' pointing to me, 'really does you damage.' He got up, his designer clothes muddy, wet and torn slightly, turned around and walked off, without so much as another word. Dave nodded to me and walked back inside. I saw him at the top of the stairs chatting to a gorgeous woman but I ended the night quite drunk and alone.

After a few months working together and developing a good relationship, Dave Powers left The Rectory. He is not the most tactful of people and, although very funny at times, he does tend to upset a great many people and eventually get kicked off or moved from most of the doors he works. The Rectory wasn't his kind of venue as he couldn't abuse and upset customers as easily as he could at other larger and more anonymous units. Those he did offend at The Rectory were generally professionals and so he got himself into all sorts of arguments and trouble. He eventually moved back into Manchester, to a large, 1,000 capacity unit targeting the 18 to 20-year-olds where he could be rude to as many customers as much as he liked with little comeback.

Andy took Dave's place and I worked with him for almost nine months. One good thing about working with Dave was that Dave wasn't the handsomest of men and standing next to him made even me look attractive – I am getting older and am no longer an oil painting. But Andy is one good-looking bastard, and every single night he worked he had women chatting him up.

Short dark hair, slim build, 5ft 8ins, fit and strong, he was also quite handy as he taught kickboxing a few nights a week. Even though he spent most evenings with women draping themselves over him, he was reliable and always there when needed. We certainly had some laughs.

One evening we stopped a thirty-something as he approached the door. He looked a little unsteady but nothing major. Depending upon his attitude and just how drunk he really was, I would have let him in as he wore an expensive suit and tie and looked quite respectable.

As he approached I stopped him and jokingly asked, 'Hi buddy, where have you been tonight?'

If there is any doubt about anyone approaching the door it is always good to stop them for just a few seconds and ask something trivial. 'Where have you been tonight?' 'Are you all together?' 'Are you meeting anyone inside?' 'Are there any more in your group?' As long as it is a question that needs to be answered. I almost always do this, especially with groups of guys that I don't know or am cautious of. In these first few seconds I can assess their manner and if they give me any bad attitude they don't get in. Any question can be asked or anything can be said, but you need to elicit an answer to see what they say and the way it is said and then make a quick judgement. And then, depending upon your initial judgement, make the decision whether to let them in or turn them away.

I just wanted to assess whether this guy was a little too drunk. So I stopped him and asked this simple question. Not a hard thing to answer, or so I thought.

'Do you know who I am?' was his immediate reply.

Now I knew most of the heads, and I knew he wasn't one of them. He didn't even look like a gangster. In fact he looked a bit like a lawyer or an accountant.

'I didn't ask you who you were, I just asked where you have been. Was that a difficult question to answer?'

I knew there and then that he wasn't going to get in but I fancied a little sport, I fancied winding him up a little.

'Do you know who you are talking to?' he said again, louder, closer to my face and more aggressively. I didn't believe it. So I replied with my standard phrase:

'Yeah, I am talking to a wanker, now piss off!' Andy smiled, as he usually does when he hears that response.

'I'm from Trafford Park,' he said, and if that wasn't enough to send us into fits of laughter he followed that ridiculous comment by saying, 'I am well connected, I will have you shot.'

I looked at Andy and we burst out laughing. I couldn't believe that someone I had stopped for looking a little drunk was now coming out with all this crap.

'Trafford Park?' I said trying not to cry with laughter. I knew heads in Cheetham Hill, Moss Side, Salford, Longsight and many other suburbs of Manchester but I had never had anyone threatening me with Trafford Park. I thought Trafford Park was an industrial estate.

'You have got no idea,' I said to him, 'now piss off home, there is no way you will be getting in here tonight, Trafford Park or not.' Andy and I must have looked bizarre as we really were trying to be serious with him and not to laugh too much, but this idiot was not making things easy for us, we just couldn't stop laughing and this made him even angrier. He started walking up the steps at the entrance as if going into the venue. I put my hand on his chest to stop him.

'I'll tell you one last time,' I was now deadly serious, 'you are not coming in tonight now go home, move away from the door.'

He looked down at my hand on his chest and looked up again and said, 'Get your hand off me you cunt,' and started to walk past.

It was no longer funny, and like with any incident I could feel the adrenalin start to rush. Had I finally met my match in this unexpected knob? Was he someone, as he certainly had the bottle to just walk past the two of us? Was he my match in the most unlikely of guises? I shoved him hard on his chest and he fell back down the step and backwards into a puddle on the floor.

No, he wasn't.

'I have been patient, now go home,' I said as he was getting up.

'I am going to have you shot!' he screamed at me, 'I know everyone. They are coming down to shoot you.' He started up the stairs again and again I shoved him hard on the chest, and he fell back onto the same spot and into the same dirty puddle.

Sitting in the puddle with his arse soaking wet he got out his mobile phone and punched in some numbers. He wasn't so drunk that he didn't know exactly what he was saying and doing. 'I am at The Rectory in Wilmslow, yes, I want all your firepower down here fast, yeah, everything you got. Bring it all, everything. Yeah, 30 minutes, great.'

I looked at Andy and we both burst into laughter yet again. He was saying all this while sitting in a muddy puddle. He got up, water dripping from his arse, with his phone in his ear, but we could not hear what he was saying. For the rest of the night he stood alone in the car park, waiting. We closed, kicked everyone out, locked the front doors, had a quick drink and finally left and he was still waiting outside. As I was leaving I asked him if his Trafford Park shooters had arrived yet and laughed to myself as I walked off. He just stood there staring at me. Maybe he was waiting for me to leave, maybe he had found a little courage to take me on one to one outside. But he said nothing as I walked on my own down the drive and away from yet another interesting evening.

Andy and I frequently gave pet names to people we banned. There was 'Sadsack', a dick-head in every sense of the word. Short, fat and ugly. He was with a group of decent friends but we had to stop him coming in because he was too pissed to walk in a straight line. He could easily have come back at another time when he was sober had he not decided to let loose a torrent of abuse. He was calling us every single thing going, and more. Even I had not heard of some of the things he said. Mark, the manager, just happened to come on the door, and Sadsack even started on him. It is one thing being abusive to the doormen, but another to be abusive to the manager. So of course he was barred for good. To our astonishment, he tried to get back in almost every weekend thereafter and was still abusive whenever he was stopped. We called him Sadsack as he really was a sad sack of shit.

There was also 'Frenchie', so-called for an incident when he was stopped for being too scruffy. Being a pretentious smart-arse snob, he decided to call me all sorts of things, but in French, thinking I was a thick doorman and wouldn't understand. However, having lived in France for a while I eventually spoke French quite well and understood most things. When I replied to him in French he had a look of utter fear on his face, impossible to describe. He knew he had fucked up, big time. I slapped him hard over the head as he was turning to run. He ran as fast as he could down the driveway.

I sometimes like to take the night off. It isn't often as generally I desperately need the money and so I have to work, but as and when I can afford to, I like to have an occasional night off.

There were not many doormen working for the company that were experienced enough to work The Rectory and had a Macclesfield badge (an official licence to run the door). For the one night I had off, the office had replaced me with Steve. He had worked with me on a couple of other occasions, filling in when the regular doormen were off. Although he made out he had been working the door for a while, he knew no-one and none of the heads. That night he was put on the front door as he was the only doorman holding a Macclesfield badge, while the other two without badges worked inside.

As usual for a Friday there was a queue, and I am sure that Steve was coping until JD arrived with his small entourage. I have known JD for many years, since Peruvia. Not a hard-man himself, he knows just about everyone and runs much of Moss Side. Fuck with him and you would end up floating on your back in the canal.

JD is a good acquaintance of mine, we shake hands, we embrace, we have a quick chat and move on. When he is not off his head on cocaine he is fine, but lately that had been rare and he was becoming unpredictable. JD never queues in any nightclub anywhere in Manchester. Everyone knows him – he has been around for a long time and is very well respected. But it seemed that the only doorman in Manchester not to know JD that particular night was Steve.

As JD approached the door, Steve blocked him with his hand and told him he had to queue.

'It is alright mate, I know Robin,' JD said.

'Sorry mate, a lot of people have said that tonight, you still have to queue.' Steve should have seen who he was with to see that he was somebody. He looks like somebody – confident and wealthy – and is surrounded by beautiful women, usually coked up and out of their heads.

JD did not want to cause any trouble. He knew I ran the door and wouldn't cause trouble at a venue I worked. And so one of the biggest heads in Manchester waited in the queue outside The Rectory for 15 minutes before being allowed in.

However, once he was in he was fuming. Mark also knew JD as he had been in before and usually spent hundreds of pounds on champagne. Mark apologized and made the excuse that Steve was a new doorman and just filling in. I would be back tomorrow. Slowly JD calmed down and they sat together for a while, drinking. It was worth Mark buying a couple of rounds that night, as there was no trouble. However Steve spent the rest of the evening shitting himself once he was told he had just made one of the biggest heads in Moss Side wait in the queue.

The next night I was back at work standing in my normal spot outside on the steps when a big black Range Rover with tinted windows screeched into the drive and pulled up directly in front of the door.

The tinted window lowered, JD poked his head out from the window and shouted, 'Do you know I waited in the queue for fifteen fucking minutes to get in here last night?' He didn't look very happy but had a sly kind of grin on his face which meant he was pissed off but joking a little nevertheless. 'If it was any other club than yours I would have fucked your doorman.'

'Yeah, I heard,' I replied gravely. 'Sorry, it won't happen again. They know who you are and any time I am not in just ask for me, you won't have a problem next time.'

'I fucking did ask for you, you cunt,' he said as he got out. He then smiled, we shook hands and hugged. I looked back at the Range Rover to see who was driving. The door opened and the driver got out and walked round the car. Immediately I recognized another familiar face, that of G, another leading head of Moss Side. An immaculately dressed black man wearing more jewellery than there is at Buckingham Palace, he walked round the front of the car, shook hands and stood chatting for a short while. Sitting in the back of the Range Rover staring at me were two of the evilest, meanest and most frightening-looking black gangsters I had ever seen. They were monsters, and sat there giving me a look that said 'touch these two and you are dead meat'.

It is so important to be respected on the doors, and in return to respect others. One time I was inside doing a quick tour. The queue was held for a while, as we were full and running 'one in and one out'. I had left a doorman holding the queue until I came back out. When I came out of the club and looked down the queue I noticed Paul standing there with his girlfriend and another equally monstrous friend. Paul used to run all the doors in a large town close by. He is big, actually not big but downright huge, with hands the size of small shovels. At one time no-one could have a club in the town without employing Paul's lads, but a few years ago the police took hold of the door situation in Manchester and all the surrounding suburbs and towns, and ended the monopoly the gangs had on the business. The police effectively forced Paul to abandon the doors and to concentrate on other business activities instead. He was waiting in the queue. As soon as I saw him I beckoned him to the front, explaining, as I had done to JD, that he never needed to queue, just to come straight to the door and ask for me. If for any reason I wasn't in just to mention my name.

People like to be treated in this way and in return will almost always be one of the first behind you if you have a problem. It is always worth showing courtesy and respect to a few select names and faces, but not to any Tom, Dick or rough-looking scrote. Only to those that really are someone, of which there are few.

It is not what they look like, but who they are. But there are a great many wankers out there who genuinely think they are somebody special and that expect to get in free to every club and pub. Most of them are nothing on their own and they rely on the power of their group to back them and to give them the confidence to front the club.

Some of the toughest guys I have met in the world were not big meatheads, but just average size, average-looking guys, but with a determination and strength of character never to be beaten. However, I always say be aware of the good-looking doorman – either he has been very lucky in his profession or he is truly that good that he has never had a good beating!

For a long while I had wanted to leave the doors and find a normal job, but there was nothing I felt I could do. I looked around but shuddered at the thought of working in some office or for some awful stuck-up, conceited boss. I could see myself getting pissed off after a week and battering him for his arrogance and attitude. I always enjoyed travelling and always enjoyed bodyguarding, but because I now tended to focus on Moscow and the Russian Federation, I had to keep coming home and back to the doors as there wasn't yet enough work for me to live over there permanently. Also there was no job other than the doors that would allow me so much time off.

On the door I am the boss. I control my own territory. On the doors and as a bodyguard I am somebody and I enjoy that feeling. I am unique and an individual and could never imagine being just a number in a big company somewhere pushing paper all day. I would go mad before my first week had ended.

Over the past few years I had also been able to effectively control my aggressive temperament. I could feel the rage rise up inside, but I fought it and controlled it and now I rarely went too far. There were times when I was younger when I would come away from a fight covered in blood – not mine. There were times when my rage was so great no-one dared to stop me. There were times when I beat people unconscious. But throughout that period of my life I was never once arrested, and never had any major retaliation. I was lucky. However, since experiencing the extremes of violence I have changed, and I now spend more time controlling my rage and reacting differently to situations and problems. I would now prefer to talk than to fight. I also realized that, at 40, it was becoming harder to keep up with the 20- and 30-year-olds, and that I would have to do more and more just to equal them. Also, in this ever-changing and increasingly violent society, people have a lot less respect than they did a few years ago and are more willing to take revenge with a knife or a gun.

I knew I would have to give up the doors and I still had a vague idea of someday living in Moscow. I had been there many times and it became my ambition to live and die in this crazy city, not on the door of some stupid pub in some stupid village in the UK.

However, I never imagined that I would be leaving the doors as suddenly as I did.

It was a Saturday night and The Rectory was packed as usual. I was working the front door with Andy while Steve, who had been filling in more and more, was upstairs on the balcony keeping an eye on both the front door and the club upstairs. The DJ was upstairs and, although there was no dance floor, people were dancing. Mark had just done his own small tour of the club and had noticed two knobheads making arses of themselves near the DJ console – dancing aggressively, banging into other customers nearby and generally pissing around. Steve was nearest, but Mark came down to the door and asked me to go to ask them to leave. I didn't think there would be a problem so I told Andy he could stay on the door while I took Steve with me.

I followed Mark upstairs, beckoning Steve to join us as we passed him on the balcony. We squeezed through the crowd, it was busy and there was always a bottleneck at the top of the stairs near the bar. I immediately noticed the two arseholes in question. Mark went up to one of them and asked him to leave. He ignored us. Mark asked him again and for the second time he ignored us so Mark – who never backed down to anyone even though he was only 5ft 6ins and about 10 stone – grabbed one of them and turned him in the direction of the stairs. Steve then took over and started to escort him downstairs.

'You have to go as well,' I shouted to the second.

'Fuck off,' he replied and turned slightly away from me as though I wasn't there.

'Listen, I am not going to argue, will you leave by yourself or will I have to escort you out?' I was being patient, but I could feel the anger rise.

'You?' he looked at me and laughed. 'Throw me out? Fuck off.' I took his arm, intending to guide him downstairs. As I grabbed his arm I could feel him tense and, in the corner of my eye, saw his fist clench. He stepped back slightly, ready to throw a punch, but I grabbed him hard by the throat and threw him onto the floor. Something inside me snapped. I grabbed him by the hair and screamed, 'Fuck with me will you, fuck around in my club?' I punched him again and again in the face while I was dragging him down the stairs by his hair. Mark tried to pull me off, but I just shrugged him away. He realized there was nothing he could do to stop me. I dragged the lad by the hair all the way down the steps, punching him repeatedly in the face and the side of his head. I could feel great chunks of bloodied hair coming out in my hands, but then I would drop him for a few seconds, grab another handful and continue to drag him down and out the front doors, all the time screaming, 'Fuck with me will you?' Everyone in The Rectory could see what I was doing.

After that night I realized that it would soon be my last night on the doors. My mind had finally gone. I had snapped and lost all control. I was crazy. I realized I could no longer put myself in that situation. It was different from planning to kill someone. If I had shot Tinker and Anthony I would have had complete control over my destiny, but losing it in a pub there would be no control and that was dangerous.

The weekend afterwards, I went back to Moscow. I had a contract which lasted one week and so I was away from The Rectory just one weekend. On the Saturday night I was away, after an absence of 12 months, Anthony K decided to visit the venue. None of the doormen stopped him – he came in with all of his friends, drank two bottles of champagne and left without paying.

Mark the manager called the office and Tony promised a strong team on the door the following weekend to stop him coming back in. Tony would also be there, as would Darren from Warrington – another hard-looking doorman who didn't give a fuck about anyone. We would tell Anthony K to his face that he was barred for good, and if he wanted a war we would give him a war.

While I was away I had made the decision to leave the doors once and for all. I knew, after that previous weekend, that my time on the doors was coming to an end. If I stayed on the doors things would never change. I would be going nowhere, struggling by week after week.

I had decided to work that one weekend and then quit. I would find another life, wherever that may be. As soon as I got back I was briefed by both the office and Mark. I decided that I would not let the guys down and would work through the confrontation. I would stand fast – do what I had to do this one last time and then leave the doors for good.

Darren and I stood on the door. Tony had to drop another doorman off at a club nearby, and would shortly return and then stay with us until the end of the night. I had an awful feeling that Anthony K would turn up again and both Darren and I hoped Tony would be back in time.

Darren and I decided that if Anthony was to come and it was too difficult to stop him on our own, we would let him in. Then we'd call Tony, who would return, bringing with him an army of North West doormen. I wanted this over once and for all. I didn't want to be fighting, not any more. I had truly had enough.

While standing on the door chatting and waiting for the night to pass we noticed the imposing figure of Anthony sauntering across the car park towards the front door with about five others behind him. Just as he reached the door, Tony Hill pulled into the driveway. There would be three of us against six of them. It would be a war, but a good war nevertheless.

Anthony grinned and held out his hand. I grabbed his hand as though to shake it and looked him square in the face. 'Sorry Anthony, you've been barred.'

His smirk turned to rage.

'What the fuck for?' he shouted. I still had hold of his hand. His other hand was in a cast from where he had been shot. I knew he could only punch with the hand I had hold of.

'Because you left without paying your bar tab and the manager does not want to let you in any more.'

He slammed his injured arm across my chest, pushing me away from him.

'I'll give you the fucking money now,' he shouted. 'I have £2,000 in my pocket, go and get the fucking bill.'

'Sorry, but it's too late,' I said, 'the manager doesn't want you in.'

'Go and fucking get him.'

'He isn't working tonight.'

'Go and fucking get him – I am coming in.' He started to walk past but we blocked his way.

'You are not coming in,' I said.

'And you are going to fucking stop me?' He screamed. My legs were shaking but I went up to his face.

'If you want a fucking war, I'll give you a fucking war,' I said. 'You take the piss out of us and you've got a shit attitude. Who do you think you are? We don't want you here. Now if you want to fight, let's do it now and get it over. Either way you are not coming in. I am too old for all of this and I don't want a war with you, but if you want a war I'll give you a fucking war you will wish you never started.'

He slammed me hard in the chest, pushing me away from him. One of his friends said, 'Come on Anthony, they are not going to fucking stop us, we are going in.' But the others crowded round and pushed him back.

We stood our ground Anthony was straining forward, the veins in his neck bulging, his face contorted with anger and his fists clenched. We stood ready for battle. I was just on the verge of jumping in, grabbing at his eyes and tearing them from his sockets when a police van pulled into the driveway.

Anthony turned and ran, yelling, 'I will be back, I will return and you, Robin, are fucking dead.' I knew this time I was marked. I understood it completely. He was a head amongst his own small gang. He would never leave it.

So I left the doors not knowing what I was going to do or where I was going to go.

AFTERWORD

Moscow, 2003

It is Thursday morning and I am due to fly back to England later today, catching the 17.05 Czech Airlines flight from Moscow Sheremetyevo airport to Manchester via Prague. I am going home for a few days to see my daughter. I miss her terribly: her smile, her hugs, her warmth, her wonderful smell and her love. Her uncompromising and absolute love.

I am lying in bed looking out of the window. It is snowing, and the snow settles lightly on the trees outside. It is the first week in April. Winters here are harsh and can get extremely cold. They last a long time, too long.

I watch as Inna climbs out of bed and walks naked across the bedroom and into the bathroom. I stare at her wonderful arse – she is just 27 years old, beautifully slim with short dark hair and a gorgeous smile. I lay watching her thinking what a lucky fuck I am.

Manchester is probably one of the toughest cities in the UK, and Moscow arguably one of the toughest cities in the world. Last year Russia was voted the third most violent country, coming after Colombia and El Salvador.

I moved to Moscow shortly after Thelma and I finally split up. Thelma was the kindest and most loving person anyone could imagine. Pretty, warm-hearted and incredibly loyal. She simply did not deserve to get hurt and I hurt her too many times. I simply got bored with being in one place and with one person. She could no longer trust me; shortly after I left The

Rectory she caught me screwing around for the third time and that – as they say – was that.

The thought of me living apart from my wonderful daughter caused me to have a nervous breakdown. I could not contemplate life without her, she was my world, and I would have preferred to die rather than be without her. It was simply impossible for me not to see her first thing every morning, or not to cuddle up with her last thing at night. I loved to sit next to her and read, or just to play and be stupid and silly. She was the only person I have ever or will ever love, and now that love was being taken away and I knew that without her I could not survive.

Thelma screamed and shouted at me as I walked out of the door, hoping it would be for the last time. It was the middle of winter, and I was wearing just a flimsy shirt and trousers. I had no money, no ID, nothing. I didn't want anything as I genuinely didn't want to come back. I would walk until I could walk no further, then I would crawl until I could crawl no further, then I was hoping to just curl up in a field somewhere and sleep for ever. I didn't want to live.

It was late in the evening, freezing cold and raining. I was soaked and shivering, I have never felt cold like it. It physically hurt. I walked from Wilmslow to Macclesfield, about ten miles. I then walked over the Peak District towards Buxton. Over the top, the rain turned to sleet and snow. An occasional lorry passed, and with each one that passed I considered just stepping in front and ending everything in one swift motion. But I continued walking, becoming more and more distressed. Tears were pouring down my cheeks and I was shaking violently with the cold. I had finally had enough and huddled in a ball on the soaking wet ground by the side of the road. I just wanted to sleep.

'I think we'd better take you to hospital,' said a voice above me.

I looked up and saw the blurred image of a man. He put his

jacket over my shoulders and helped me into his car and took me the short distance to Buxton Hospital. I had walked over twenty miles. Later that morning I was transferred to Macclesfield Psychiatric Hospital where I spent a week in relative solitude.

Thelma found me and brought Daniella to the hospital. I returned and spent a couple of months sleeping in the spare room until I finally decided to move to Moscow and build a new life.

I never wanted to hurt Thelma, she was the mother of my daughter and I understood that by hurting her I have hurt my daughter and have changed my daughter's life forever. And yet she doesn't understand, she only knows that she misses her daddy.

I cannot live a normal life in England, in a normal job. I need constant excitement, both personally and professionally. I could never resist something different, a new woman, a new job, a new environment and a new challenge. Neither could I stand not being able to influence my daughter in exactly the way I want to and believe in. There are those around her that influence her life in ways I absolutely and fundamentally disagree with and I could never compromise my basic beliefs and values. So I have decided to move, to build a new life and maybe to eventually find harmony, happiness and above all contentment.

I love it here in Moscow – it is exactly the sort of lifestyle that I adore. Moscow is a harsh, challenging and cruel environment. No-one really cares or has much time for each other, and no-one really knows what is going to happen in the next hour let alone the next day. Everyone lives for the moment, which makes it a fast, aggressive, determined and cut-throat place to live in, where only the strongest survive.

Moscow is also a beautiful, culturally outstanding and enchanting city, with a diverse, interesting yet incredibly sad history based upon tyranny, cruelty and dictatorship. When I walk down the boulevards I look around and marvel at what has happened to this monstrous country over the last ten years and wonder what will befall it over the next ten.

Crime is dominant. Like an octopus, the Russian mafia have their ruthless and cold-blooded tentacles in almost every single business, from street traders selling shoelaces to multinational organizations. You pay protection, you pay extortion, you pay to be allowed to trade, for the right papers and permits and if you don't pay you get shot – simple.

It is virtually impossible to start any sort of business in Moscow without encountering the mafia. The mafia is a collective word for organized crime. There isn't one mafia family but hundreds of small crime syndicates running their own small empire within their own small territory. The local police are closely connected to every crime syndicate and are just as corrupt – in fact one of the most corrupt police forces in the world. I have travelled to many places yet I have found that the police in Moscow are a particularly awful and hostile group of individuals whose aim is to stop everybody, all the time, not because they need to but because they are eager to find the slightest thing wrong with documents and papers and so elicit an illegal payment down some dark street.

A lot of crime here is never reported and that which is tends not to be investigated and those that are investigated seldom reach court. Someone gets paid off somewhere along the line, or gets shot and so the case just disappears.

According to statistics, there were 579 business assassinations in Russia last year, and 299 bodyguards were killed. Out of the 579 business assassinations, only two were investigated. Which means if you have money, you can pretty much do what you want.

Criminality is accepted as normal behaviour, as the only way of making money, of surviving. Only ten per cent of the population pay the correct amount of tax so it seems that everyone practises some forms of illegality. No-one uses credit, everything is cash and cash is easily hidden. I pay for my apartment in cash and of course the landlord does not declare it. When I work with Russian bodyguards I pay them in cash, and of course they don't declare it. When I get paid it is in cash and of course I don't declare it.

But crime thankfully tends to just be centred on the Russian business community and westerners are seldom targeted for extortion and assassination. But the risks are still there and are still very high. The last high-profile foreign business assassination was an American hotelier who part-owned the Radisson. His Russian business partner wanted to buy him out – he refused and was shot dead. But that was a few years ago and there hasn't been a high-profile western assassination since, although westerners have certainly been killed but it is thought there were other factors involved rather than just extortion.

From what I've seen it seems that the Russian government simply cannot control corruption and crime – they seem to leave the mafia alone as long as the mafia leave western businesses alone. For without western investment the Russian economy would collapse. This happened in the crisis of 1998. Most foreigners pulled out, the rouble collapsed, banks closed, companies went bankrupt and many people were left without work and any income. It was the worst time since the fall of communism and no Russian wants to go through that again. But Russia is slowly changing and there is renewed investment and confidence.

Personal security is big business and being in Moscow is a bodyguard's dream. It is virtually impossible for a foreigner to get a licence to operate legally as a bodyguard so there are almost no foreign operational bodyguards in Moscow but there are foreign 'security consultants' and very many well-trained Russian guards. Almost all the bodyguards operating in Moscow at the moment are from a Russian Special Forces background; they are tough, incredibly skilled and very well trained. Ironically, most assassins are also from the Special Forces. Depending upon an individual's morals and ethics, when they leave the Special Forces they become either bodyguards or assassins, but there is more money to be made as an assassin. An assassin could earn US$3,000–5,000 per hit and a skilled assassin might get four or five jobs a year. A Russian bodyguard earns about US$5 an hour, which is a very good wage in Moscow but the average lifespan for a bodyguard in Moscow is about two years.

But, as you walk down Tverskaya Boulevard towards the Kremlin and Red Square it is great to see the executive vehicle convoys, the armed drivers and the bodyguards going about their daily business protecting their principal and always keeping guard. Just recently there was another high-profile assassination in Red Square and a separate kidnapping nearby.

I am now over 40 and finally I am sure I know what I want in my life and exactly how I want to lead it. I know myself better than I ever have; I know my capacities and my limits. I know what I like and what I hate, I know what makes me happy and what really pisses me off. I have been around the world, delivered aid for children and fought in a war. I have beaten arseholes senseless in nightclubs and cried for the disabled and the injured. And I am also psychologically wrecked. I am scared – an emotional timebomb.

My life has been a real rollercoaster. I have had two failed marriages and more engagements and live-in girlfriends than I can actually remember. It seems as soon as I meet someone I move in and live with them, and as soon as I have moved in I fuck off. I just wake up, pack my bags and leave without warning.

I have never had many possessions and didn't want anything except my freedom. And this has been my life for the past 25 years: always searching for something, new relationships, and excitement, something interesting, challenging and different. I got so bored with everyday existence and was always searching for the new, for the next big adventure. I have lost count of the number of times I walked away from everything. I leave absolutely everything behind; friends, possessions, photographs but I do love my books and some of them come with me everywhere.

And of course Moscow is one of the few places a 40-year-old like me can still find a beautiful, slim, intelligent 27-year-old. Here in Moscow I have slept with some of the most beautiful women in the world. But be warned, Russian women are also the most predatory; they know exactly what they want and go out to get it. There are a great many women here in Moscow whose only goal is to meet a foreigner and to settle down with him. Like all women, Russians desire a good standard of living and lifestyle, which sadly many Russian men cannot provide. Unless they have their own business or work for a western company, Russian men have little opportunity to earn a good salary. The average wage is about US$300 a month. And so it is easy to see why many western men fall in love with Russian women. They really are beautiful, they take pride in their appearance and they are generally very well educated. Most can cook and most, once they have found a partner, are very loyal and trustworthy.

As I lie here I realize I finally like my life. I have a beautiful woman keeping me company. When I am not with Inna I write, and when I am not writing I still have the occasional bodyguard contract and run the occasional close protection training course. I still love to travel and doubt I will ever stop. Travelling is the best experience that anyone can ever have and without experiences we are nothing, we learn nothing. However, being on your own has its lonely times. To experience something beautiful, magical and interesting by oneself is not really an experience – it is just something that happened. An experience should be discussed, thought about and explored and shared. An experience is not just something that has happened but something that has a deeper meaning and understanding and it is hard to achieve this by oneself. So I explore with Inna. We have lots in common, lots to discuss.

When it comes to violence I am as hard as anyone. I have seen and been involved in extreme violence, and yet when it comes to relationships with women I am as weak and as simple as anyone could ever be. I have destroyed so many women with my fake promises and lies. I have set out to build up false relationships, I have manipulated their feelings to adoration and love and then I have just walked away, and destroyed everything. I have done it time and time and time again.

Doing the doors has changed my life immeasurably. I occasionally go back to my hometown of Norwich, reminisce a little, look up old friends and think of who I was back then and how I have changed so much, from my first donning of that notorious yellow jacket at Ritzy nightclub 18 years ago in a job I knew nothing about to my life here in Moscow. There are still those I went to school with that are in the same job, doing the same thing at the same office as they were 20 years ago. Maybe, had I not been desperate for a job, I might have turned out the same as them.

But lying here in bed in Moscow looking at Inna's gorgeous behind, around at my apartment and at the snow falling outside, I realize what a wonderful and exciting life I have had, and looking back I wouldn't change a thing.

Sure I have seen and done some crazy and horrible things but I am what I am because of them, and I like the way I am. I am mad. I am crazy and have been extremely violent and am certainly very unstable but I am also kind-hearted and warm, thoughtful and considerate. I would do anything for anyone – I would give away my last penny, or travel to the other side of the world. I don't need possessions or a home, I don't need to speak to my mother and I don't really need much money. I can live in a shed as long as I feel inner contentment and inner happiness. I don't need or want for anything apart from the adoration of a woman. Maybe in Moscow I will finally settle, finally find the life and the person I have spent my life searching for. Maybe someone will be strong enough to tame me – maybe I can escape this life of emotional turmoil and misery and find some stability and security. Maybe I can finally find love and be loved. Maybe then, and only then, would my violent past be forgiven and forgotten and I can start my life afresh. They say life begins at 40. Maybe it is true.

I jumped out of bed; after all I had a flight to catch.

'Inna, will you be long in the bathroom?' I called.

'Not long,' she called back. I stood at the window looking down to the streets below.

'Darling . . .' she said, walking back into the bedroom.

'Yes,' I turned to her.

'. . . I love you – my husband.'

Yesterday we got married.

APPENDIX

The Doors

Here is a complete list of venues that I have worked as a doorman and occasionally as a manager, over 18 years.

Ritzy – Norwich
Hy's Nightclub – Norwich
Hector's House – Norwich
Bedford's Wine bar – Norwich
St Giles Wine bar – Norwich
Henry's Cafe bar – Norwich
Rick's Place – Norwich
Hog in Armour – Norwich
Peppermint Park – Norwich
Snooker Hall – Norwich
Ronnelles International – Cambridge
The Millionaire – Peterborough
Easy Street – Preston
Digby's – Mansfield
Gables and Raffles – Wellingborough
Starbucks – Corby
Le Central – Paris, France
Coppid Beech – Bracknell
Ritzy – Guildford
Henley's Nightclub – Henley on Thames
Cinderella's – Kingston-upon-Thames, London
Broadway Boulevard – Ealing, London

The Mill – Reading
Equivino (Peruvia) – Wilmslow
The Mirage – Standish, near Wigan
Loaf – Manchester
Old Monk – Manchester
The Academy – Manchester
The Rectory – Wilmslow

The Worldwide Federation of Bodyguards can be contacted at TheWFB@aol.com.

Robin Barratt can be contacted at BarrattAssociates@yahoo.co.uk